Frank :
May hockey open your eyes to the world !

HOCKEY
MY DOOR TO
EUROPE

DENIS GIBBONS

28-09-18

◆ FriesenPress

Suite 300 - 990 Fort St
Victoria, BC, V8V 3K2
Canada

www.friesenpress.com

The majority of the photographs in this book were taken by Denis Gibbons

Cover design by Geoff Soch, FriesenPress

ISBN
978-1-5255-0803-5 (Hardcover)
978-1-5255-0804-2 (Paperback)
978-1-5255-0805-9 (eBook)

1. SPORTS & RECREATION, HOCKEY

Distributed to the trade by The Ingram Book Company

Table of Contents

ACKNOWLEDGMENTS

There is no way this book could have been published without the support of my wife Chris, who has served as secretary for my international hockey interests for the last 25 years, prepared me for journeys to the Olympics and looked after my health care while I recuperated from triple bypass surgery in 2006.

We were married on May 25, 1991, the day the Pittsburgh Penguins won their first Stanley Cup.

I also want to thank my sister Mary Kay, my nieces Pauline and Sarah, as well as my nephews Nathan and Nolan for all their encouragement. I add a special prayer for my cousin Garry Gibbons, a loving father who passed away before he had a chance to read the book.

The man responsible for launching my career in the newspaper business was Hartley Coles, who at various times was editor of *The Acton Free Press*, *Georgetown Independent*, *Acton New Tanner* and *Listowel Banner.*

Coles, who died in 2010, doubled his own workload and encouraged me to go on my first trip behind the Iron Curtain — a three-week study tour to Moscow in the spring of 1974.

Growing up in Acton, Ont., my best friend was Brian McCristall, who also had a huge influence on my decision to go into the business. McCristall became publisher of several community newspapers in British Columbia's Lower Mainland and was a vice-president of Black Press when he retired.

My father Neil showed me the fundamentals of the game and, together with my Uncle Tom, took me to my first NHL game on Feb. 26, 1949, at Maple Leaf Gardens when the Toronto Maple Leafs and Chicago Black Hawks skated to a 2-2 tie.

Only 5 at the time, I remember the goaltending duel between Turk Broda and Sugar Jim Henry. I recall being fascinated by the red, black and white barber pole-striped jerseys of the Black Hawks, the beautiful white and blue cardigans worn by the ice-resurfacing crew and the whiteness of the Gardens ice.

I saw my father play only once.

On Valentine's Day 1952, the Acton Minor Hockey Association held its annual Booster Night. The feature attraction was an oldtimers game between the Acton Tanners, OHA Intermediate champions in 1938-39 and the 1929-30 version of the town's intermediate club, the first to win a group championship for Acton.

I was slightly embarrassed when my father, so happy to be on the old blades again at age 48, continued to skate around and warm up while the band played the first few notes of *God Save the King!*

King George VI had just died and Booster Night, originally scheduled for Friday, was moved ahead one day on the calendar out of respect for the late King, who was to be buried on Friday.

Although he was towards the end of his career and did not see any action in the playoffs, my Uncle Frank Gibbons had played some regular season games for the OHA champions of 1938-39.

A defenceman of some note as a junior, Uncle Frank had caught the attention of New York Rangers general manager Lester Patrick, who while the Blueshirts were playing in Toronto one night, made a special trip out to Acton to try to convince him to sign a minor league contract.

However, his mother managed to convince him that faraway fields look green and he declined Patrick's offer, winding up his amateur career in Acton.

The younger 1938-39 champs, with Uncle Frank in uniform, prevailed 5-3, but the older group, with which my father played, put some pressure on in the final minute by comically icing a 12-man power play!

Much earlier, my father had been schooled in hockey by Ken Randall while playing junior in nearby Georgetown.

Randall, who was playing for the defending Stanley Cup champion Toronto St. Pats at the time, would come out from Toronto, as long as the St. Pats didn't have a game, to coach the juniors.

The NHL schedule was only 24 games long. He had an assistant coach who would take over on the occasions of a game conflict.

Incidentally, the 1922-23 season was the year the Georgetown Memorial Arena opened. It had an ice surface measuring only 175 feet by 74 feet, so it was easy for defencemen to contain attackers in the corners. It closed only a few years ago, and I believe was one of the oldest arenas in Ontario, right up there with the Galt Memorial Gardens, which is still used for hockey. The building in Galt also opened in 1922.

Randall, known as the 'Pepper Kid', played in the first NHL game ever in which the Montreal Wanderers outlasted the Toronto Arenas 10-9 in Montreal on Dec. 19, 1917. He also played in the first game at Madison Square Garden in 1925 and the first NHL game broadcast on radio on Valentine's Day 1923, with the legendary broadcaster Foster Hewitt calling it.

Another supporter was my father-in-law, John Ivanco, who was born in 1928 in the village of Vilag, Czechoslovakia, within walking distance of the border of Poland.

He was born the same year the Toronto Varsity Grads won both the Olympic and World Championship gold medals for Canada in St. Moritz, Switzerland.

John died in 2016 at the age of 87, but I am grateful for the insight he provided into life in the 'old country'.

A huge tip of the hat to Tim Whitnell, who edited the book, and Igor Kuperman, who handled the fact-checking.

Whitnell worked for me as a reporter at *The Burlington Post* and has won many awards for his work during the 30 years-plus he has been there.

Kuperman, a native of Moscow, was the leading hockey statistician in the Soviet Union until he accepted a job with the Winnipeg Jets in 1991. He moved with the team when it transferred to Phoenix.

Vlasta Candra, who was born in Ceske Budejovice in the former Czechoslovakia, was responsible for translating my secret police files, which I was able to obtain as a result of a new policy implemented by the government of the Czech Republic.

Alex and Mila Khayutin, former residents of St. Petersburg, Russia, also have served as volunteer translators and helped improve my Russian language skills.

Frank Buchanan, former president of the Burlington Lions-Optimist Hockey Association, got me involved in four hockey and cultural exchanges with clubs in Europe.

I've always admired the work of broadcaster Mike Emrick, with whom I have worked as a researcher at four Olympics. 'Doc', more than anyone in the television world, has given my information wide exposure.

Bill Fitsell, who founded the Society for International Hockey Research, always has been a mentor.

My mother Kay, who brought me into the world in 1943 and my Aunt Dean, honored as Acton's Citizen of the Year in 1962 for her good deeds in the community, deserve tributes.

I also give a big shout-out to Gord Miller, Dan Hamilton, Steve Dryden, Brian Costello, Jason Kay, Gus Matsos, Kevin Shea, Greg Oliver, Lloyd Davis, John Shannon, Kevin Nagel, Richie Zyontz, Draggan Mihailovich, Len Kotylo and Jimmy Doyle.

My book preparation included researching articles in *The Toronto Star, The Globe and Mail, The Toronto Sun, The National Post, The Hockey News, Sovietsky Sport, Sport Express, Izvestia, The Daily Telegraph, USA Today, The New York Times* and *St. Petersburg (Russia) Times.*

INTRODUCTION

In Father Vince Morgan's world, rooting for any hockey team other than the Toronto St. Michael's Majors was bordering on mortal sin.

That's why as an altar boy at St. Joseph's Parish in Acton I followed Father David Bauer's Majors religiously.

When the Majors won the Memorial Cup in 1961, the team budget was so low that a darning needle and hockey tape often were used to prolong the life of their uniforms.

After he coached St. Michael's to the Memorial Cup championship in 1960-61 Father Bauer, a Basilian priest, was transferred to St. Mark's College in Vancouver, where he became head coach of the University of British Columbia Thunderbirds.

In the fall of 1963 the Waterloo, Ont., native founded the Canadian national team. That's when my interest in international hockey really begins.

Father Bauer stressed the importance of education, not just hockey.

"He is a Canadian legend," said 1961 team captain Terry O'Malley, now a citizenship court judge in Saskatchewan, "not only in an academic sense, but in preparing for life."

While most of the players on the championship squad went their separate ways following the 1961-62 season, in which the Majors played in the Metro Junior A League, seven players – O'Malley, Barry MacKenzie, Billy MacMillan, Paul Conlin, Terry Clancy, Rod Seiling and Gary Dineen – went on to play for Canada and Father Bauer in Olympics and World Championships in the 1960s.

During Memorial Cup Week in Mississauga in 2011, the 1961 champs finally got their due when all players were presented with championship rings and replica jerseys inscribed with the school's famous block letter 'M'.

My allegiance followed Father Bauer, and at the age of 20, I literally broke down in tears when the Canadians lost to the Soviet Union by the narrow margin of 3-2 at the 1964 Olympics.

As a Grade 8 student at Robert Little School in Acton eight years earlier, I remember the shock I got when I heard the Kitchener-Waterloo Dutchmen, representing Canada, had lost to both the Soviets and Americans at the 1956 Winter Olympics in Cortina d'Ampezzo, Italy, and finished third.

Nevertheless, as a boy of 12, I was still looking forward to the day the team bus was to pass through Acton on its way from Malton Airport back to Kitchener.

Principal Pat McKenzie let all students out in the middle of the afternoon to walk down to Main St. There was a good chance, we were told, the bus would stop for a few minutes.

My friends and I anxiously lined up along the street, hoping to get autographs, but when the bus came through Acton team officials were so embarrassed they told the driver to just keep rolling and all the youngsters were disappointed.

Life has its ups and downs. Such was the lesson both I and the Dutchmen learned!

While he loved hockey, Father Bauer never forgot his primary vocation as a priest. Hans Dobida of Austria, a former member of the IIHF council, told me a great tale about Bauer when he coached the national team of Austria towards the end of his career.

The Austrians were preparing for a crucial match against Switzerland, with the loser facing relegation at the B Pool World Championship.

"Father Bauer came to me and said, 'Hans, you must make it possible for me to celebrate Mass in the pilgrimage church of Maria Trost'.

"All players and persons in charge attended. We won the game and remained in Group B."

When the Soviets continued to win against Canada, albeit without NHL players, in the years following the 1964 Olympics, I began to question reports blaming the referees for most of the Canadian losses.

They lost six years in a row at Olympics and World Championships and I knew it couldn't be the referees' fault every time. When the Summit

Series took place in 1972, and the Soviets almost beat Canada's best pros, I knew they were for real.

I had no interest in their country or politics at that point, but I was immensely interested in their scientific approach to hockey.

Canada's successes and failures in international hockey have been well documented in other books. While I will touch on them in this tome, it's my intention to focus more on the global perspective of the game.

I have tried to give readers a behind-the-scenes look at seven Olympic hockey tournaments I worked at between 1988 and 2014. I missed the 2006 Games in Torino, Italy, when I had triple bypass surgery.

I have recalled my experiences as related to five startling events that occurred while I was in Europe on hockey business.

The first was being detained by the Czechoslovak secret police in 1983, the second the nuclear plant explosion in Chernobyl in 1986, the third the defection of Soviet hockey star Alexander Mogilny following the 1989 World Championship, the fourth the fall of the Berlin Wall in November 1989 and the fifth the conflict in Ukraine in February 2014 that led to Russia's annexation of Crimea.

On my first visit to the Soviet Union in the summer of 1974 I had no knowledge of the Russian language and was baffled by the Cyryllic letters adorning signs and stores in Moscow.

When I returned to Canada, I bought a Berlitz language book and started to teach myself a few words in my spare time. It was enough to allow me to start reading Russian newspapers like *Sovietsky Sport* and *Futbol-Hokkei*, which I purchased at the Troyka bookstore on College St. in Toronto.

Finally, in the fall of 1979, I decided to take a Russian language course in the evening at McMaster University with the hopes of landing a free-lance assignment at the 1980 Olympics in Moscow during my holidays.

I was told that the first-year course was offered only in the daytime and I was still working at my regular job as news editor of *The Burlington Post*.

Disappointed, I came up with another idea, asking if there was any chance I could start in second year, which was offered in the evening.

Professor Simeon Cioran was initially flabbergasted, but luckily for me he decided to give me chance and offered me a deal.

"You can sit in on the classes and audit them, we won't charge you a fee and you can write the tests and exams, and we'll see how you do," he said.

The first month left my head spinning and wondering if I should pack it in. That thought seemed like a good one when I scored five out of 100 on the mid-term fall test.

However, I kept plodding along. My mark improved to 35 per cent at Christmastime, still well below the passing point of 50.

On the winter mid-term test I managed a mark of 65.

At that point, I approached the professor and asked him if I could now pay my tuition and take the course for credit.

Professor Cioran made a special request to the Dean of Arts and Humanities, who granted me permission.

The climax of my rags-to-riches story came in early June when Cioran took time to call me personally and congratulate me on scoring 95 on the final exam.

The following year I took third-year Russian under the tutelage of Professor Nina Kolesnikoff, and continued to drive to Toronto once a week to pick up Russian newspapers, until the dawn of the Internet. After that, I started reading them online.

However, without a fundamental knowledge of Latin and all its declensions and verb conjugations, learning Russian would have been almost impossible.

My introduction to Latin came as a result of serving as an altar boy. Then, during my first year at Acton District High School, I took French and Latin and was identified as having a gift for languages.

With my improving knowledge of the Russian language, I started slowly translating hockey articles from newspapers like *Sovietsky Sport* and *Futbol-Hokkei* in the 1980s and mailing the translations to Canadian national team coach Dave King.

Every Soviet player I talked to in those days was amazed that Soviet newspapers could be purchased in Canada.

I was only a spectator at the 1980 Olympics in Lake Placid, N.Y., rising at 3 a.m. to catch a bus from Montreal, where I was staying, to the Olympic Arena south of the border two hours away.

Everybody remembers the Americans' 4-3 Miracle On Ice upset of the Soviet Union, but few recall that Canada came within a hair of also beating the Big Red Machine.

The Soviets trailed the team Father David Bauer had assembled, mostly from the university ranks, 3-1 with 13 seconds remaining in the second period when Alexei Kasatonov scored a goal for the Soviets that turned the tide.

Led by Captain Boris Mikhailov, the defending Olympic champions were on fire in the final period, scoring four goals to win 6-4.

In 1987 Donald Beauchamp, then director of communications for Hockey Canada in Calgary, recommended me to ABC as a researcher, a year before the 1988 Olympics.

Draggan Mihailovich, chief of research for ABC Sports, came to Hamilton to meet with me during the 1987 Canada Cup tournament, and I was hired.

I was chief researcher for the book *The Red Machine: The Soviet Quest to Dominate Canada's Game,* by Lawrence Martin, who at that time in 1988 had just finished a stint as Moscow correspondent for *The Globe and Mail.* I gathered much of my information during a one-week stay in the Soviet capital in November 1989.

I was lucky enough to get interviews with Alexander Yakushev, the Soviet star of the Summit Series, as well as Vladimir Lutchenko, Yuri Liapkin, Evgeny Zimin and Yuri Lebedev who also played in it.

I worked with Ken Dryden at the 1988 Olympics in Calgary and did a small amount of research for *Home Game,* one of his many outstanding books.

Since then I have worked at six more Olympic hockey tournaments, four of them as chief researcher for Emrick.

My contacts increased immensely when I became a member of the Society for International Hockey Research (SIHR) in 1996.

For the last 26 years SIHR has made a major contribution to publicizing hockey history and correcting many mistakes that have been made in books and magazines over the years. The society has experts in virtually every aspect of the game.

Preservation of player statistics has been equally important for SIHR.

Ernie Fitzsimmons, a retired air traffic controller from Fredericton, N.B, was responsible for compiling most of the original data found in the SIHR player database, with the help of Toronto's John Paton and Pat Conway of Syracuse, N.Y., who both are deceased.

James Milks of Gatineau, Quebec, a past president of SIHR, built the online player database in 2003, at which time the database used to create the book *Total Hockey*, published by Dan Diamond and Associates Inc. of Toronto, was imported. Another Canadian, Dave Weigum, also of Fredericton, joined SIHR in 2004, and gave the project a huge boost when he shared his stats, pushing it past the 10,000-player mark.

Today, thanks to the efforts of many members, the database has stats dating back to the 1886-87 season for various pro, semi-pro, European and amateur male and female leagues. The collection includes 313,263 players, along with more than one million lines of individual statistics and 82,666 photographs.

CHAPTER 1

Fred Shero visits Moscow to learn the Russian way

Fred Shero's Broad Street Bullies brought Philadelphia its first Stanley Cup in 1974, largely through intimidation and physically hammering the hell out of opponents, although the Flyers had great leadership with Bobby Clarke as captain and exceptional goaltending with Bernie Parent.

Less than a month later, the off-beat Flyers coach was defending *himself* against a 'brutal beating' in the confines of a Moscow steam bath.

"I've never gone through anything like it before," Shero said. "First there was a steam bath, then a dip in a cold pool, then they started feeding us the vodka. After that, more steam.

"Then they brought out the cognac. I thought we were finished so I started to put my clothes on when two guys grabbed me by the arms and took me over to a massage table. They were pounding the hell out of my back and asking me how it felt. Well, it hurt like hell, but I didn't have the nerve to tell them!"

The Soviets sometimes had a strange way of showing their hospitality, but Shero played the perfect guest in his first visit to the Soviet Union with a group of hockey coaches and physical education teachers from North America.

Organized at Montreal's Concordia University by former B.C. Lions lineman Ed Enos, founder of the university's Institute of Comparative Physical Education, the three-week study tour offered participants return airfare, three weeks' accommodation, all meals, one full university credit, tickets to the Moscow Circus, Moscow Symphony, ballet, international rowing competition and Premier League soccer match, as well as an official reception at the Canadian Embassy, a visit to the Soviet Exposition of Economic Achievement and a side bus trip to the Russian Orthodox monastery in Zagorsk, just outside of Moscow, for a bargain price of $850.

Little was known about Soviet training methods at the time, except that they were much more rigid than those in North America. There was a lot of debate about whether that was beneficial or detrimental to the players over the long run.

Most Stanley Cup-winning coaches would have been on the golf course and lazing on the beach soaking up the sun at this time. Yet 'Freddie the Fog' and Ron Ryan, then GM of the WHA's New England Whalers, took advantage of the opportunity to expand their horizons and learn something new about the game. Enos said Al Arbour of the New York Islanders was the only one of the NHL's 15 other coaches who even bothered to call to enquire about the study tour.

However, there were several prominent college coaches like John MacInnes of Michigan Tech, Bob Crocker of the University of Pennsylvania, Bob Boucher of St. Mary's of Halifax, Paul Arsenault of Concordia, Pierre Page of Dalhousie and Grant Standbrook of Dartmouth on the list of summer students.

Page, who later coached the Minnesota North Stars, Calgary, Quebec and Anaheim in the NHL, submitted a paper on the structure of specialized training programs for hockey in Canada and the Soviet Union.

We studied at the Central Institute of Sport and Physical Culture and took on-ice lessons from members of the Soviet national team, including Vladimir Vikulov and Alexander Ragulin.

Shero also lectured and told the Soviets one of the reasons the Flyers won the Cup is that he had adopted the Soviet system of quick counterattacks, rather than having a defenceman take the puck behind the net and set up a break-out play. By that time, Shero argued, the defensive team already is set up and waiting for you.

The Soviets, who trained at a break-neck pace for 11 months of the year, were anxious to know how an NHL practice works.

Making light of the carefree attitude in the NHL and the power of the NHL Players Association under Alan Eagleson, Shero explained how he conducts a practice.

"The first thing I do," he said, "is call all the players over to one corner of the rink, where we kid each other and tell a few jokes to loosen up. Then I ask them if they'd like to do some work. If they say yes, we start!"

Shero admitted North Americans could learn a lot from the Soviet system of training coaches, which called for candidates to attend schools and write exams before becoming qualified.

Asked why he came to Moscow just two weeks after winning the Stanley Cup, Shero replied:

"Because I needed to know more about hockey and I believe the Russians know more about hockey than anyone else in the world."

Flyers coach Fred Shero and author Denis Gibbons watch Soviet hockey drills in Moscow in 1974.

Shero said he could not consider the Flyers true world champions until they had beaten the Soviets' best club team. His visit to Moscow was a precursor to the first Super Series between NHL and Soviet clubs, which was held in December 1975 and January 1976.

There even were discussions with high officials of the Soviet Ice Hockey Federation about the possibility of a six-game series between Philadelphia, if they were able to repeat as Stanley Cup champs in 1974-75 and the champion of the Soviet Elite League.

The Flyers did win their second straight Cup and Central Red Army came out on top in the USSR. Somewhere in-between Eagleson stepped in and arranged the inaugural Super Series, which involved the Red Army and Wings of the Soviet each playing four exhibition games against NHL clubs.

Shero was a goodwill ambassador on the trip. He was available for interviews with the Soviet media whenever they asked him.

Near the end of our three-week stay, he sold one of his Philadelphia Flyers club rings and took about 10 of us out to dinner at The Prague Restaurant with the proceeds.

Boris Mayorov, a two-time Olympic gold medalist, diagrammed the Soviet system for defending three against five when their team is short-handed. In those days they pressured the puck, placing two men out front and only one in front of the net at the vortex of an inverted triangle.

This conflicted with NHL clubs, who had one man on the puck and two guarding the net. Over the years these patterns have emerged into a moving diamond shape.

Because they believe the ankle should be used more in skating than many coaches who think hip movement is more important, the Soviets recommended players not lace up the top two eyelets of their skates to permit the ankle to move more freely.

On-ice training demonstrations were held at the Sokolniki Arena, home base of the Spartak Moscow Hockey Club, with instructors putting players from the Soviet national junior team through their paces.

The only disappointing aspect was that Anatoly Tarasov, the godfather of Soviet hockey, was on vacation in Bulgaria at the time.

At that time the city had only four covered ice arenas. The largest was the Luzhniki Ice Palace, site of the 1972 Summit Series, with seating for 12,000. Sokolniki, in the northeast sector of the city, accommodated about 5,000, the Central Army Sports Club arena in the northwest had about 3,000 seats and the fourth, the tiny Kristall Arena in Luzhniki had none; it was simply a practice rink.

But as impressive as the Soviet system appeared, its players were by no means perfect. Ragulin was the first Soviet player I ever saw smoking a cigarette and it shattered my dream of these guys as pure athletes. When we arrived at the Sokolniki Arena for our first on-ice session, he was leaning against a car taking a drag.

We stayed at the Hotel Neptune, a boarding school for elite swimmers in Moscow's northeast quadrant. It was a Spartan existence with three people to a room in narrow single beds, barely two feet off the floor.

My roommates were Bruce Andrews, a long-distance runner of some note who was a silver medalist in the one-mile event at the 1962 Ontario high school championships, placing second behind Toronto's Bruce Kidd, and Doug Darling, director of aquatics for the City of Sudbury. Kidd had competed for Canada at the 1964 Summer Olympics.

It was Andrews, a physical education teacher at Acton District High School and graduate of Seton Hall University in East Orange, N.J., who alerted me to the tour.

I was so exhausted from the overseas flight and stressed out from a harsh experience at Soviet customs, in which our bags were turned upside down, that I didn't sleep a wink the first night. In fact, if there had been a taxi waiting outside, I would have taken it right back to the airport and flown home.

"What am I doing here?" I kept asking myself.

But I toughed it out and the short trip that saved me from total emotional collapse occurred two days later when we were bused to the hockey arena.

We had been asked to bring our skates, and the minute I started lacing them up to go on the ice and observe workouts, I started to unwind and feel at home.

On the last day of the tour, we had the thrill of a lifetime when we were given a chance to suit up and play a controlled scrimmage – with no body contact – against the Soviet national junior team. Among them was Valery Bragin, then only 19, who has since coached Russia to the gold medal at the 2011 World Junior Championship in Buffalo.

I borrowed a stick from the Soviets, and when I started to play with no gloves, a young boy watching from the sidelines noticed it, quickly ran either to a dressing room or his apartment building and returned with a pair of worn-out mitts for me to wear.

The Soviet juniors dazzled us with their speed and passing, but with players like Bob Boucher, Bryan O'Byrne, Trevor Fahey and Ron Naud on our side, we managed to keep the score down to a reasonable count.

Boucher had played for the St. Michael's Majors on the same line as Frank Mahovlich. His father Billy scored the first goal ever at the Montreal Forum while playing for the Canadiens in November 1924.

O'Byrne was a star defenceman at St. Mary's, who had played junior for the Peterborough Petes and Montreal Junior Canadiens. Fahey, a former Guelph Royals junior, had played one game for the New York Rangers in 1964-65 and at that time was starring with the St. Francis Xavier Huskies in Antigonish, N.S. Naud had played for Peterborough and captained the team at Dalhousie University.

On graduation night at the Hotel Leningradsky, we received a certificate indicating we had completed the first course conducted under the terms of the 1972 Soviet-Canadian exchange agreement, signed by Prime Minister Pierre Trudeau and Soviet Premier Alexei Kosygin.

I had hardly been in the giant GUM department store on the edge of Red Square for five minutes when I was offered 25 rubles (about $20 U.S.) for the blue Acton peewee hockey jacket I was wearing. Later, I had chances to unload my Adidas shoes and tracksuit, which in those days were not available to Soviet citizens.

I recall we sometimes had to pay for lunch, which amounted to 35 kopecks – the equivalent of about 18 cents in Canadian money.

The more adventurous among us washed it down with kvass, a traditional fermented drink made from rye bread, which was available in vending machines on many street corners in Moscow. It was tasty, the health risk involved drinking out of the same plastic glass as the person before you before it was washed!

Trying to flag down a taxi is another story. No matter how much you waved in those days, the cabs just kept flying by. However, on a subsequent trip to Russia in 2014, I discovered that ordinary citizens now will stop and give you a lift for a fee to earn extra income.

The danger there, though, is you don't have a clue who is at the wheel or where you're going to end up.

Enos also organized a Physical Education in Europe study tour in the summer of 1975, but it very nearly had to be cancelled.

I was among the group that had dinner at the Belvedere Motel in Montreal before what was supposed to be our flight across the pond.

Shortly after we boarded the bus for the airport Wendy Awde, a teacher from Richmond Hill, Ont., went into convulsions and was rushed to Lachine General Hospital. Since none of us knew each other, it was assumed she had suffered from this throughout her life.

The bus left the motel parking lot, but the assumption proved wrong when a second member of the group also started convulsing. One by one the same thing happened to almost all of us and we actually were at the airport waiting to board the plane when my turn came.

All I remember is blacking out and waking up in a bed at Lachine General with a backache that was killing me.

The first and only visitor I had was Victor Malarek, a young reporter with *The Montreal Star*, who had been assigned to cover the story. By that time more than 20 members of the contingent had suffered convulsions and the flight took off without any of us. Today, Malarek is the host of the CTV's acclaimed public affairs program *W-5*.

About 20 police officers and ambulances were sent to the airport to make sure the victims got to the hospital as quickly as possible.

We were kept overnight, but luckily doctors gave us clearance to fly to Sweden the next day.

A subsequent investigation showed that we had all consumed coleslaw, made from cabbage, which had been sprayed with a bug repellant but not washed properly in the kitchen before it was served.

While the 1975 tour focused more on sport for the masses, I did manage to take a train to Tyringe, Sweden, where former Swedish national hockey team coach Arne Stromberg was operating the country's first hockey school.

I also traveled to Moscow for the 1986 World Championship on an excursion organized by former NHL referee Bruce Hood's travel agency and headed by Billy Harris, the former Toronto Maple Leafs centre who coached Team Canada (WHA) in its eight-game series against the Soviets in 1974.

We stayed at the giant Cosmos Hotel, which has a lobby almost large enough to land a 747. The hotel, which contains more than 1,700 rooms and about 60 suites, opened in July 1979 specifically to accommodate visitors for the 1980 Summer Olympics. It also housed the main press centre for the Olympics.

Harris was almost alone in prognosticating that the Soviets would give the NHL version of Team Canada all they could handle in the 1972 Summit Series. He predicted the Soviets would win the series 6-2 and, although he was laughed at and turned out to be slightly off-base, he won praise for his knowledge of the Big Red Machine.

One day Harris, a student of history and culture, invited me to take a walk around the northwest sector of Moscow. We decided to go into a Russian Orthodox Church just to take a look. As we were entering the narthex, we looked to the left and were surprised to see an open casket with a body laid out. The church was empty, but apparently a wake had either been held there or was about to be.

It was another revelation of longstanding Soviet customs.

In a corner bake shop not far from the Cosmos, I watched Muscovites using what looked like a metal tongue depressor to test the freshness of bread on the shelves before they bought it. Then after going through that exercise, the ones without shopping bags carried the unwrapped loaves down the street with them like a football. Stores did not provide wrappings.

Traveling behind the Iron Curtain for the first time helped me form my own impressions and reduced the possibility of my swallowing everything I read in the media as the gospel. That fall, Gordie Howe's wife Colleen came home from the 1974 series between the Soviets and WHA, claiming the Canadian group was horded around like a bunch of cattle.

But I found out that as long as tourists mind their own business they could travel around Moscow on their own without any problems. The subway is one of the best in the world.

In Canada we were used to seeing Soviet players rarely smiling and often with frowns on their faces, even when they scored a goal.

My take is that they were following orders not to get too friendly with the locals, who might encourage them to defect.

I attributed the dour looks on the faces of Muscovites to the over-crowded streets in the huge city and having to jam their way on to subway cars at rush hour.

No matter where you go in the world the less space people have to move around, the more stressed they become. The smaller the Soviet city, the friendlier the people.

However, Russians have an established reputation for taking tourists by the hand to exactly where they want to go, if they get lost. And I found a lot more people there with a little knowledge of English than I did Canadians who knew some Russian.

During my travels I have learned that Canada is not the only country that takes immigrants, all Swedes are not blonde and that there are a large number of Asians and Muslims living in Russia.

I am fascinated by the overlapping of culture and language. A lot of Russians live in eastern Finland, for example, a lot of Hungarians in Slovakia.

Also in 1986 I met Igor Kuperman for the first time at Luzhniki. A top-notch writer for the *Sovietsky Sport* newspaper, he emigrated to Canada five years later, with the help of Ken Dryden and Lawrence Martin, the latter Moscow correspondent for *The Globe and Mail*, and was hired by Winnipeg Jets general manager Mike Smith.

Smith, who had been part of a similar study tour to Moscow in the summer of 1975, was fond of Soviet players, so much so that he drafted two in 1990, four in 1991 and nine more in 1992 at a time when most NHL clubs were still shying away from them. So Kuperman was the perfect fit in helping new arrivals acclimatize to life in North America and in recom-mending draft choices for the future.

Igor and his wife Natasha invited me to dinner at their apartment, where I learned another good cultural lesson, namely not all people in the Soviet Union are starving.

As we talked at the dinner table for what seemed like a half-hour, I filled up on salad, thinking that was it for the evening. Little did I know, it was just the first course, and unlike Canadians, Russians don't worry about the clock when they're dining.

I could hardly make it to the subway after polishing off the beef, chicken, potatoes, vegetables and dessert that followed. By that time it was midnight.

The 1986 World Championship was the first held after the tragic accident in which Slava Fetisov's younger brother Anatoly was killed in the car Slava was driving in Moscow.

Muscovites at the 1986 Worlds told me Fetisov was in a deep depression following the accident. However, it didn't bother his performance on the ice. He led all defencemen in the Soviet Elite League in scoring in the 1985-86 season, then sparked the Soviets to a World Championship gold medal by averaging better than a point per game to finish third in the tournament in individual scoring and earn the award as the best defender.

The Los Angeles Kings had missed the NHL playoffs, so after being named coach of Team Canada, Pat Quinn selected eight players from his own club, including Marcel Dionne and Dave Taylor, to the roster even though the Kings had finished with the second worst record in the NHL.

Nevertheless, the Canadians managed to win the bronze medal by edging Finland 4-3, mainly through a superb effort by Islanders centre Brent Sutter.

Our tickets were for seats located high in the southeast corner of the arena with no curves at the corners, so we were required to twist our necks to the right and hold them there just to see the game. When I got back to the hotel, I was looking for someone who could twist mine back to its normal spot.

Two of the Soviet stars of the Summit Series reacted quite differently to small inconveniences in the pressroom.

I remember Alexander Yakushev's reaction when someone bumped into him and splattered the ice cream cone he was eating all over his new three-piece suit. He booted what was left of the cone on the floor down the hallway, narrowly missing one of the babushkas working as an usher.

Children load up on ice cream cones at the Moscow Circus.

Oleg Spassky, the famous Soviet hockey writer, arranged for me to interview former national team captain Boris Mikhailov. I was stunned when, after the interview had barely begun, the young lady helping me with the translation explained that Mikhailov was excusing himself to get a good place in the lineup at the souvenir counter to buy a puck.

"In Canada," I replied with a grin. "Wayne Gretzky goes right to the front of the line!"

When Boris returned with the puck bearing the gold lettering and logo of the 1986 World Championship, I asked him why he had to line up.

"Well, Gretzky lives in Canada," the legendary winger said with his customary quick wit. "Over here, everybody's equal!"

The confusing incident had a happy ending, though, when Mikhailov presented me with the puck as a memento to take back home.

Goalie Vladislav Tretiak, who less than two years after the Summit Series was almost as popular in Canada as he was in the Soviet Union, provided another valuable interview.

Today Tretiak, now 65, might be the busiest man in Russia.

Elected to the State Duma, the lower chamber of the Russian Parliament as a member of the United Russia Party in 2003, Tretiak still holds his seat 13 years later.

Besides chairing the State Duma Committee on Physical Culture, Sport and Youth, he maintains the job of President of the Russian Ice Hockey Federation.

So huge is his popularity that when he came up for re-election for a third term as president in 2014, he defeated runner-up Fetisov, also a Russian hockey legend, by a landslide vote of 125-11.

If that doesn't keep him busy, Tretiak can turn his attention to his duties as a council member of the International Ice Hockey Federation, representing Russia. He has held that position since 2012.

Up for re-election to the council in May of 2016, he received the highest number of votes among male members seeking another term.

Tretiak founded the Friends of Canada organization to foster good relations between Canada and Russia and, as a result, became the first Russian to be awarded the Meritorious Service Medal by the Governor General of Canada.

A foundation named for Tretiak has aided in saving the lives of Russian children. It arranged to bring medical experts from North America to perform surgeries for children.

The Soviet Union went 10-0 in winning the gold medal at the 1989 World Championship in Sweden as Fetisov, Alexei Kasatonov, Vladimir Krutov, Igor Larionov and Sergei Makarov all played together as a unit for the last time. I filed radio reports for Broadcast News on CFRB, Toronto, from the sparkling new Globe Arena.

The Soviets' second line of Slava Bykov, Valery Kamensky and Andrei Khomutov outscored the famous Krutov-Larionov-Makarov (KLM) troika, signaling the start of a new era for the national team, which had relied so heavily on the latter trio for almost a decade.

I flew to Stockholm with Dave Norton, who had played hockey in The Netherlands and Spain after a stint with the Junior B Burlington Mohawks. Sadly, Dave was killed in 2006 when the aircraft he was piloting collided with another plane north of Toronto.

April 30 was an off-day, so the two of us took the train north to Uppsala, where we experienced all the fun associated with the annual celebration of the 'First Day of Spring'. It's called that in Sweden, even though traditional calendars mark the first day of spring on March 21.

The streets of Uppsala were absolutely jammed with people, many of them with a beer or glass of spirits in their hands to welcome the new warmer season.

My hockey travels have resulted in many more surprises. In the fall of 1989, I was about to dine in what appeared to be a classy restaurant near Moscow's Mayakovskaya Square, but changed my mind after seeing workers unload a carcass of beef from an unrefrigerated truck and slide it down a sawdust-lined ramp into the basement at the back of the building.

Instead, I ate dirt-cheap at one of the many joint-venture restaurants nearby where I was able to get meat, potatoes and red cabbage for less than $5 U.S.

While having lunch at a Japanese restaurant in Riga, the capital of Latvia in January 2011, I ordered an iceberg salad with 'Gretzky Orekh', which translated from Russian means 'walnuts'. It reminded me that Wayne Gretzky's grandfather Anthony was born in the nearby Soviet republic of Byelorussia, which now is Belarus.

The same year I hopped over to St. Petersburg, Russia, to watch the annual KHL All-Star Game.

On an off-night I took a cab to watch the local club SKA-1946 club play a Molodozhnya Hokkeynya Liga (MHL) game against Spartak Moscow. It's Russia's equivalent of the Canadian Hockey League for junior players.

While the dream game drew more than 12,000 fans to the Sports Palace the next day, the junior contest was squeezed into the practice rink of the old Yubileny Arena, where fewer than 500 fans attended, a far cry from the 9,000 the London Knights of the Ontario Hockey League have been averaging in recent years.

This is in a gigantic city of 4.5 million people, but with a world of cultural activities going on every evening. Attendance at junior games in the eastern part of Russia, where community spirit is more evident, was averaging 2,000.

Author Denis Gibbons surrounded by the huge pillars and
ornate gold décor of the Hermitage Museum in Leningrad, now
St. Petersburg.

The rink, with seats for 1,200, is attached by a tunnel to Yubileny, site
of the 1983 World Junior Championship, the only one in which Mario
Lemieux played.

The first clue I was not in an Ontario Hockey League arena surfaced
when I entered the lobby. Six security officers from the Ministry of Internal
Affairs wearing helmets directed fans through metal detectors and asked
them to have their bags scanned.

A recent suicide bombing at Moscow's Domodedovo Airport, which
killed 36 people, had created a new sense of insecurity in Russia.

The club charged no admission for games. That was my second clue.
Even teams who chose to sell tickets were offering them at a price of
between 50 and 100 rubles, which amounted to about $3 U.S.

Many of the fans were relatives or friends of the players, there to
watch the home team eke out a 2-1 victory on a hybrid ice surface, which

measured 59 metres by 28, slightly smaller than the regulation international size of 61 by 30, but still larger than the pads used in North America.

The calibre of play appeared to be middle-of-the-table Tier 2 Junior A and there was no sign of the amusements that have been introduced into Canadian rinks to entertain fans.

Pucks deflected into the stands were thrown back onto the ice to save money in a league with a very tight budget. It seemed there were more Internal Affairs Ministry officers on duty than there were fans. And in the stands some fans were catching up on their sleep during the peak of the action.

But the trip to the junior game was worthwhile. After the match, I interviewed St. Petersburg goalie Dmitry Shikin, who had backstopped Russia to a gold medal at the 2011 World Junior Championship in Buffalo only a couple of weeks before.

Shikin and SKA-1946 teammate Georgy Berdyukov were rewarded for the victory with a new Mercedes B180, one which he said he had not had time to drive yet.

"I used to have a Mazda, but I didn't like it," Shikin said. "The model I had was for girls!"

Shikin was one of nine players from the MHL who earned gold medals in Buffalo. All members of the team also received monetary rewards of varying amounts from the Russian Hockey Federation, based on their individual performance. Shikin's share was 700,000 rubles – about $25,000 U.S.

Russian junior goalie Dmitry Shikin signs an autograph for a
young fan.

In the Siberian city of Novokuznetsk, national junior team gold medalists Dmitri Orlov and Maxim Kitsyn were promised apartments by the
mayor of the city. Kitsyn later played for the Mississauga St. Michael's

Majors of the Ontario Hockey League and Orlov, a first-team all-star at the World Juniors, is now with the Washington Capitals.

None of the top 10 scorers in the league made the national junior team, indicating Russia has a lot more depth of junior talent than a lot of NHL scouts let on, nor did any of the best 10 goalies get a trip to Buffalo.

NHL clubs are reluctant to draft Russians, since there is no official transfer agreement between the league and the Russian Ice Hockey Federation.

Spectator support for the new league might be lacking but millions of Russians viewed the gold medal game on Russia's Channel 1 station.

That is, except for one.

Shikin's mother Natalia has always been afraid of her son's suffering a serious injury.

"I sat in the bathroom with the door closed," she laughed. "I watched the replay of the game only!"

Still, the MHL is the development ground for the Kontinental Hockey League (KHL).

The MHL started in 2009-10 with 22 teams. By 2016-17 it had grown to 31. In fact, Russia now also has a 28-team junior league for smaller cities. MHL clubs compete for the Kharlamov Cup, named after the legendary Russian star Valery Kharlamov.

Vladimir Yurzinov, recognized as one of Russia's all-time best hockey teachers, is a consultant for the junior league.

"The MHL was created to develop young players and coaches," he said. "We can see that it's working already. Now we have a gold medal."

By the year 2020, when the MHL has a decade of operation under its belt, Russian coaches fully expect a string of gold medals. The logic is that, starting in 2002, hockey in Russia began to improve again. Since then a record number of new arenas have been built.

Russia experienced a dying population, poverty and a war in Chechnya in the 10 years prior to that, which made it difficult to put more resources into sport.

Dmitry Efimov, the league's managing director, said he had contacted Dave Branch about setting up some exhibition games with Canadian Hockey League clubs, but when I asked him the CHL President couldn't recall ever receiving such a request.

"We want to play major junior teams from Canada, but they don't want it," Efimov told the newspaper *Sovietsky Sport*. "I can only conclude from this that they are afraid of losing."

Both junior leagues in Russia have an age limit of 21, one year higher than in Canada. Hockey Hall of Famer Sergei Fedorov believes the MHL could do an even more effective job of developing talent by extending the age limit as high as 25.

"Some guys are late bloomers," he said. "They don't reach their physical peak until the age of 25. I hate to see players disappear after they reach their 21st birthday."

When Slava Fetisov won a gold medal with the Soviet Union at the first official World Junior Championship in 1977, the country had no official junior league. During his term as Minister of Sport between 2005 and 2008, 300 new indoor hockey rinks were built.

Now Russian junior prospects are competing in anywhere from 50 to 60 games annually.

When the World Junior Championship became an IIHF-sanctioned event in the 1976-77 season, communications and transportation routes were still not fully developed in the Soviet Union, a country that spans 11 time zones. As a result, top prospects from cities and towns in the Far East sometimes were overlooked in the national team selection process.

In fact, prior to the 2009-10 season, the USSR (Russia) won 13 gold medals, for the most part using players developed in a regional, tournament-style national junior championship in which some might play as few as 25 games.

Before the 2018 World Juniors, the USSR (and later Russia) had a winning record against Canada.

The Soviets lost two World Junior Championship gold medals in a matter of just 16 seconds in 1990 and 1991. They could have clinched the gold medal by beating Sweden on the final day of the 1990 tournament in Finland.

Instead, Patrik Englund of Sweden incredibly scored with just one second left in the game in Helsinki to produce a 5-5 tie. Meanwhile in Turku, on the other side of the country, Canada rallied to beat Czechoslovakia and win the gold, backed by the standout goaltending of Stephane Fiset.

The Soviets launched a protest that Englund's goal was scored after the final buzzer had sounded, but it was rejected.

The Canadians and Soviets finished in a first place tie at 5-1-1, but Canada was awarded the gold medal because it beat the USSR 6-4 earlier in the tournament.

In 1991, with Pavel Bure starring, the Soviets needed only a win over Finland at the Regina Agridome to clinch the gold. However, the Finns tied that game 5-5 with only 15 seconds to play and the gold medal went again to Canada, which defeated the Soviet Union 3-2 on a third-period goal by John Slaney in Saskatoon.

While the youth teams of the elite clubs in Moscow got lots of practice time in the old days, house leaguers as we know them in North America rarely saw the inside of an arena. The entire Soviet house-league system, known as The Golden Puck Tournament, was played on outdoor rinks, most of them constructed in quadrangles surrounded by apartment buildings.

The Soviets used to put together a team for the World University Games every two years, but often some of the players were from the Elite League. They classified them as students because they were taking courses while playing.

Today, Russia forms its World University Games team by selecting players from the Russian Major League, which is one level below the KHL. Canada, meanwhile, is represented strictly by full-time university players who do not play professionally.

At the 2017 World University Games in Kazakhstan, Russia defeated Canada 4-1 in both the men's and women's gold medal games. The Russians used their national women's team.

The U.S. was represented by select teams from the American Collegiate Hockey Association (ACHA) club hockey league, which offers no athletic scholarships.

Meanwhile, during the skills competition at the KHL All-Star Game, the winner in the shooting accuracy competition surprisingly was Chris Simon, who although he scored 144 goals during his 15-year NHL career, mostly played the role of a goon. Simon nailed four out of five targets.

In his first season in Russia the pugilistic native of Wawa, Ont. led the KHL in penalty minutes with 236 in 40 games, an average of almost six minutes a game. He trained with Valery Belov, the coach of Russian heavyweight boxer Alexander Povetkin, who at that time had 12 knockouts in 16 professional fights

The owners of Simon's Vityaz Chekhov club had a curious reaction to his on-ice shenanigans. They made him team captain next season.

The truth is for a short time the league's image was tarnished by the hooliganism of North American players on the very weak Vityaz club. They were signed purposely to fill the arena by disreputable owners because Russian fans were becoming fond of fighting.

Vityaz, which translates into English as 'Warriors', lived up to its name in 2009-10 by instigating a brawl in a game against Avangard Omsk that resulted in a record 840 minutes in penalties. The game was eventually suspended.

The bad blood began to flow after former Washington Capitals tough guy Darcy Verot fired the puck at an Avangard player before the opening whistle.

Later in the season Verot and former NHLer Josh Gratton were questioned by police and suspended for 12 and 15 games, respectively, following another free-for-all against Avangard that started after only six seconds of play.

Simon showed no regrets.

"This is hockey, guys! We hate (Avangard) with pride," he told the website *sportbox.ru.* "We will always show emotions in matches against this opponent. This is real fighting spirit!"

Ironically, the Vityaz club's slogan is, "Who comes to us with the sword shall perish by the sword."

In an interview published last year on the Russian Hockey Federation website Boris Mayorov, a two-time Olympic gold medalist and former Soviet team captain, said Verot's tactics are nothing new.

"In my time (1960s) the Canadians quite often pulled such tricks before games with the Soviet team," he said. "They skated across the red line to purposely grab you, push you or block your way."

The night before the 2012 KHL All-Star Game in Riga, the capital of Latvia, teams of Latvian and Russian oldtimers faced each other in an exhibition game. Helmut Balderis, nicknamed *Elektrichka (the Electric Train)* because of his speed in earlier years, starred for the Latvians and one of the best Russians was 61-year-old Slava Anisin, who played in the 1972 Summit Series.

Because his last name sounds like the brand name of a popular over-the-counter medication, and also on account of the trouble it gave Team Canada, Anisin's line with Yuri Lebedev and Alexander Bodunov was dubbed the 'headache line' by Canadian sportswriters.

Prior to the All-Star Game, the media was allowed access to the dressing rooms of both teams while the Zamboni resurfaced the ice.

Being selected to play was very significant for Russian winger Slava Kozlov, who at the age of 39 was playing in his first dream game.

A two-time Stanley Cup champion with the Detroit Red Wings, Kozlov produced 356 goals and 853 points in 1,182 NHL games during a career that spanned 16 seasons with the Wings, Buffalo and Atlanta.

He still owns a share of the Detroit team record with Steve Yzerman and Johan Franzen with 12 game-winning goals in the playoffs. Yet he was never selected to play in an NHL All-Star Game.

Hockey is part of the fabric of the Kozlov family. During his days in Detroit, Kozlov's nephew Vladislav Namestnikov, now with the Tampa Bay Lightning, lived with him for awhile and often came to Red Wing practices. Namestnikov's mother Marina is Kozlov's sister. His father Evgeny 'John' was drafted by Vancouver in 1991 and played 43 NHL games for the Canucks, Islanders and Nashville.

Before the game, Anisin's son Mikhail gave a beautiful rendition of the old Italian favourite *O Sole Mio* on the ice. As a boy he had heard Luciano Pavarotti sing it at the La Scala Theatre when his father was winding down his career as a player-coach in Italy.

Mikhail then went out and scored three second-period goals for Team Ozolinsh in a 15-11 loss to Team Fedorov. The younger Anisin stands only 5-5 and weighs just 150 soaking wet, but he is lightning on skates and has a marvelous voice.

Anisin's daughter Marina Anisina, from his first marriage to figure skater Irina Chernayeva, teamed up with Gwendal Peizerat to win the gold medal in ice dancing for France at the 2002 Olympics in Salt Lake City. She was inducted into France's Legion of Honour Order, the highest award the country presents.

Slava said Misha loved karaoke, learned to sing by himself at home and performed everywhere he could. When he was just six years old he and his mother Tamara met a friend who was a singing teacher at the famous Bolshoi Theatre. She invited him to a competition there. He was successful, but said he preferred to be a hockey player.

Also in uniform for the Latvian oldtimers was former NHLer Sandis Ozolinsh, who built the Ozo Golf Club, the first 18-hole golf course in Latvia. It opened in 2002.

Ozolinsh actually didn't start playing golf until his adult years when he was with the San Jose Sharks.

He fondly recalled a visit American golfer Fred Couples made to the dressing room while he was playing for the Colorado Avalanche. On another occasion, pro Craig Stadler presented all players on the team with a new pair of golf shoes.

Kevin Dallman, a diminutive but highly-skilled defenceman from Niagara Falls, Ont., who had been drafted by Los Angeles after starring in junior with the Guelph Storm, was used as a winger during the dream game. He volunteered for the job after a last-minute injury left his team short one forward. His linemates were Fedorov and Evgeny Kuznetsov.

Dallman was playing for the Barys club in the city of Astana, Kazakhstan, at the time. The Kings had not renewed his NHL contract but he earned a lot more money in the KHL than he would have in the AHL.

He became a local hero, but eventually had to transfer to another club SKA St. Petersburg for the 2012-13 season after his wife Stacy had her visa lifted for criticizing the government of Kazakhstan on the Internet.

Slava Fetisov, considered the greatest defenceman Russia has produced, held the league record for points by a rearguard with 49 in 44 games with CSKA Moscow in 1983-84 until Dallman came along and set a new mark of 58 points in 53 games for Barys Astana in 2008-09.

In spite of his wife's difficulties, Dallman said he often wonders why more NHL players with contract disputes do not choose to play in the KHL.

"They always hear rumours about the tough living conditions and whether or not they're going to get their money," he said. "But it keeps getting better over there. I don't really know what's the negative with a lot guys going over. I don't want to knock the AHL, but this league's one step ahead of it."

Dallman and his family lived in a luxury three-bedroom apartment, which he says would likely rent for $5,000 a month in the U.S. Their children attended the American Embassy school.

He said Astana is very Americanized and life in the city is nothing like the movie *Borat,* which portrays Kazakhstan as a backward nation. The team has its own private jet, provided by the government.

However, Dallman said the local police need to lighten up a little.

"They pull you over for no reason over here," he said. "They indicated my car wasn't clean and motioned with their hands that I should make sure I get it washed."

Matt Ellison, a native of Duncan, B.C., said to make things easier he obtained a police badge, and whenever he was pulled over for an alleged offence, he just flashed the badge and was waved on.

While Dallman became a franchise player in Kazakhstan, using too many Canadians cost Vityaz Chekhov a bundle.

The club was fined 500,000 rubles (about $18,000) for using more than four imports in the same game, contrary to KHL rules. At one point Vityaz had five Canadians – Nathan Perrot, Derrick Walser, Ahren Spylo, Simon and Verot on the ice at the same time.

Vityaz officials didn't realize they had made a mistake until after the game and tried to strike Walser's name off the game sheet, but it was too late.

Coach Sergei Gomolyako, a Calgary Flames draft pick in 1989, said that in the summer when the team was signing Canadians to contracts, nobody told him about the regulations.

It was a big blow to the club's bank account coming shortly after it had been fined for not having an ambulance at the arena the night New York Rangers prospect Alexei Cherepanov, playing for Avangard Omsk, collapsed on the bench and later died.

CHAPTER 2
Meeting the secret police in Czechoslovakia

In 1983, when the Burlington Cougars midget reps paid a visit to Šumperk, Czechoslovakia, for a tournament, I was beginning to feel my oats as a continental traveler. Just when I thought the secret police was as big a hoax as the Loch Ness monster, they grabbed me.

Šumperk, a town of about 30,000, is located only a few miles from the Polish border. In those days the Soviets liked to locate their military bases near the borders of two Warsaw Pact countries, which would allow them to move either way quickly in case of an uprising.

The first three words of the Czech national anthem, 'Kde domov muj?' translate into English as 'Where is my homeland?' It's a reference to a country always trying to determine its own identity, since it has so often been occupied.

The words were written almost 180 years ago for the opera *Fidlovacka* when the Czechs were only an ethnic minority in the Austrian Empire, where the German language dominated.

Longtime citizens were more than used to political change. In 1918 the Czechoslovak army had occupied Šumperk, at that time part of what was called Sudetenland.

Many years later in 1945 the Soviet Red Army liberated Šumperk from Nazi control not long before the end of the Second World War.

By 1968, it is said, a statue of Stalin in Šumperk was the only one left in the country. Legend has it that one of Stalin's hands was cut off by a revolutionary during the uprising that summer.

Russian soldiers, the story continues, fastened it back on using glue and, after they caught the culprit, they made him stand and hold the hand in place for two hours.

In February of 1969 Jan Zajic, an 18-year-old student of the Šumperk industrial secondary school, set himself on fire in Prague and died to show his opposition to the occupation of his country by Warsaw Pact soldiers.

U.S. President Ronald Reagan publicly declared the Soviet Union an evil empire as tensions heightened in the cold war in 1983. In response, Reagan was compared to Hitler by Yuri Andropov, general secretary of the Communist Party of the Soviet Union.

The Soviets feared a nuclear training exercise, carried out by NATO, was a serious threat to countries in the Eastern Bloc. As a result, nuclear missiles were moved from the Soviet Union to sites where they could be launched in Europe, if necessary.

Adding fuel to the fire, the Soviet Union had shot down a South Korean airliner with 269 passengers on board on Sept. 1, 1983, and was condemned by almost the whole world.

Milan Janecek, a friend who moved to Burlington from the town of Martin, Czechoslovakia in 2000, told me when he was serving his compulsory two-year term in the Czechoslovak army it was mandatory for him and all the other soldiers to sit and watch the funerals of Soviet leaders Yuri Andropov in February 1984 and Konstantin Chernenko in March 1985.

Janecek said they were supposed to sit and look sad, but in any case most of them viewed it as a day of rest from having to do heavy training outdoors in the winter.

A Soviet team was scheduled to play a six-game exhibition series against the U.S. Olympic team in American rinks in 1983 but pulled out of the series because they feared reprisals.

Also, for the same reason, the Hamilton, Ont., Huskies bantam team, which was headed to Europe after Christmas to play in the Finnair Cup, dropped the Soviet portion of the tour and replaced it with a visit to Sweden.

However, the Cougars had raised funds in advance and decided to go ahead with a planned tour of Czechoslovakia in November.

It was a Saturday morning and Burlington was scheduled to play its first game in the Great October Revolution Tournament that afternoon.

The Burlington Cougars midgets and Czech national midget team
at the opening ceremonies of the tournament in Šumperk.

We'd already been in Czechoslovakia for four days and had played games in the Bohemian region of the country, south and west of Prague. Šumperk, known as the Gateway to the Jeseniky Mountains, was to be our home for the next six days.

In those days the Soviet Union had 100,000 troops stationed in Czechoslovakia alone, to say nothing of their deployments in other Iron Curtain countries like Poland and Hungary. That's more than the entire Canadian Forces, which had only 87,000 men and women in uniform.

The 375th tank regiment of the Soviet Army was based in Šumperk.

The morning after we arrived, I set out on my usual solo tour through town, snapping shots of stores, shoppers, churches etc.

About noon hour I dropped into a restaurant named 'Pod Kaštany' where I struck up a conversation with a couple of Soviet soldiers having a beer. We chatted for a short time about their life in the region and their interest in hockey.

Later I was wandering near the base when all of a sudden a uniformed officer came out of the compound and indicated I should not take photos of it.

Then a small Skoda automobile pulled up and a plainclothesman with a flat top hat, looking like someone out of the Bowery Boys, got out and produced some credentials.

When the mysterious man asked to see my passport, I told him I had left it at the hotel. I further explained that I had not taken any photos of the military installations and had no intention of doing so.

He did not speak English. Naively, I thought the guards had sent for a taxi to help me get back to the hotel, but the officer told me I would have to accompany him in his car to the hotel.

We arrived at an intersection near the hotel when he suddenly told me we would be going directly to the local police station instead. It was not until then that it registered with me that I was in the hands of the STB, the Czechoslovak secret police.

Doing my best to keep cool, I continued to make various requests which included permission to go to the hotel and show my passport first and a chance to call the hotel and ask to speak to our group interpreter.

We'd been at the police station about 15 minutes debating the matter when he finally agreed to drive me to the hotel and get my passport. A woman at the desk, who spoke very good English, explained to me they suspected I had taken photos of military objects and if I turned over the film from the two cameras around my neck, the matter would be finished.

I handed over the films and the officer put them in a special envelope marked that they should be returned to me later.

For the next six days I was on pins and needles, in effect under house arrest. I was never jailed, but the STB officer visited me a couple of times for further questioning.

Two days later I was having lunch at the hotel with Canadian Consul-General Darcy Thorpe, who had made a special trip from Prague to support the Cougars. I got up from the table to retrieve the latest copy of *The Hockey News*, which the Trail, B.C., native had requested for afternoon reading.

As I passed through the hotel lobby on the way to my room, I was surprised to meet the same officer who had picked me up two days before. He told me I was to report to the police station the next day to meet with authorities.

My so-called mini-trial was held in a second-floor office, where I was questioned through an interpreter and was finally cleared after promising never to go near a Soviet military base again. They believed that I was in the country, strictly on hockey business.

I had asked to have a representative there – either a lawyer or Jan Janda, our Czech guide, but was refused.

The day I was detained I was wearing a bright orange and blue jacket, sporting the colours of the Burlington Lions-Optimist Minor Hockey Association (BLOMHA). I am convinced one of the deciding factors in the decision not to prosecute or jail me was that the Czechoslovaks came to the conclusion no self-respecting spy would go out on the streets wearing an orange and blue jacket!

Slezan Opava, the local team, prepared a dinner for the Cougars in connection with their next game in Opava. Just before we were about to start eating a woman I suspect was a secret police agent, switched seats with another man so she could be closer to me. This time I was smart enough to keep my mouth shut.

The Cougars lost 7-3, and after the game we took the red-eye bus directly back to Prague, where we arrived on the outskirts at 4 a.m. and spent the night in a dormitory.

The next day at the Hotel International Janda told me in no uncertain terms to remove all things suspicious from my room. Later, while we were sightseeing near Prague Castle, another mystery man carrying a briefcase appeared and, trying not to tip his hand, kept an eye on me from about 40 yards away.

When we left the country, a passport official at the airport made a special note of my personal information.

Following the Velvet Revolution, the peaceful end of Communism in Czechoslovakia, the Soviet army left Šumperk in May 1990.

You can imagine how happy I was when Vaclav Havel took over as president of the country and fired all the STB agents. Shortly after that, almost all of the 100,000 Soviet soldiers packed up and headed home.

In 2015, I applied to the new Czech government to view my secret police files and on Jan. 6, 2016, a letter arrived at my home from the Security Services Archive in Prague, informing me they would send them for a fee of $50. I never saw my films again, however.

Burlington made it to the bronze medal game of the Šumperk tournament before losing 4-2 to the Slovak selects.

From that team Dan Currie went on to lead the AHL in goals twice and played briefly with the Los Angeles Kings on a line with Wayne Gretzky. Defenceman Paul Constantin was one of the sparkplugs of Lake Superior State University's NCAA championship victory in the 1991-92 season and was named MVP of the Frozen Four tournament.

Team captain Mike Moes played four years at the University of Michigan for Red Berenson and became captain of the Wolverines. Tom Neziol, a seventh-round draft pick of New Jersey in 1987, played college hockey at Miami of Ohio for four years.

The nucleus of the club had won the OMHA championship the year before as minor midgets, recording an overall record of 58-6.

Jim Smillie, the midgets' mentor, had coached the Burlington bantams led by Lance Nethery, to the Loblaw's Cup championship, the all-Ontario title for bantams in the 1975-76 season. Nethery later played for the New York Rangers.

The 1983 midget team was quartered in a cozy country inn called Znamek Sobotin, not far from Šumperk. There they dined on tasty chickens, which were so big coach Smillie swore they had four legs. It was just a coincidence, I suppose, that the sponsor for his championship bantam club in 1976 was a fast food outlet called 'Big Chicken, Little'!

In Šumperk, I visited a family that built its own house for $35,000. In those days there were no land taxes required for new houses for the first 25 years. An 800-square-metre lot could be leased from the government for 100 years for only $800.

Older citizens were hard-working but the younger generation, born under a Communist government which guaranteed everybody a job, was getting used to simply showing up for eight hours a day and drawing a paycheque. There were clerks in every aisle of the grocery stores, but if you asked them to find something for you in another aisle, they wouldn't leave their post. It was almost as if they were employing a zone defence!

When the American film *Coal Miner's Daughter* played in a small Czechoslovak town, the title was changed to *The First Lady of Country Music*, not as a tribute to singer Loretta Lynn but because promoters feared the locals would think it was about work and stay away in droves.

Jaroslav Holik, a former national team star and the father of Bobby Holik, who won two Stanley Cups with the New Jersey Devils, offered a different point of view in an interview with *The Toronto Star* in January 2002.

"Czechs are very handy," he said. "We are used to building our own homes ourselves. We know how to bring water into the houses, how to repair something, things like that.

"My impression of Americans is that they can barely cut their grass themselves. They order professionals in to do everything.

"Children at school here know much more than American children, in general, not just in hockey. We know how to play the clever game.

"But it's not about being colourful. America is built on a system of individualism. Since we know we are a little nation, the only chance we have is to work together, to co-operate and use our brains."

The Czechs had just finished an incredible five-year stretch of international hockey success in which they won an Olympic gold medal, three World Championships and two World Junior Championships. The elder Holik was head coach of both junior championship teams in 2000 and 2001.

In the town of Kadan, with a population of 26,000, Burlington played on a floodlit outdoor rink, where 'Papa' Klima, the father of future NHLer Petr Klima, drove the Zamboni. Snow and wind made it difficult for the players to see where they were going. The temperature was -10 C.

There was so much coal dust in the air that handkerchiefs turned black when fans blew their noses. But coal was king in Czechoslovakia in those days. It fueled power plants, heated most apartment buildings and homes during the winter and, just by coincidence, kept laundry ladies in business washing once lily-white hankies.

In Pribram, where uranium-mining was the major industry, the Cougars game with the host club drew only 300 fans in a renovated 6,000-seat arena because Czechoslovakia's national soccer team was playing Italy on national TV in a qualifying match for the 1984 European Championship.

While walking across the Charles Bridge in Prague, I encountered a young woman promoting literature for the Jehovah's Witness movement. I pinched myself to see whether I really was just a few blocks from the Czechoslovak Communist Party headquarters.

Filing my radio reports to CHML in Hamilton was not an easy task. In the town of Kadan, for example, I had to book the call at the desk in the lobby, then run back up to my room on the second floor to wait for the connection. When I got it, the lady suggested it would be better for me to take it in an office in the lobby, so I ran back down again.

It took anywhere from 15 minutes to an hour for the connection to be made from the time I booked the call and made it clear that I wanted it to be collect. The quality of the line ranged anywhere from very good to almost non-existent.

The previous year in the Soviet Union I had to pay $50 American up front for each call because long-distance collect calls were not permitted.

Czechoslovak children were required to learn Russian as a second language in school, so they could converse in the language to a certain extent. But their parents, because of the Soviet invasion of Czechoslovakia in 1968, resented being spoken to in Russian.

However, after I explained that my first language is English and I was a student of languages in Canada, they accepted Russian as a way for us to communicate. Older folks, who lived through the Second World War, still spoke some German.

By the 1990s a new generation had arrived and a Russian – defenceman Alexei Yashkin – was actually named captain of the Vsetin club in the Czech Extraleague. He won six league championships in the Czech Republic, after concluding his career in Russia in 1993 and finally retired in 2005 at age 39.

During his final home game against Karlovy Vary, he was given the honor of playing with his older son Mikhail, who was only 13 at the time and the youngest player ever to appear in a league game.

Yashkin's younger son Dmitri was drafted by St. Louis in 2011 and now plays for the Blues.

There were six major stages to go through in exiting Czechoslovakia at the airport in 1983. First was a lineup to show your passport and visa. Next we had to haul our luggage over to the scales to be weighed. There was a second passport control at which visas, now invalid, were taken away.

The fourth step was to pass through electronic doors, which checked us to make sure we weren't carrying any weapons. Fifth was the third and final passport control. The sixth and final stage was a personal search of hand luggage and a once over lightly with a hand-held electronic detector.

All this 18 years before 9/11 in the U.S.

Grey political clouds also hovered over the seven-game tour of Czechoslovakia, made by the 1980-81 edition of the Cougars.

Canadian Embassy officials revealed they had been on a 'red alert' during the Burlington club's visit because of a tense situation in nearby Poland. Staff at the embassy were under instructions to assist in every way if it became necessary for the Burlington group to leave the country early.

Frank Buchanan, head of the Burlington delegation, said he had been told of a buildup of Soviet troops in the area of Tabor, 65 miles south of Prague, when the team traveled there for an exhibition game.

Colonel Michael Zrymiak, at that time the Canadian Forces attache to the Canadian Embassy in Prague, took the time to root for the Burlington midgets on two occasions in January 1981. The first was a 6-5 victory over the local club in Tabor, the second a 3-2 loss to the Prague Selects at the Julius Fucik Sports Hall.

Shortly after the team arrived back in Canada, Colonel Zrymiak was arrested and questioned for more than eight hours after being stopped by police while driving near Tabor. He was accompanied by Wing Commander Oliver Knight, the British air attache, who was accused of spying and evading police.

We didn't win many games behind the Iron Curtain because we were often matched against all-star teams, or in a couple of cases, the national team for that age group – 15, 16 or whatever. There was always a debate among us internally whether the Eastern Europeans did this on purpose so that they would always win and give a boost to communism or whether they acknowledged from the beginning Canadian teams were stronger and they had to do this to make the games competitive.

On the 1980-81 tour Burlington won just two of seven games. However, two of the losses were to the national Under-17 team and two more to the national U-16 squad.

When we faced the U-17 team in Sobeslav the hosts, with future NHLer Petr Klima in the lineup, romped to a 17-3 victory.

Future Stanley Cup winner Petr Klima, then just 16, scores against Burlington on New Year's Day, 1981.

Two days later, on New Year's Day 1981 in the same rink, the Burlington kids played an immensely improved game, bowing only 4-1 to the same team even though several Canadian players were out of the lineup with severe colds.

Just two years later Klima was playing for Czechoslovakia in the World Junior Championship. He defected to West Germany in 1985 while the Czech national team was training there and eventually signed with the Detroit Red Wings. He was the first Czechoslovak player to defect to a U.S.-based team.

David Volek and Leo Gudas suited up for the national U-16 team. Volek later scored 95 goals in six seasons with the New York Islanders and notched the winning goal in overtime to eliminate the two-time Stanley Cup champion Pittsburgh Penguins from the playoffs in 1992-93.

Gudas, a bronze medalist at the 1992 Olympics, is the father of Radko Gudas of the Philadelphia Flyers.

Petr Briza, the Czechoslovak U-17 goalie, also became an Olympic bronze medalist in 1992, earning himself a shiny new Skoda automobile with the rest of his teammates.

The star of the 1980-81 Burlington team was Mark Jooris, who went on to win an NCAA championship with Renselaar Polytechnic Institute (RPI) in Troy, N.Y., in 1984-85, playing on the same line with Adam Oates and John Carter. The line produced 97 goals in just 38 games. Jooris' son Josh is now in the NHL with the Carolina Hurricanes.

Jeff Johnson from the 1980-81 midgets earned a scholarship to Cornell where he played football for the Big Red before spending two seasons as a pro in the CFL, one with Hamilton and the other with Calgary.

Most of the players on the 1980-81 Burlington midget team had played on the Burlington bantam club that lost to Brian Bellows and St. Catharines in the OMHA finals two years before.

When the midgets played their first game against the Prague Selects at the Slavia Arena on Dec. 28, 1980, about 30 staffers from the Canadian and British embassies were among the crowd of 2,000.

Crowds generally were in the 800 to 1,500 range. Exceptions were 2,000 for the opener and 3,000 at a sparkling new arena in Slany against Czechoslovakia's national midget team.

In those days many Czechoslovak arenas had seating on only one side. In fact, the top half-dozen rows on the other side were equipped only with railings, so fans in that area stood for the whole game.

Ushers wearing red armbands personally directed spectators to their seats in Prague, and if they objected, they were told in no uncertain terms they had to sit there. Ushers were the most powerful people in the arenas.

A few years later a man accompanying a team from British Columbia was charged with assaulting an usher under similar circumstances and was held by Czechoslovak police for two months before being released.

Before and after the games Czechoslovak children crowded around the Burlington team bus to trade their hockey club pins for scrumptious 'Zhvatzhky z Kanady' – bubblegum from Canada.

"We have our own (bubblegum) here," explained one of the young chompers, "but it is not so fine."

Since there was a scarcity of material goods in the Eastern Bloc in those days, Czechoslovaks looked forward to gifts from North America. However, when we met with local officials at City Hall, there never seemed to be enough to go around for the number of people.

When one official in Tabor didn't get the hockey stick his colleagues were presented with, he frowned and snapped, "It's OK, I've got a Russian one, anyway!"

We stayed at the International Hotel, which resembled a Soviet-style building, and were surprised to meet a few staff members from African countries like Libya and Nigeria. The International Hotel was the largest building in Prague built in the mode of Stalinist architecture with a giant red star on top. In 1968 Soviet tanks rolled right past the front door on their way to quell a political uprising.

Today it is called the Crowne Plaza and is a prime location for movie shoots.

A mother and child out for a stroll in Prague in December 1980.

I filed radio reports to CHML in Hamilton from Czechoslovakia. The most important words I relayed to the hotel operators in the Iron Curtain country were 'Kanada zahplahteet' – translation – 'Canada will pay', assuring them I was reversing the charges!

In Czechoslovakia, the national dish is veprzhova, knedlik, a zeli – pork with sauerkraut and dumplings. It's as popular as fish and chips in Canada.

Walter Sedlbauer, the father of former NHLer Ron Sedlbauer, accompanied us in 1980, returning to the country where he was born. While there, he was presented with the pin of the soccer club he played for in the town of Zlin many years earlier.

Our boys, who come from one of the richest cities in Canada, learned a good lesson about how the other half lives. They had been told before they left home that, if their hosts gave them as much as one orange for dessert, they should be thankful.

Nevertheless, there was a friendly atmosphere even in the days of communism. When we played at a new arena in Slany, all the Canadian mothers were presented with flowers and ushered to seats in the VIP section.

In the winter of 1980-81, there was little of appeal in smalltown grocery stores. Oranges, imported from Africa were shrivelled. There might be two bags of potatoes, perhaps a turnip and about a dozen assorted vegetables, most of them looking dried out.

There was a shortage of beef in Czechoslovakia and 75 per cent of our meals included pork in some form.

The team stayed in the tiny Park Hotel in the village of Hluboka, a building normally used only during the summer months. The hotel was opened specifically to house our Canadian contingent, but it took three days for the heat to come on fully.

While spending New Year's Eve of 1980 there, we enjoyed a full turkey dinner and watched celebrations on TV until midnight.

But at the stroke of 12, the screen switched to something more political. One by one the leaders of all socialist countries appeared on the tube to bring greetings for the new year.

It was a sad reminder to the country's 14 million people of the bureaucratic snares that awaited them along any imaginary path of New Year's resolutions they may be dreaming about to improve their lives. It meant more standing in line to buy meat and vegetables, spending their life's savings for just one holiday outside the country and elections with just one party to vote for.

"I am not happy that I cannot travel very much," a Czech acquaintance, who saved for five years for a trip to Cuba, told me. "But on the other hand, we cannot be unhappy all the time, so we just have to make ourselves happy."

Czechoslovakia's Communist government provided free daycare, and parents took full advantage of it.

Czechoslovakia, we learned, has mostly cloudy and humid weather in the wintertime. However, there is one area near the border of East Germany, nicknamed 'Siberia', which had a ton of snow.

On the coldest day of January in Prague the thermometer was scarcely below zero centigrade (32 F), but a tremendous amount of moisture in the air made it feel much worse and the cold cut through you like a knife. The dampness and coal dust in the atmosphere made breathing more than just an average task.

In 1981, car prices in Czechoslovakia started at 80,000 crowns ($8,000), but workers averaged only about $300 per month in take-home pay.

That's one reason the metro system in Prague was excellent. The standard fare in Prague was just one crown (10 cents).

Almost everybody in the group was wandering around hacking and coughing. The standing joke was that we put an extra sweater on when we were inside and took it off again when we went outside!

Parents of the players paid $1,423 for the 15-day excursion to Czechoslovakia and Denmark. The Czechoslovaks paid the land expenses of OMHA teams for an official party of 30, plus six crowns a day for spending money per person.

In 1989, I spent a week in Czechoslovakia, where I watched the Czechoslovak and Soviet national teams play a three-game exhibition series in Ostrava, Gottwaldov and Prague. It was the first time in seven years the Soviets had played without the Famous First Five of Igor Larionov, Sergei Makarov, Vladimir Krutov, Slava Fetisov and Alexei Kasatonov.

After landing in Prague on Saturday, Oct. 28, I took what I thought would be an uneventful cab ride to my downtown hotel. As the driver neared the Ambassador Hotel on Wenceslas Square, the traffic started to back up and I could see smoke rising from the square.

The entrance to the square on all sides had been barricaded after security forces used tear gas to disperse a large group of demonstrators, pushing for the end of communism in Czechoslovakia.

I paid the driver and got out of the car three blocks from the square, checked with a receptionist at a smaller hotel to see if things had quieted down and had to carry my heavy bags on foot to the Ambassador.

Security forces in full riot gear and carrying rifles were still on the streets, although the crowd had dispersed by that time.

This was the beginning of the Velvet Revolution, which led to the overthrow of the Communist government and the arrival of former dissident playwright Vaclav Havel as president.

The museum in Prague at the top of Wenceslas Square still has marks where the shells from tanks made an impression during the uprising in the summer of 1968.

On the way into the city from Ruzyne Airport in May 2004 for the World Championship, the cab driver pointed out hundreds of lilac trees and told me, ironically, the Czechoslovaks had welcomed the Soviets with lilac branches in 1945 when they came to liberate them from the Nazis.

When the war ended in 1945, both the Nazis and Allies left a lot of military equipment like tanks, trucks and motorcycles with sidecars there. While in the western part of the Czech Republic Lucie Seifertova, a driver working for Czech tourism, took me to a spot in the country near Plzen, where her husband was taking part in a Second World War battle re-enactment.

I also visited Karlovy Vary, where by that time rich Russians had bought up almost all of the spa hotels. Czech citizens can get a prescription from their doctor entitling them to free treatment at the spas. However, they must pay for their travel and accommodation.

The air went out of the World Championship tournament at the well-appointed new Sazka Arena when the Czechs were upset 3-2 by the United States in the quarterfinals, just two nights after they had dominated Canada in a 6-2 win.

Because of the early exit of the Czech team, people were trying to unload tickets and there were even plenty of empty seats at the gold medal game in which Canada rallied from a 3-1 deficit to beat Sweden 5-3.

While at the tournament I interviewed Otto Jelinek, Canada's former minister of sport and a world-class figure skater. Jelinek, at that time head of Deloitte Touche for Western Europe, was helping the arena to book events and also touting it as part of a bid to bring the 2020 Summer Olympics to Prague. However, the bid never was made and the 2020 Games have since been awarded to Tokyo, Japan.

A native of Czechoslovkia, Jelinek defected in 1948 when the Communist government took over his father's factory.

Otto and his sister Maria won a World Championship gold medal for Canada at Prague in 1962. They did it under tremendous pressure because there always was a chance they would be arrested because of their earlier defection.

It was a significant event in figure skating history for another reason. The 1961 championships were scheduled to be held in Prague but were cancelled after the entire figure skating team of the United States was killed in a plane crash in February 1961 on its way to the Czechoslovak capital.

Jelinek was appointed Canada's Ambassador to the Czech Republic in August 2013.

On the Charles Bridge I witnessed one of the negative side effects of the change from communism. A group of British hooligans, who had flown to Prague at a dirt-cheap rate for a bachelor party, were kicking the living daylights out of a homeless person who was laying on the ground.

I stayed in the Husov Dum pension near the centre of the city. It was named after Jan Husov, who led a reformation against the Catholic Church in the days when indulgences were being sold.

Beer, the national drink, was so cheap in Prague that if you ordered a $5 combo at Kentucky Fried Chicken you had your choice of drinks – soda pop or beer. Statistics show Czechs lead the world in drinking their most famous product, averaging 157 litres per person a year, placing them ahead of Ireland and Germany.

Richard Moravec, whom I met at the tournament, is a fine example of a young Canadian who went abroad to seek his future.

Even though he had a diploma in broadcasting and communications from Niagara College in Welland, Moravec could not find a job, save a short stint as the play-by-play man for the Junior C Caledonia Corvairs and Glanbrook Rangers on Cablenet in Hamilton.

His parents, Jan and Jana, were born in the former Czechoslovakia. So he followed them when they moved back to the Czech Republic and started work dealing with the heads of multinational corporations who were establishing headquarters in the former Communist country.

Under communism, the state owned 97 per cent of all businesses in Czechoslovakia. By 2004 that figure dropped to less than 20 per cent.

The Moravec family had inherited land from relatives that had been confiscated by the former Communist government. Richard's parents left Czechoslovakia as newlyweds in 1967 for political reasons.

"One of the inspirations that led me to come to Prague was that when I graduated in Canada student unemployment rates were between 40 and 50 per cent," he said. "The salary was terrible, but because I spoke English I was hired in public relations."

Prague is the crossroads of Europe, a link between western Europe and the former Eastern Bloc. Both the mountains of Austria and beaches of the Mediterranean are within easy access for skiers and sunbathers, respectively.

For young women behind the Iron Curtain, marrying a hockey player instantly provided them with a better standard of living. Marcela Kadlecova said that, after marrying Czechoslovak national team defenceman Arnold Kadlec at the age of 19, she was surprised to hear her closest friends finally speaking to her in very formal Czech.

CHAPTER 3
Facing off against Soviet youth teams

It wasn't long after the Soviet Union had proved it could play with the NHL's best players in 1972 that its ice hockey federation indicated an interest in testing youth hockey players against North American teams.

In the 1970s, Soviet midget teams started to tour Canada, playing mostly in Quebec, but the Ontario Minor Hockey Association wanted no part of them. OMHA secretary-manager Vern McCallum said in 1979 the Soviets wanted a guarantee of $4,000 a game to play in Ontario. He said the OMHA was having enough trouble breaking even on its Finnish and Swedish team tours.

McCallum said the Soviets would not even guarantee that an Ontario club would get a return visit to the USSR, although the champion of the Wrigley Cup national midget championship tournament was being sent overseas starting with the Verdun Maple Leafs in the 1973-74 season.

The Maple Leafs then played a series of games in the Soviet Union. There were only two television channels there at the time, but the national viewing audience for the last game of the tour was reported by officials in Moscow to be 100,000.

The Wrigley Tournament was the predecessor of today's Telus Cup.

The same season, the Soviets sent the midget club of the Central Army Sports Club over for a series of exhibition games in Quebec. They went undefeated on the tour but Toronto Maple Leafs owner Harold Ballard, who was not fond of them, was so upset that he convinced the Soviet team to stay for one more game.

Ballard agreed to host it at Maple Leaf Gardens with the Soviet midgets facing a team of players made up of midget-age (16-year-old) players who were playing with the Junior A Toronto Marlboros and Junior B Markham Waxers.

This time, the Canadian team won 4-1 before a sellout crowd. Future NHLers John Tonelli, John Anderson, Mark Napier and Greg Millen were on the team. Although they were playing junior, they were only 16 just like Slava Fetisov and the other Soviet players.

Ballard was satisfied he had countered any arguments that the Soviets were producing better hockey prospects than Canada.

By 2002, when a team of 13 yearolds from Spartak Moscow came to Burlington for an exhibition game, Russian officials had been allowing their boys to be billeted in Canadian homes for some time. It wasn't long before a game of hide-and-seek developed with all the boys on Autumn Hill Crescent, where Burlington defenceman Evan Zych lived, joining in.

Most of the Spartak kids spoke English, and because they grew up following the breakup of the Soviet Union, they were far more familiar with Western ways than I had envisioned.

In the fall of 1982 the Burlington Cougars bantam club strengthened Canada's position as the world's No. 1 hockey nation by winning a four-team tournament in the city of Minsk, capital city of Byelorussia, one of 15 republics in the Soviet Union. The Cougars became the first OMHA team below midget (16) age to play in the USSR.

A poster advertises the first tournament involving youth teams
from Canada and the Soviet Union in Minsk in 1982

The team lost only one game on its European tour – that by a slim margin of 10-9 to a Soviet team strengthened by five players who were one year older.

In an article, headlined 'Byli zharkimi lyedoviyeh batal' ('There were hot battles on the ice'), the newspaper *Vyechyerny Minsk* previewed the tournament in these words:

"Taking part in it are three Byelorussian teams – Yunost, Dynamo and Burvestnik, along with our guests from the city of Burlington. All of them are 13 and 14 years old, but when they put on their 'suits of hockey armor' and go out on to the ice, then they appear much older. Their courage is the same, if not more, than that of adult teams. Evidence of that is the hot battles which have taken place during three days on the ice of the arena of the Yunost Hockey School."

Burlington's Paul Constantin was named best defenceman in the tournament and teammate Jeff Boose the best goalie.

At the closing ceremony the Burlington kids, unaccustomed to Soviet traditions, accepted the championship trophy and captain Rod Anthony, who stood only five feet tall and weighed 100 pounds soaking wet, raised it high over his head in celebration.

It turned out to be a samovar (Russian teapot) and the lid came off, tumbling down to the ice and just missing Rod's head!

Burlington captain Rod Anthony hoists the Russian samovar in
Minsk. On the right are tournament award winners Jeff Boose
(jacket) and Paul Constantin.

A decade later while playing at the University of Windsor, Anthony
received the Olympic Shield as the school's Athlete of the Year.

Later that season (1982-83) the bantams made it all the way to the
OMHA Triple-A finals before losing to the Peterborough Petes.

Five years later Dmitry Medvedev, one of the Burvestnik overage players,
was playing for the Soviet Union at the World Junior Championship in
Czechoslovakia and took part in the famous bench-clearing brawl in a
game against Canada at Piestany.

Dan Currie was only 14 when he first faced goalie Alexei Scheblanov at
the tournament. Burlington won that game against Yunost Minsk 5-4, with
Currie scoring one of the five goals.

Six years later the two faced each other again in the key game of the
1988 World Junior Championship at Moscow's Luzhniki Arena. Although
Currie didn't score, Canada also won that game 3-2, behind the spectacular goaltending of Jimmy Waite who made 38 saves. The Canadians

went on to win the gold medal and Currie averaged a point per game in seven matches.

By this time my knowledge of the world was growing, but at the same time my world was getting smaller, in a sense. Here were two lads from Canada and two from the Soviet Union, living 10,000 miles apart but meeting through sport time and time again.

Burlington Cougars players stand at attention for the Canadian national anthem in Minsk.

In what is now Belarus, our boys found out there was little cola to drink and that the most popular drink was birch juice. But they loved the ice cream and found out that they were being hosted by extremely hospitable people.

After Burlington won the tournament, local fans actually stood in the cold outside the old Gorky Park ice rink to applaud our players as they made their way to the bus. We all shouted back 'bolshoy spahseebah' (thank-you very much) to acknowledge the applause.

I discovered that most locals were far more interested in the success of the Dynamo Minsk football club, which had surprised all the experts by winning the USSR championship, than they were about ice hockey.

Since they couldn't find a bottle of cola anywhere in Minsk, they drank the Pribaltiskaya Hotel in Leningrad almost dry of the stuff when they arrived there for a stopover on the way to Finland for more games.

At the same hotel our 14 yearolds rushed into the dining room towards what looked to them like chocolate cake. Much to their disappointment, it turned out to be liver pate!

It was while I was in Leningrad with the bantams in 1982 that I got a behind-the-scenes look into the lifestyle of Soviet Elite League players. I had heard that Moscow Dynamo would be practising at the Yubileny Arena, so I took the subway there to have a look.

As I approached the sports palace, I was shocked to see Dynamo star Alexander Maltsev, who holds the all-time record for games played with the Soviet national team at 321, riding on a huge pile of hockey equipment bags in the back of an old truck.

He gave all the appearances of a humble man living on a shoestring, relative to players of similar talent in the NHL, albeit one with an excellent sense of humour.

When I was introduced to Maltsev as a Canadian, he replied through an interpreter wryly, "If he's a Canadian, how come he's not drunk?"

Maltsev was recalling the 1972 series when many of the Canadian fans who traveled to Moscow for the final four games were wandering around the streets of the city inebriated after Paul Henderson scored the winning goal in Game 8.

Sadly, in later years thieves broke into Maltsev's Moscow apartment and made off with memorabilia, which included his gold medals, trophies and souvenirs from the 1972 Summit Series.

During the SKA practice, I was introduced to the famous Soviet hockey song 'Trus ne igrayet v hokkei' (Cowards Don't Play Hockey), which in those days was played at every league game as the teams skated onto the ice.

It was written by the famous Soviet composer Alexandra Pakhmutova, who was kind enough to mail me a copy after I wrote her a letter.

Aggie Kukulowicz, who was Team Canada's official interpreter at the 1972 Summit Series, owned the Canadian rights to distribute it, but it never happened.

Kukulowicz spoke Russian, French, German, Polish and Ukrainian and was highly respected by the Soviets since he had been stationed and lived in Moscow for five years as an employee of Air Canada Cargo

During visits to Leningrad in both 1982 and 1985, I visited Abram and Svetlana Kagan and their family, who lived in an apartment not far from the Akademicheskaya metro station in the northern part of the city.

At that time the Kagans were feeding a family of four on a monthly income of about 400 rubles (then about $235 U.S.), and they were living above average by Soviet standards.

Before leaving home, I had arranged to visit them and drop off some goods from their relatives in Canada. Normally, I would have taken the subway directly to their apartment but this time I took the precaution of going to an outside pay phone and calling them first just in case the phones in the hotel were bugged. Soviet citizens were not allowed to enter international hotels.

Quality goods could be purchased in the Soviet Union at Beryozka shops and in Czechoslovakia at Tuzek shops with Canadian and American dollars. However, locals were not allowed to shop there.

Kagan, who was subject to monitoring by the KGB because he was Jewish and had indicated an interest in emigrating to North America, then came downtown by tram, met me and took me to their apartment.

They had a simple four-room flat. The largest room, used for dining during the daytime, doubled as a bedroom in the evening.

"Fifty rubles of my monthly income is taken off in taxes," Kagan said. "And I must pay 30 for the apartment. The rest all goes for food."

Needless to say the family had no car, which in 1982 would have cost them 6,300 rubles – almost two years' salary – for even the cheapest model.

But public transportation was cheap in the city. Five kopecks – about a dime – would get you a ride anywhere in Leningrad on the modern Pushkin subway system. At rush hour, though, you had to be ready to use your arms and elbows for protection as you pushed your way on to the car and just plain got carried by the flow.

Later the Kagans moved to the U.S. and Abram became a professor of mathematics at the University of Maryland. He also is a highly skilled chess player.

U.S. Congressman Jack Kemp, the former Buffalo Bills quarterback who later became Bob Dole's Republican running mate in the 1996 presidential election, Senator Bill Bradley, a former All-American in basketball at Princeton and pro with the New York Knicks and Senator Bill Armstrong of Colorado, chairman of the Republican Party Policy Committee, had already visited the family in an effort to hasten the procedure for their emigration to the U.S.

Svetlana and her daughter Clara had been sent an invitation to come to Canada by her sister Mila Khayutin of Hamilton

While Moscow streets were full of men in Army uniforms going back and forth to office jobs carrying briefcases during my first trip to the Soviet Union in 1974, Navy personnel dominated the streets of Leningrad, which is a port on the Baltic Sea.

Moving on to Finland, the Cougars played in a tournament in Rauma, a shipbuilding town on the west coast. The town has a population of about 30,000 and in those days the largest industry was Rauma Repola, which built icebreakers for several countries, including the Soviet Union.

Canals that criss-crossed the town were so popular that when a citizen of Rauma died the first question asked was, "What kind of a boat did he have?" and the second, "How's the family doing?"

Burlington established strong ties with Rauma, dating back to 1973 when a juvenile team from the Finnish town played in Canada.

With gasoline prices too high in Finland in 1982, many residents of Rauma traveled back and forth to work on bicycles, even in the snow. We saw youngsters arriving at the arenas with their hockey bags securely fastened to the back of their bicycles.

With only five million people, Finland is such a small country that you're liable to see anybody on the street. One night I was out walking along Alexander Street in Helsinki when I passed the president of Finland, Mauno Koivisto, out for a stroll with his wife.

Paul Talvio and his son Risto operated Kisapuku Oy, a sporting goods company in Rauma. Both were excellent hosts for the Burlington kids on off-days, taking them around to see the sights. The younger Talvio also served as host for the U.S. team at many of the IIHF World Championships held in Finland, taking three weeks off without pay from his regular job.

Jaana Sarkola and Petri Moisio of Tampere, Finland, check out the Suomi jerseys at the 2016 World Cup of Hockey in Toronto.

Swedish, the official second language of Finland, is spoken mostly on the west coast. English is taught in all schools.

Two 16-year-old girls I met at a Finnish League game in Helsinki were studying a list of English terms between periods for a test they were having at school the next day. The list included idiomatic expressions like 'paint the town red' and 'if worst comes to worst'.

In those days Finnish citizens could obtain weekend visas very quickly to visit Leningrad in the Soviet Union and many of them took advantage of the situation to travel there, buy cheap vodka and get drunk.

Russian trains ran on a daily basis between Leningrad and Helsinki, but the gauge of the railway lines was different in the two countries and the wheels on the train had to be altered at the border.

In Finland, I discovered the law requires all drivers to have their headlights on 24 hours a day. In the dead of winter, there are only about six hours of daylight in the Helsinki area. By contrast, there's almost no darkness in the summer, yet the same law about headlights applies.

Police at that time also were completely intolerant of drinking and driving. One or two beers was enough to land you in jail the same night, if you were caught. All the big hotels and bars had coin-operated breathalyzers to allow party-goers to make sure they were not over the limit.

In Sweden in 1985 Bruce Evans, one of our hockey parents, was invited to dinner at the home of the family who was billeting his son Jamie. All adults in the room had drinks except for the father, who had to drive him back to the hotel in Stockholm.

Bruce was told it was not uncommon for one-third of the workforce to be in jail for a week at any one time. The laws against drinking and driving were that strict.

Smokers were required to step outside arenas to indulge in their habit, and this was more than 20 years before the same rules were initiated in Ontario and Quebec.

When we landed at Pulkovo Airport in Leningrad in January 1985 on a separate excursion, the aircraft stopped in the middle of the tarmac and we were picked up by a terminal transfer bus, which was right out of the 1950s.

It was minus16 C and the bus had no heat, meaning the windows were completely frosted.

"There you go," cracked one Burlington parent. "We've been here five minutes and already they don't want us to see anything!"

Another parent joked that if a passenger in a hurry had left a bagged lunch on the bus by mistake it would still be good a week later!

Leningrad's trams had no heat except for the very small driver's cabin, which was closed with a door. The windows of the tram were frosted and riders were shivering in the below-zero temperatures, despite being bundled up. At rush hour, however, they were jammed into the vehicle like sardines and that provided some body heat.

I took four Burlington parents, Wally Beevor, Mike Moir, Bob Stanbury and Evans on the blue line of the subway for a tour of Nevsky Prospect and downtown Leningrad. Beevor, who was director of education for the Halton public school board, also came to dinner with me at the Kagans. His son Sean was a defenceman with the bantam team.

The junket down to Nevsky Prospect, the city's main street, was a real eye-opener for the parents.

There were sporting goods stores, but we couldn't find a single one that carried hockey jerseys with lettering or logos on them. Today, St. Petersburg has tons of them.

But the trip was worthwhile when I discovered a bandy stick for sale and purchased it for a souvenir. Russian hockey, of course, evolved from bandy, a game played with field hockey sticks and a ball on a soccer pitch covered with ice.

A visit to Leningrad's major department store Gostiny Dvor was an adventure that almost made us sick when we visited the washroom and were choked by the stench.

At Ploschad Vostanya, a major transfer station for the subway lines, while thousands of people jammed together like sardines in a tin shuffled ahead at the rate of about 10 feet per minute, a pleasant female voice on the public address system gave them reassurance they were not far from where they were headed to catch the next train.

Although it was freezing, residents of what once was the Soviet capital were very co-operative in giving me directions and in more than one case actually took me by the hand to my destination if it was not too far away.

We found out that the same Russians who look so stern when they're riding the subway, laugh and kibbitz with each other in their own apartments the same as Canadians do. Although the living conditions were far below what Burlingtonians were used to, family life was just as important.

Beevor was surprised to learn how much more the Soviets knew about politics in Canada than we know about them. They were anxious to know, for example, how relations were between the people of Quebec and the rest of the country.

In 1974, we were advised to pack Tang crystals to make our own drinks because North American soft drinks were not available, but by 1985 the Soviets had their own orange juice and there was plenty of Pepsi-Cola.

Blue jeans and pantyhose were the best bartering tools at one time, but by the mid-1980s they were worthless because the Soviets were importing these goods from India.

At Pulkovo Airport, tour leaders Ray McLay and Cliff Martin were irked when they were charged $1,300 for overweight baggage when the team left the country, after bringing in far more in the way of gifts and souvenirs than they took out.

Later, in 1989, when I boarded a plane from Prague to Moscow, I also was charged $95 by Czech Airlines for overweight baggage.

However, it was nothing compared to the shock the two Burlingtonians got when Aeroflot oversold our flight from Helsinki to Leningrad and they were required to stand for the entire 50-minute flight, including takeoff and landing, completely contrary to aviation regulations.

The Cougars faced Izhorets, a team sponsored by a large excavating equipment manufacturer, on an outdoor rink in Kulpino, a suburb of Leningrad. It was freezing, forcing everybody to wear gloves, and I needed both hands to steady my camera to take decent shots of the game.

Local police were on duty discouraging locals from trading for North American goods. The snow was piled very high over the top of the boards around the rink, and several children were standing on top of the snow to get a better look at the game.

Resurfacing of the ice between periods took me back 25 years to the days when I learned the game on the natural ice of the old Acton Arena. Snow was cleared from the surface by about six men, each pushing scrapers, and the ice was flooded with a hose. But there were cracks in the ice, the likes of which I had not seen since I was 12 years old and playing peewee at home.

I met what seemed to be a nice young couple on the snowbank surrounding the rink and asked them if they would hold a plastic bag full of Russian souvenirs I had purchased for a minute so that I could take a few photos. That was the last I saw of the souvenirs.

On another occasion, I took my gloves off and put them on a table in the lobby of the Hotel Evropeyskaya in order to change film in my camera. As soon as I turned my back they were gone. It seems good gloves were hard to come by in the cold Russian winter.

There were a limited number of indoor ice rinks in Leningrad then, and that's one of the reasons the game was played outdoors. The temperature was minus 16 C with a very stiff wind blowing when the puck was dropped at the unusually early time of 11 a.m.

The Izhorets club won 5-2. After the game, Burlington coach Frank Buchanan said his lads weren't used to such conditions.

"In the third period some of them couldn't even hold on to their sticks, it was so cold," he said.

By that time many of the Burlington parents had decided to view the third period through the windows of their heated Intourist bus.

Some of the Soviet players were bigger. There was no way of proving how old they were, but one of the locals I spoke with in Russian indicated at least one player might be 15 or 16. The Burlington boys all were 14.

A girl at the Pulkovskaya Hotel told me how Soviet Elite League star Nikolai Drozdetsky got his start in hockey at the nearby 'Myaso Kombinat' – which in English means 'meat factory', the sponsor of the team.

Drozdetsky was generally among the leading scorers in the league in the 1980s, but Viktor Tikhonov rarely called him to the national team. One of the occasions he did was for the 1981 Canada Cup, and the big, strong winger helped them win the tournament.

But Drozdetsky's health had never been very good and, sadly, he died in November 1995 at the age of just 38, as a result of complications from diabetes.

After the 1983 episode in Czechoslovakia when I was detained by the secret police, I was nervous about entering the Soviet Union.

It was common knowledge that the state security services of Iron Curtain countries shared information with each other. So before going I sent a letter to Darcy Thorpe, who had been the Canadian consul general in Prague when I was detained there in 1983. By this time Thorpe was First Secretary at the Canadian embassy in Stockholm.

Thorpe sent this reply:

"We did indeed try to get your two rolls of film back from the police in Šumperk. We contacted them regularly, but had no success, and never did get a satisfactory explanation. I doubt the prospects for success at this stage, given the time that has gone by.

"I have no way of knowing what effect the incident might have on your travels to other East European countries and the Soviet Union. However, you would undoubtedly be wise to advise the department concerned of your travel plans and to register on arrival at the embassy as a visiting Canadian journalist."

The bantams played a few games in the Stockholm area first and luckily I was able to have lunch with him and give him the dates of my arrival in and departure from Leningrad, as well as the name of the hotel where we would be staying. He, in turn, relayed the information to the Canadian Embassy in Moscow.

Before leaving Canada I had talked to the *Toronto Star's* Gerald Utting, a former correspondent in Czechoslovakia, and was told it was not uncommon for journalists to be issued visas again, provided they have had no charges laid against them.

Fortunately, I had no problems in the Soviet Union. I passed through passport control and cleared customs in the shortest time I can ever remember. When I left the country, I was asked to open only one of the five bags I had with me.

On the same excursion the bantams played in the Finnair Cup in the Helsinki area, facing Jokerit Helsinki and its 14-year-old star Teemu Selanne, who in 1992-93 would lead the NHL in goals with an incredible 76 as a rookie with the Winnipeg Jets.

The future Finnish Flash scored three goals in an easy 7-1 win by the Finnish club, but Selanne's team lost 2-0 to cross-town rival IFK Helsinki in the gold medal game.

Jamie Evans, who scored three goals on the European tour, later was a pitcher with Canada's national junior baseball team in two World Youth Championships, was signed by the Houston Astros and played minor pro ball. In the spring of 1995 during spring training, he pitched for Houston's team of replacement players while the major league strike was going on.

I roomed with OMHA rep Jim Pollard of London at the Hotel Presidentti in Helsinki and kept him awake pounding out stories for *The Globe and Mail* from the 1985 World Junior Championship, also taking place there, on a typewriter borrowed from the front desk.

It was one of the strangest tournaments in history. Canada won the gold medal, but only because of a third-period goal by Wendel Clark on Dominik Hasek that gave them a 2-2 tie with Czechoslovakia on the final day. There was no overtime in those days. The medals were decided on the basis of the final standings.

Canada and Czechoslovakia both finished with five wins, no losses and two ties, but the Canadians had a better goal differential.

Meanwhile, in the final game of the tournament the Soviet Union rallied from a deficit to edge host Finland 6-5 to claim the bronze medal.

That left the Finns with the distinction of being the only team in tournament history to lose only one game and not get a medal. Finland finished at 4-1-2 for 10 points, but the nod went to the Soviets, who were 5-2-0, also for 10 points, because they beat the hosts head-to-head.

One night in Sweden I had to wait 45 minutes for the telephone operator to make a connection to Canada so that I could file my radio report with Al Craig and CHML in Hamilton. Another night I made my report from a room on the ninth floor of a ship, the Silvia Regina, which essentially was the captain's communications room. We were sailing from Helsinki to Stockholm.

At the same time, I interviewed Burlington defenceman Kevin Sneddon, the son of former NHL goalie Bob Sneddon. Kevin was only 14 then, but he went on to win an NCAA championship at Harvard in 1989 and serve as team captain in 1991-92, his senior year. Later he became head coach at Union College, then the University of Vermont.

During an outdoor game in Balsta, a suburb of Stockholm, Sneddon scored one of the prettiest goals of the tour, stickhandling his way past several Swedish defenders. Instead of announcing the goal in the traditional way, the public address man simply said, "Kevin Sneddon has just given us a lesson in hockey."

The Burlington kids were delighted to find out there were ice lanes directly from their dressing room to the rink and they were able to skate there.

Sweden is so dark during the winter that the Lulea Bears of the Swedish Hockey League installed a series of bright white lights in their dressing room to improve the mood of its players.

In Lulea, located 100 kilometres south of the Arctic Circle, there are 21 hours of darkness in the peak of winter and three more hours of what can best be described as greyness.

Nevertheless, the region has groomed some quality NHL players like Mikael Renberg and Mattias Ohlund.

A study showed that almost 10 per cent of Finland's population of five million suffer from depression at that time of the year.

The use of lights, called luminotherapy, has been effective in 80 per cent of cases of depression.

When the Cougars took on the Huddinge club from Sweden at the Finnair Cup, the Swedish players added a sweet touch to the affair by hurling Snickers chocolate bars, courtesy of their sponsors, into the crowd as they skated onto the ice.

CHAPTER 4
Summit Series opens floodgates from Europe

Fred Shero knew there are a lot of headaches associated with coaching in pro hockey. There was one problem, however, he never thought he'd have to solve when he was behind the bench of the New York Rangers' Central Pro Hockey League farm club in Omaha, Nebraska.

The Rangers signed promising young Swedish prospect Ulf Sterner, who had played at the 1960 Olympics when he was only 19. Word got around the league and many players were not fond of the idea of a player from Europe stealing one of their jobs.

"I knew we'd have trouble keeping opposing players from running at him," Shero said, "but I never dreamed it would also come from our own players at practice."

Just two weeks after coaching his first Stanley Cup champion in
May 1974, Philadelphia Flyers coach Fred Shero meets Andrei
Starovoitov, secretary-general of the Soviet Ice Hockey Federation
(centre), in Moscow. In the background is Concordia University's
Ed Enos, who arranged the sports exchange.

Sterner made his NHL debut with the Rangers on Jan. 27, 1965, but
lasted only four games before being assigned to Omaha. At the end of the
season he returned to Europe for good.

Still, it was a significant development along the path to bringing more
European players to North America.

The St. Louis Blues, working through official channels in the
Czechoslovak government, brought winger Jaroslav Jirik to the U.S. for the
1969-70 season. However, he was already 29, played only four NHL games
and spent most of it with Kansas City of the Central Pro League returning
to Czechoslovakia in the spring.

More Canadians viewed the 1972 Canada-Soviet Summit Series on TV
than the news program that showed Neil Armstrong of the United States
becoming the first man to walk on the moon in 1969.

Alex Khayutin remembers that in 1972 a lot of people who went to work in Leningrad lived in dormitories. He watched most of the games in one of them, where a co-worker from the Nevsky Plant kitchen lived.

Khayutin recalled about one-third of city residents had a black and white TV set in those days, but they were state-of-the-art, compared to the model in the dormitory.

"The screen was about 12 centimetres square and we had to put a large magnifying glass in front of it so that we could see what was happening," he said.

Each of the more than 25 fans crammed into the small room was holding either a beer or a glass of vodka

Khayutin said Soviet fans were disappointed that their team lost Game 8, but the mood in the workplace the next day was not even close to as sombre as the time Czechoslovakia defeated the USSR twice at the 1969 World Championship in Stockholm.

Canada won the Summit Series by the skin of its teeth, but an even more positive result of the event was that it demonstrated top level European players were as good as those in the NHL and it, for all intents and purposes, marked the beginning of the transfer of quality talent destined to make it a stronger league.

The Detroit Red Wings already had made arrangements to bring over Swedish defenceman Thommie Bergman for the 1972-73 season. Borje Salming and Inge Hammarstrom of Sweden followed in 1973-74 when they signed with the Toronto Maple Leafs.

However, the Communist governments in Moscow and Prague were not at all ready to release star players, developed under their tutelage.

Czechoslovak star Vaclav Nedomansky took matters into his own hands by defecting to play for the Toronto Toros of the WHA in 1974. Nedomansky had been absolutely dominant in Europe, scoring 163 goals in only 220 matches with the national team.

More than once the speed of his wrist shot had been measured at in excess of 90 miles per hour. At that time, most players weren't even propelling slapshots at that speed.

When the NHL expanded from six to 12 teams for the 1967-68 season, almost every minor leaguer was bidding for a shot at the big time. Yet expansion did not tap into the vast pool of European talent, especially in the Soviet Union.

The Soviet government's refusal to grant exit visas to its stars from that era prevented them from playing in the NHL. In fact, it wasn't until 1989 that Soviet players were allowed to leave.

Ironically, the Soviet national team that won nine consecutive World Championship gold medals between 1963 and 1971 might have been the strongest of all time. NHL scouts scrutinized them when the Soviet team toured North America and even drafted some stars with the hope that someday the government would change its mind.

Vladislav Tretiak never played in the NHL, but the Montreal Canadiens did take a flyer on him in the draft of 1983 towards the end of his career.

As far back as 1964, the Soviets asked New York Rangers general manager Muzz Patrick for some exhibition games, but Patrick declined and it took eight years before most of Canada's best pros and the Soviet Union clashed in the Summit Series.

Bobby Orr, the NHL's best defenceman, did not play because of an injury and Bobby Hull, who had already scored 604 goals for the Chicago Black Hawks, was not selected because he had jumped to the WHA to play for the Winnipeg Jets.

After watching Soviet superstar Valery Kharlamov play in 1972, Toronto Maple Leafs owner Harold Ballard said he would offer him $1 million to play for the Leafs. Kharlamov, who brought fans at the Montreal Forum out of their seats with two brilliant goals in the first game in 1972, a surprising 7-3 win for the visitors, had three skating speeds and used quick dekes to beat defenders.

In 1974, the Los Angeles Kings were pursuing Anatoly Firsov, one of the greatest Soviet stars of all time, but failed when officials in Moscow learned through other sources that he was considering defecting.

On vacation at a resort near the Black Sea, Firsov was summoned to the Soviet capital instantly.

He had played in the 1972 Olympics in Japan, but because of his advancing age was not selected to play against Team Canada that fall.

Firsov contined to play for the Central Red Army club in the Soviet Elite League in 1973 but never made it to the NHL.

By the mid-70s, the demand for experienced players was on the rise in North America. There were now 18 teams in the NHL and 14 more in the WHA, which began play in 1972.

Anders Hedberg, Ulf Nilsson, Lars-Erik Sjoberg and Curt Larsson, stars of the Swedish national team, joined the Winnipeg Jets for the 1974-75 WHA season. The Jets won two Avco Cup championships with Hedberg, Nilsson and Sjoberg in the lineup. Later, Sjoberg became Winnipeg's first NHL captain, when the Jets switched to that league in 1979.

Good timing and luck can make the difference between success and failure. Viktor Khatulev was blessed with neither, and it cost him a chance to be the NHL's first Soviet superstar.

The Philadelphia Flyers selected Khatulev 160th overall in the 1975 draft, but he never played an NHL game. He became an alcoholic and died a drunk's death in the streets of Riga, the capital city of Latvia, at the age of 39 in 1994.

Khatulev was the first Soviet player ever drafted by an NHL club. He, in fact, didn't even know he'd been chosen until three years after the fact.

A rock-solid 6-3, 203-pound winger at age 19, he was the star of the Soviet team that beat a squad of Western Hockey League all-stars 4-3 to win the gold medal at the 1975 World Junior Tournament in Winnipeg, He won the award for best forward and also made the first all-star team.

While the calibre of play was not as high as today's World Junior Championships, two future Hall of Famers, Bryan Trottier and Peter Stastny, played for Canada and Czechoslovakia, respectively, and Kent 'Magic Man' Nilsson was one of Sweden's stars.

Eric Coville, eastern head scout for the Flyers, talked to Khatulev following the gold medal game in Winnipeg, but he declined the scout's offer to sign him to an NHL contract, saying he would be well enough looked after in Russia.

The Soviet players had been allowed a few beers to celebrate their championship victory and later that night Khatulev went back to Coville and asked to see the money.

"You'll get your money," Coville told him, but then the government interpreter grabbed Khatulev by the arm and whisked him away.

Keith Allen, who was general manager of the Flyers at that time, recalls there were some doubters when the draft choice was announced.

"Mr. Snider (team owner Ed) might not have been too pleased with me for making the pick," he said.

Khatulev's father-in-law was the one who always kept him in check when he got out of line, but when his father-in-law died he went off the deep end. In 1979, he got into an on-ice fight with Red Army star Vladimir Vikulov. The referee tried to separate the pugilists but Vikulov was struck in the face, and Khatulev was suspended. Some thought the punch was an accident, but league officials in Moscow saw it differently.

The suspension later was lifted but, in 1981 at the age of 26, he was suspended for life for rough play and other off-ice shenanigans.

Khatulev's wife Inasa had been killed in an auto accident and his father died from a heart attack at an arena while he was watching a game in Riga. The responsibility of raising a baby daughter fell on the beleaguered defenceman.

Some Flyers like Bobby Clarke, who broke the dynamic Kharlamov's ankle in the 1972 Summit Series, detested the Soviets. When Clarke became general manager in Philadelphia, he didn't sign Russian players for many years, finally inking his first, Andrei Lomakin, in 1991.

However, today Clarke says he never discriminated against Soviet players.

"It was a time when you didn't know if you would ever get them out of the country," he said. "The Soviets were producing some great players, but the next level below the greats were below mediocrity.

"We just thought we would be better off with Canadians."

Khatulev's only visit to the old Spectrum, where the Flyers won back-to-back Stanley Cups in 1974 and 1975, was on Jan. 2, 1979, when the Soviet Wings tied the Flyers 4-4 in an exhibition game.

Khatulev became a taxi driver after he finished playing, but struggled with alcoholism. Former Soviet national team winger Helmut Balderis, who played with him in Latvia, said Khatulev also worked cutting the letters into tombstones for cemeteries with a hammer and chisel and for a time was a bouncer at a bar.

Nevertheless, the NHL gained some bigtime talent through defections from the Eastern Bloc.

Peter and Anton Stastny left their Czechoslovak club team, Slovan Bratislava, surreptitiously, after competing in the European Cup tournament in Innsbruck, Austria in August 1980.

"It was midnight after the final game we played against the Soviet Red Army team," Peter said. "We were staying at the Holiday Inn. The bus was waiting to take the team back to Bratislava, but the Nordiques had a car waiting for us. I looked for Anton, but I couldn't find him. I wondered to myself, 'Did they catch him?'

"Our clubs always were surrounded by secret police. My imagination started to work overtime. It was a most difficult time for me. I was afraid for my brother.

"It came to be 12:30, then 1, then 1:30. I was still looking around and hoping for the best, but every minute it was getting worse and worse. Finally, at 1:30 I said, 'We have to go. He's smart enough to find his way. They were watching us. We couldn't wait there forever. We had an appointment in the morning in Vienna.'

"While we were driving through the streets of Innsbruck, I saw the silhouette of a man, and I knew right away it was my brother. It was like a miracle. I saw the body language of my younger brother. I was so happy.

"It shows the importance of communication. He thought we were supposed to meet at the hotel of the Nordiques people. I maybe aged five years worrying that night.

"We had to drive through the mountains. It's a high, mountainous region. You climb up, then down. It adds two or three hours to your trip to Vienna, but we had to do it. There is a short-cut through Germany, but we didn't have visas for Germany.

"The driver, whom they called '007', was going as fast as he could. He was afraid we might be followed. Finally, we got to Vienna where there was a room reserved for us at the Intercontinental Hotel.

"We had been asleep for 20 minutes when the phones started ringing everywhere. They told us to please not open the door to anyone, because there were reports from the Austrian police that they (STB – Czechoslovak secret police) were looking for us.

"Then the Nordique guys came to the door with about a half-dozen military men with machine guns. They cleared out the whole lobby of the hotel. They took us straight to the car and we went straight to the Canadian embassy where papers were being prepared for us. All the precautions were just unbelievable.

"We had an Austrian police escort in front of us and behind us. The driver was even driving up on the walkway, almost going between trees. He even went down a one-way street.

"Finally we got to the airport, got on the plane and were able to relax.

"Gilles (Leger) had a pile of $100 bills. Every time somebody helped us, he gave them 100 bucks. He tipped the Austrian police for clearing out the lobby.

"Darina (Peter's wife) wasn't supposed to go to Innsbruck. She was pregnant and we didn't want to endanger our first child, but finally the doctor gave his approval. She came on a poor bus with no air-conditioning. It was a 10-hour trip. With a late pregnancy, she could have delivered the baby right there.

"I didn't contact the Nordiques' people until after she had arrived in Innsbruck."

A third brother, Marian, stayed behind because he had a wife and three children.

"Marian was devastated. He took the news that we were leaving very, very hard. When he went home, he was suspended, couldn't find a job and none of his friends would talk to him.

"At the summer Olympics in Munich in 1972, some Eastern Bloc athletes tried to defect. But they were drugged up and reappeared in the Soviet Union. There was reason to fear they would try to do something like that to us if they found us – either convince us to change our minds or use force.

"An agent assigned to our team had come to our room the night before we left to check and see if there were any signs that we were going to go. But, of course, we said nothing. In fact, even at that late stage, we still weren't sure. It was only 50-50.

"The Czechoslovak federation was even more careful after we left. On the other hand, it gradually became easier for players to leave. Even while we played there, it was possible for players to leave, but they had to be at least 34 years of age. Gradually, they dropped the limit down to 32 then to

30. The players had to have played at least 100 games for the Czechoslovak national team. All of a sudden, the NHL was an option for our players.

Eventually the Nordiques negotiated with Czechoslovak officials to bring Marian over as well.

"What they didn't want was more players defecting. They had declared themselves a most democratic society. When famous people defect, it sends a strong signal; people start questioning the system.

Peter said after he arrived in Canada the Czechoslovak government sentenced him in absentia to two years in prison and Darina to 12 months.

The Stastnys would have had to be granted an official pardon if they had gone back while the Communist government was still in power. Luckily for them the Berlin Wall fell in 1989 and they were able to return to their homeland for a visit in 1990.

The capital cities of Bratislava, Slovakia and Vienna, Austria, are right across the Danube River from each other. In the days of Communist government in the former Czechoslovakia, some Czechoslovaks paddled their way to freedom across the river.

George Gross, former sports editor of *The Toronto Sun*, used this method on his way to freedom and launching a new career in Canada.

In 1981-82, former national team captain Ivan Hlinka and defenceman Jiri Bubla were the first Czechoslovak players to play a full season in the NHL with the blessing of their government, both signed with Vancouver. In 1982-83, high-scoring Milan Novy joined the Washington Capitals and veteran blueliner Miroslav Dvorak the Philadelphia Flyers.

Hlinka and Bubla also became the first players from Czechoslovakia to play in a Stanley Cup final, although the Canucks lost to the New York Islanders.

NHL general managers and scouts began to pay closer attention to prospects behind the Iron Curtain and to their personal data. Anton was the first player born and trained in what is now Slovakia ever drafted by an NHL team. Philadelphia selected him in 1978, but it was later discovered he was not old enough. He had to re-enter the draft in 1979 and the Nordiques grabbed him in the fourth round.

Finally in 1992, Roman Hamrlik became the first player from Czechoslovakia to be chosen first overall in the draft. He went to the Tampa Bay Lightning.

Nevertheless, after democracy came to Czechoslovakia and the two republics split into two new countries, Peter became the first ever flag bearer for Slovakia at the 1994 Olympics in Norway. Later he became general manager of the Slovak national team.

He was elected to the European Parliament representing Slovakia in June 2004, after being personally asked to run by Slovak President Rudolf Schuster.

Peter Stastny went on to score 450 goals and 789 assists in a 15-year, Hall-of-Fame NHL career that included stops in New Jersey and St. Louis before his retirement in 1995. Anton also had a strong career, recording 636 points in a nine-year career with the Nordiques.

Only Wayne Gretzky recorded more points in the 1980s than Peter.

The Stastny brothers also played a huge role in creating a torrid rivalry with the Montreal Canadiens, who essentially owned the province's hockey fans prior to the arrival of Les Nordiques.

When Czechoslovak players started to defect, their career stats at home were no longer published in magazines and newspapers there. However, years later officials had a change of heart and allowed them to be recorded again.

In that respect Czechoslovakia was light years ahead of the Communist government in Cuba, which even now refuses to allow players who have defected to play in the Major Leagues to represent the country in the World Baseball Classic.

Peter Ihnacak was in his fourth season with Sparta Prague when he decided to defect following the 1982 World Championship in Finland

Finland and Russia are neighbours, and at that time Finland had an agreement with the Soviet Union to return defectors to their native countries, in Ihnacak's case Czechoslovakia.

Two of Ihnacak's sisters, Magdalena and Maria, had already escaped to the United States; older brother John made it three when he defected to West Germany, and eventually wound up in the U.S.

As a result, almost every time the Czechoslovak national team traveled to the West Peter was left at home for fear he also would turn his back on his country.

Tensions between the East and West increased when the Soviet Union invaded Afghanistan in December 1979. Ihnacak thought he had been selected to the Czechoslovak national team for the 1980 Olympics in Lake Placid. However, at the last minute authorities told him he had been dropped from the team.

In a similar display of distrust, officials with the Czechoslovak Ice Hockey Federation left him off the roster for the Canada Cup competition in September 1981.

His passport was taken away, with the explanation that he was viewed as an enemy of the state because his siblings had already defected. But it was later returned because the federation wanted him to play in the 1982 World Championship.

With the help of his brother John, who flew to Finland from New York, Ihnacak grabbed what he could following a practice in Helsinki and flagged down a cab.

John was smart enough to know agents of the secret police would be watching the airport, so he managed to purchase a pair of tickets on a small ship that sailed between Finland and Stockholm, Sweden.

From there, he continued on to North America and signed with the Toronto Maple Leafs.

Ihnacak's younger brother Miro was still playing for Kosice in the eastern part of the Slovak region of Czechoslovakia. Because of Peter's defection, his passport also was confiscated. He was not even allowed to travel to Eastern Bloc nations.

Eventually, though, Miro also defected and signed with the Leafs.

The first Soviet-trained player to play in the NHL – Viktor Nechaev – arrived in 1982, making his debut with the Los Angeles Kings. He did not defect, rather he was allowed to leave the USSR because he married an American girl.

Nechaev had never played for the Soviet national team in a World Championship or Olympics, but had skated briefly in the Soviet Elite League for SKA Leningrad, one of the weaker teams.

He met his wife Cheryl Haigler, a student at Yale, in a park in Leningrad. Since Nechaev was not a superstar, the Soviet Sports Committee was not as anxious to hang on to him. Nevertheless, it took him a full year to get an exit visa to the U.S.

George Maguire, at that time general manager of the Kings, said selecting Nechaev in the seventh round, 132nd overall, of the 1982 draft was worth trying because he already was in the United States.

As it turned out, Nechaev was a flop. He played only three games for the Kings.

Wearing two hats as head of the NHL Players Association and chief international negotiator for Hockey Canada, Alan Eagleson continued to negotiate with officials from the Soviet Union in an effort to convince them to allow some of their best players to pursue NHL careers. But during the 1987 Canada Cup tournament, a discouraged Eagleson told the media he didn't believe there ever would be more than 10 Soviet players in the world's best league.

It's not that he didn't think they were good enough, rather that the bureaucracy in the Communist country would prevent it.

In fact, a member of the Soviet national team did not play in the NHL until late in the 1988-89 season when the Soviet Ice Hockey Federation finally agreed to release Sergei Priakhin to the Calgary Flames.

In January of 1989, Ken Dryden made a trip to the Soviet Union to do a documentary. There was all kinds of speculation about who would be the first national team player to come to North America.

Most of the speculation was about star players nearing the end of their careers. A major candidate was Vladimir Zubkov, a big defenseman who played for the Red Army team. Eagleson had suggested this, I suppose from his own conversations with the Soviets. Zubkov rarely played with the national team, but he was very good, played a clean game and carried himself well off the ice.

But, swearing me to secrecy, Dryden told me when he got back to Canada he had been told in Moscow it was going to be Priakhin. He was rather an average player and only a fourth liner on the national squad, although he had played in the 1987 Canada Cup

I said nothing and did not write about it until one Saturday night in March 1989 when I was in Barrie at the old Dunlop Street Arena for a game between Dave King's national team and the touring Moscow Selects.

Before the game, I was chatting with a Canadian player Ray Cote, who was not dressing for the game. I was surprised when he pointed out Cliff Fletcher in the stands and said "'I guess he's here to watch Priakhin and sign him."

Flames special assignment scout Gerry McNamara also was in the building.

Realizing the secret must be out by now, I immediately fought my way through the crowd up to Fletcher and asked if it was true he was there because Priakhin was going to stay in Canada and play for the Flames.

"Well if he is, I don't know anything about it," he replied.

"I'm here to see Daryl Olsen, who was an all-star college player at Northern Michigan. We're talking contract with Olsen's agent."

I rushed to a phone to call Dryden, interrupting him in the middle of dinner, and told him what I had heard, saying I would like to file the story with *The Toronto Sun* for its Sunday edition.

He released me from my promise not to tell anyone, so I filed the story indicating there was a rumor Fletcher was there for that purpose.

The Sun was the first publication in Canada to have the breaking news.

The next day I was reamed out by King for writing the story. He scolded me for speculating on what were very touchy negotiations with the Soviet Ice Hockey Federation.

"I don't know if that deal's going to go through now," King said.

In spite of what Fletcher had told me, the Flames made me look good on Monday morning by inking Priakhin to a contract.

Calgary had taken a flyer on Priakhin by making him the very last pick in the 1988 NHL draft, in the 12th round, 252nd overall.

Priakhin played 49 NHL games for Calgary, including playoffs, over three seasons. The Soviets said they released him first because he was a model player – a gentleman on and off the ice. They had been afraid that their reputation might be spoiled by a player coming over and getting into trouble.

The Soviets allowed him to have only $1,200 a month from the $500,000 contract he agreed to.

As early as the 1970s the Soviets were bartering players over the age of 30 to Austria in return for downhill skiing coaches.

Igor Dmitriev was one of the first to be granted permission to play abroad in Klagenfurt, Austria in the 1974-75 season.

Dmitriev had played for Wings of the Soviet, was very fond of Canada and made friends easily wherever he traveled.

Unfortunately, he died in December 1997 from a brain tumour, but he is remembered in Canada as a guy who was always smiling, spoke English and a person who had earned the trust of Canadian coaches and media.

Educated as a civil engineer, Dmitriev worked as a bridge builder for a while. He was to have been Russia's head coach at the 1996 World Cup of Hockey, but was told by doctors only three weeks before the tournament that he must have surgery.

The Russians had also tabbed him to be head coach of their Olympic team in Nagano, Japan in 1998, if he recovered from his operations, but he died before that.

He actually came back to coach Russia at the 1997 World Championship in Finland following one of the surgeries.

With his excellent sense of humour, Dmitriev said he wanted to have the surgery in Russia because the country had lots of experience in neuro-surgery, since "Russians are so often shot in the head!"

Alexander Yakushev, the Soviets best player in the 1972 Summit Series, went to Kapfenberg, Austria in 1981 and Valery Bragin, current coach of the Russian national junior team, left to play for Rodovre in Denmark in 1989.

When the Soviets faced the best Canadians in the WHA two years later, Bobby Hull described Yakushev as the best left winger of all time.

Japan also recognized the value of Soviet expertise in hockey and invited Vladimir Shadrin and Yuri Liapkin from the 1972 team to go there as player-coaches.

One of the first veteran Soviet players allowed to play in another country was Evgeny Mayorov, a Spartak winger who played on a line with his brother Boris and centre Slava Starshinov.

Evgeny Mayorov first played for VehU Tampere in Finland in the 1968-69 season. He is believed to be the first Soviet player to play in another country.

The avalanche of players from the USSR to other countries really started after a new law was passed in the summer of 1989 allowing Soviet artists and athletes to negotiate contracts with other nations on their own.

The fall of the Berlin Wall in 1989 signaled the end of communism in many Eastern Bloc countries. The following summer almost every player over the age of 30 from the 12-team Soviet Elite League left to play abroad for more money. A handful of stars made it to the NHL, but even run-of-the-mill players from non-playoff teams found new jobs in countries like Italy, France and Bulgaria.

Yet Russia was able create a new league from scratch.

According to the book entitled *Larionov*, published by former Soviet national team centre Igor Larionov, before the 1988 Olympics coach Viktor Tikhonov had promised the army players on the national team that if they won the gold medal they would have more freedom. Tikhonov, he said, also guaranteed that training camps would be shortened and players and their families would be able to spend more time together.

In fact, they also were allowed for the first time to go to the NHL.

While veteran stars Larionov, Slava Fetisov, Sergei Makarov and Vladimir Krutov signed with NHL clubs, fringe players emigrated to places like Italy, France and Germany. Czechoslovak star Igor Liba, who had played briefly with the Calgary Flames, was demanding $100,000 to re-sign with his Italian club. But a young Russian named Mikhail Vasiliev came along and said he would play for $40,000.

Vasiliev was just as good, he was very happy with $40,000 and the Italian club got a bargain.

A report published by Simon Fraser University MBA grad Haizley Trevor-Smith in 1998 claimed Czech and Russian players earned an average of $55,000 less on the first year of their NHL contracts than North American players and those from other European countries.

Trevor-Smith concluded the players from the Eastern Bloc were just happy to get into the league, because the lower salary level was far more than they had ever earned before.

One of the most interesting defections occurred on Canadian soil when Petr Nedved left his Czechoslovak midget team after it won the Mac's Milk midget tournament in Calgary in January 1989. He was only 17 at the time. With 17 goals, he was the leading scorer in the tournament.

Nedved had only $20 in his pocket when he entered a police station in Calgary on Jan. 2, 1989, telling officers it was his wish to remain in Canada.

The Seattle Thunderbirds of the WHL signed him, and he tore up the league scoring 65 goals and 145 points in just 71 games.

The following summer he was selected in the first round, second overall, by the Vancouver Canucks in the 1990 NHL draft.

Nedved eventually played for seven different NHL clubs and finished his career with 310 goals.

He became a Canadian citizen and played for Canada at the 1994 Olympics in Norway, earning a silver medal.

Canadian newspapers reported the government in Czechoslovakia ordered Nedved's mother and father to call him regularly over the next 10 months pleading with him to come home.

Over the years, Canadians have played a large role in the advancement of the game in Europe. At any one time there are in the neighbourhood of 500 Canadians playing hockey there. Coaches from Canada are employed everywhere on the continent.

Goalie Vincent Riendeau, a veteran of 184 NHL games with Montreal, St. Louis, Detroit and Boston, was the first Canadian to play in Russia in the 1998-99 season. American Todd Hartje, a graduate of Harvard, had played for Sokol Kiev in Ukraine in 1990-91.

In the 2008-09 season, the Shelburne (Ont.) Red Wings came up with a new idea by icing a team made up mostly of Russian players in the Greater Metro Hockey League (GMHL).

Wealthy Russian businessmen paid thousands of dollars to send their sons over to learn the game the Canadian way.

But there was a huge controversy about their playing in Canada. Hockey Canada voiced its displeasure about foreign players taking up roster spots on the Shelburne club, which could be filled by Canadians. Some parents in the town didn't fancy the idea of foreign players taking up icetime that could be used by local groups.

However, because the GMHL is an independent league, Hockey Canada had no authority over it.

In 2008, Hockey Canada ruled that the GMHL and other new leagues starting up were 'outlaw organizations.'

In 2011, Alexander Medvedev, president of the KHL, said Russian agents who send players to North America were making a big mistake.

"Of the 150 players who left Russia to play juniors and in the minor leagues, only five per cent managed to stay in hockey at all," he said.

"Many agents are just hunting for some quick bucks. We should take a lesson from U.S. college hockey, where agent activity is forbidden."

A notable exception to Medvedev's criticism is Ivan Provorov of the Philadelphia Flyers, who was just 14 when he emigrated to the U.S. to play for the Wilkes-Barre/Scranton Knights bantam club in Pennsylvania. He later played one season with the Cedar Rapids Roughriders of the USHL before signing with the Brandon Wheat Kings of the WHL when he was 17.

In 2015 and 2016 he earned silver medals playing for Russia in the World Junior Championship. He also was named best defenceman in the WHL in 2015-16 and made his NHL debut with the Flyers in the fall of 2016.

In March 2017 four representatives from the Swedish Ice Hockey Association attended a meeting of NHL general managers in Boca Raton, Florida to request that their clubs leave young prospects in Sweden to develop longer before bringing them to North America early to play in the AHL. Tommy Boustedt, secretary and CEO of the Swedish Ice Hockey Federation, said Sweden, in a sense, is losing a full team every year.

In Russia, meanwhile, Russian Ice Hockey Federation President Vladislav Tretiak said too many spaces in the KHL are being taken up by foreigners and Russian boys do not have the opportunity to develop.

In 2012 there were 18 goaltenders from outside Russia playing in the league.

It is basically the same thing Hockey Canada and parents in Shelburne were complaining about.

Besides the breakup of Czechoslovakia Slav Lener, head of all coaches for the Czech Ice Hockey Association, said the poor results of Czech and

Slovak youth teams in international championships recently can be attributed largely to a softening in the desire of young people.

In the last decade, the Czechs have not won a single medal at the World Junior Championship and the Slovaks have only one bronze.

In the same period Canada and the U.S. each have captured three gold medals.

During communist times, their only way out of the country was to work their butts off and hope to get a contract elsewhere. Today, with the change of government, the standard of living is higher, kids are given more and they no longer have the same desire to leave for North America.

In 1959-60, only three of the 153 NHL players were American. That's just two per cent. In 2016-17, a total of 250 players from the U.S. played in the league.

In 2000, a record 30 Europeans were selected in the first three rounds of the NHL draft. Hockey Canada, tired of Europeans taking the spots of Canadians on Canadian teams, followed Don Cherry's advice and ruled that in the future no European players would be allowed to play in Canada below the Major Junior A level.

A record 300 Europeans played in the NHL in 2003-04. Seventy-six of them were Czech, 64 Russian, 53 Swedish and 35 Finnish.

More than a decade later, in 2015-16, 87 of the 993 players who played in at least one NHL game – or 8.8 per cent – were Swedish. That was a record level for one European nation.

In the 2014-15 season, Europe surpassed the U.S. in the number of NHL players. There were 243 players from Europe who played at least one game and 237 from the U.S. Europeans represented 24.9 per cent of the NHL total and the Americans 24.3.

The European total for 2015-16 was 263 players. Canada had its lowest total ever with 490 players, which represented 49.2 per cent and the United States 241 for 24.3 per cent. It was the first time Canadian players made up less than half the league.

With the KHL in its eighth season, Russia had only 41 players in the NHL, the Czechs and Finns 39 each, and Slovakia just 12. Slovakia had reached its peak in 2003-04 with 35.

Switzerland had 15 players, its most ever.

The number of Canadians had peaked during the 1956-57 season, when 98.6 per cent of all players were from north of the 49th parallel.

Americans are the group that has grown the most over the two decades from 1995-96 to 2015-16. By then there were 242 Americans in the NHL, or 24.1 per cent of the total of 1,003 players.

Fifty years ago players were very wary of jet lag and one trip to Europe per season was plenty. In today's world, aircraft have become just like automobiles for them.

For example, between June and September 2014 David Pastrnak, who was drafted in the first round, 25th overall, by Boston that year, crossed the Atlantic four times. He attended the draft in June, returned for Boston's summer development camp in July, in August he was in Montreal with the Czech national junior team, then in late August for the Bruins rookie camp and regular training camp.

Pastrnak and William Nylander, now with the Toronto Maple Leafs, played on a line together with Sodertalje in Sweden before both came to the NHL.

To a lifelong student of Russian hockey, the printing on the back of the striped jersey was unmistakable.

Spelled out in 11 capital letters, almost making it too long to fit, was the name 'Kudryavtsev'. It seemed so out of place in the tiny 700-seat Appleby Ice Arena in Burlington, where I was covering a Family Day matinee junior game between the Burlington Cougars and Toronto Lakeshore Patriots.

Linesman Denis Kudryavtsev displays the jersey of the Russian club
Khimik Voskresensk.

Denis Kudryavtsev, 31, was born in Tver, Russia, near Moscow. He
played for Tver and Spartak St. Petersburg in the Russian Major League,
but had to retire early because of back and neck injuries.

Kudryavtsev came to Canada in 2006 with his wife Tatyana and the
following year he obtained his Level 3 certification at an Ontario Hockey
Association clinic in London.

After obtaining his Level 4 certificate he eventually started getting
assignments as a linesman in the OHA.

Kudryavtsev has officiated in the Ontario Junior A League, Ontario University Athletics league and Ontario Senior League.

While growing up in Tver, Kudryavtsev played with Ilya Kovalchuk, Ilya Nikulin, Alexei Tereschenko, Denis Denisov and Alexander Yeremenko, all of whom went on to play for the Russian national team, and Alexei Ponikarovsky, who now plays for Ukraine.

Sweden's Marcus Vinnerborg was the first European to referee in the NHL. He officiated in 40 games over two seasons before returning to his native land in 2012. Vinnerborg helped destroy the myth in Canada that European officials are incompetent.

CHAPTER 5
Soviets reach peak of their game

There's no greater compliment to a team's legacy than to say it completely changed the way hockey is played.

Igor Larionov, nicknamed 'The Professor' and an authority on the subject because he was one of the Soviet national team's best centres, said the Big Red Machine was at its peak between 1981 and 1984.

The Soviet entry at the 1983 World Championship in West Germany was so dominant, it secured all six spots on the all-star team, with Vladislav Tretiak in goal, Slava Fetisov and Alexei Kasatonov on defence and Vladimir Krutov, Igor Larionov and Sergei Makarov on the forward line as it won the gold medal easily.

"For us, the best of times – a string of continuous successes – were the four seasons between 1981 and 1984," Larionov wrote in his book, entitled *Larionov*. "The time flew by as one happy moment. It seemed that this is how it would be forever."

The Soviets toyed with a Canadian team with 19 NHL players in its lineup, trouncing them twice by the same score of 8-2.

The Soviets went through the tournament winning nine of 10 games and outscoring the opposition 60-10, an average winning margin of five goals a game, breezing to their 19th World Championship gold medal.

Their 1-1 tie with Czechoslovakia was played at a lightning tempo and described by many sportswriters as the greatest World Championship game of all time.

"The Soviet teams of that era were so damn good they made us change the way the game is played," former Canadian national team coach Dave

King said. "We were all still trying to play a forechecking game against them. We could do it for about 10 minutes, then they'd break it with a long pass and score."

"After that, teams started to lay back and play the 1-2-2, 1-3-1 or 1-4. That's where all the traps in hockey came from."

King told his players to slow the game down and control the tempo. But although there were two 50 goals-plus scorers – Marcel Dionne and Michel Goulet – on the Canadian roster, the Soviets were far superior.

Dionne, Charlie Simmer and Dave Taylor formed the Triple Crown Line with the Los Angeles Kings, the highest-scoring unit in the league. Goulet had scored 57 goals for Quebec, Dionne 56 for the Kings and Darryl Sittler 43 for Philadelphia.

The only consolation for Canadians was that, through a quirk of fate, the World Championship trophy remained in Canada.

Bill Warwick, a member of the Penticton Vees who beat the Soviets to win the gold medal in 1955, had kept it all these years.

Warwick recalled the trophy was falling apart when IIHF President Bunny Ahearne presented it to him in Krefeld, Germany.

He had a replica made and sent it back the next year with the Kitchener-Waterloo Dutchmen, who represented Canada in a tournament at Cortina d'Ampezzo, Italy, which was held jointly as an Olympics and World Championship.

When the Russians struck gold in that tournament, Warwick had the last laugh.

"I saw the Russians skating around, holding up my phony trophy," he said. "I knew they had fallen for it."

The 1972 Summit Series confirmed the USSR's best players were on the same level as Canada's top pros.

Skepticism about the Soviets' prowess still existed, nevertheless, when NHL clubs and teams from the USSR began playing exhibition games in the 1975-76 season. But at last count, there had been 117 of these encounters with the Soviets winning 61, losing just 46 and 10 games ending in a tie.

It is widely reported that Canada was the first country to use active NHL players at a World Championship, namely the 1977 event in Vienna.

However, the U.S. beat the Canadians to it when they iced a team with four NHLers at the 1976 Worlds in Katowice, Poland. Canada did not compete because it was still at odds with the IIHF over the governing body's refusal to allow the use of minor league pros at the 1970 World Championship.

The American roster included Peter LoPresti, Lou Nanne, Mike Antonovich and Steve Jensen, all of the Minnesota North Stars. Goaltender Mike Curran, who sparkled in a 2-0 shutout victory over Sweden, joined the U.S. team from the WHA's Minnesota Fighting Saints.

When the Canadians finally returned with a full roster of NHL players in 1977, all hell broke loose. They were ruthless in their tactics, intimidating the Europeans, but winding up without a medal. In fact, in two games against the Soviets they were outscored by a total of 19-2.

An 11-1 loss in the first game was the worst defeat Canada had ever suffered in international action.

Spearing and high-sticking their opponents, Team Canada left itself shorthanded for most of the game. But Alan Eagleson saw it another way, claiming the referees were to blame for over-reacting to hockey played the good old Canadian way.

Phil Esposito went a step further. His idea was to give the officials a token of the match by presenting them with a Soviet flag!

Muzz Patrick laughed when Anatoly Tarasov, known as the godfather of Soviet hockey, asked the New York Rangers GM for a few exhibition games in 1964.

Patrick thought he was being kind in declining the challenge, because he honestly thought the Soviets would be embarrassed beyond belief.

More than a decade before that the Soviets made their first appearance at a World Championship in Stockholm.

Canada seriously underrated them and sent the East York Lyndhursts, a Senior B club from Toronto, as its representative.

CAHA President George Dudley of Midland, Ont., had said beforehand he believed the European clubs the Soviets had defeated in exhibition play were no better than Intermediate 'B' calibre in Canada.

The Soviets defeated the Canadian amateurs easily 7-2 to win the gold medal.

While the Lyndhursts breezed their way to a perfect record in earlier games, the Soviets had been tied 1-1 by the host Swedes in a game played in such a heavy snowstorm the ice was invisible to the spectators a few minutes after the opening faceoff. That game, and the Canada-Soviet contest, were played outdoors in Stockholm's Royal Stadium before a crowd of 16,000.

The Hockey News edition of the day carried a dramatic quote from Canadian coach Greg Currie.

"The worst thing that ever happened to me was standing on the blueline in pouring rain and watching that Russian flag go up," he said. "A lot of guys were crying. They felt they'd let Canada down."

One of them, Eric Unger, celebrated his 90th birthday on Dec. 28, 2016

"Our ego was really hurt," said Unger. "At the end of the game they wanted to exchange sticks with us. I felt like beating them over the head with a stick for beating us. I don't think a guy on our club exchanged sticks."

Russ Robertson was selling cars in Milton, Ont., when I interviewed him in 1977 about his experience playing against the Soviet Union that day.

Robertson said the Canadian players were so embarrassed by the loss that when the players returned to Toronto by train, after sailing home on the French liner 'Liberty', some of them wanted to get off one stop before Union Station, where a few fans and a band were waiting to welcome them.

Conn Smythe, owner of the Toronto Maple Leafs, wanted retribution. Sending his NHL team over when the schedule was finished to settle the score would please all Canadians, he said.

In stark contrast to today's system where players are catered to, the Lyndhursts had to pay for their own jackets to go over, were given only $20 expense money a week and two players eventually lost their regular jobs because they took time off for the tournament.

The Lyndhursts traveled to Europe on the original 'Queen Mary' ocean liner, with most of the players getting sea-sick sick during the rough six-day voyage.

By 1987 the Soviets still were providing a tough test, although Canada beat them by a narrow margin in the Canada Cup tournament. Mario Lemieux scored the winning goal as Canada rallied from a 4-2 deficit to win 6-5 in the deciding game of a best- of-three series in Hamilton.

For the first time in history the Soviets agreed to have a Canadian, Don Koharski, referee the deciding game. It was a decision they would regret.

They cried foul when Koharski disregarded what looked like an interference penalty against Canada just a few seconds before the winning goal.

In the 21st century, however, Canada's best players have been superior in major competitions against Russia.

The temperature was 75 F in southern Ontario on May 22, 2016, the day Canada won its second straight World Championship gold medal in Moscow. It's difficult to say how many fans actually watched the game.

It was hardly as important to them as the Olympic gold medals achieved by Canada in Vancouver in 2010 or Sochi in 2014.

Russian President Vladimir Putin, who had attended the U.S. win over Russia at the 2014 Olympics, this time made a surprise appearance at the end of the gold medal game to present the Cup to Canadian captain Corey Perry and make a speech in which he thanked the fatherland of hockey for giving the world such a dynamic sport.

While the Soviets changed the face of the game, it was left to Canada and the U.S. to alter the ridiculous system of deciding medals in a round-robin system, with goals for and against differential breaking ties.

At the 1991 World Championship in Finland, Canadian coach Dave King and Tim Taylor of the U.S. engaged in a hilarious chess match with their goalies as pawns.

Going into the final weekend, the Soviets and Swedes had three points each, Canada two and the U.S. none from the medal round, meaning the Canadians' only hope for a gold medal was to beat the Americans by at least five goals and hope the Soviets and Swedes tied.

Canada was scheduled to take on the United States on Saturday, with the Soviets facing Sweden on Sunday.

The Americans, on the other hand, were already out of the gold medal race but would win bronze if they beat Canada.

Canada led 6-4 with less than three minutes to play at the new Typhoon Ice Hall in Turku when Steve Thomas scored to boost the Canadian lead to three goals at 7-4, bringing the gold medal dream closer to reality. It had been exactly 30 years since Canada last won a World Championship gold medal.

The Americans still needed to score four goals in less than three minutes to win the bronze.

Canadian hopes sagged when Murray Craven took a penalty at 17:48. Surprisingly, Taylor pulled goalie John Vanbiesbrouck in what he would later say was an effort to stage a come-from-behind win. He didn't care that Canada was still in gold medal contention. His aim was to bring a bronze medal back to the U.S.

The move backfired, however, when Steve Larmer fired a long shot into the empty American net making it 8-4.

The Canadian bench then went wild when, with 'Beezer' back in the nets, Jamie Macoun scored with one second left on the clock making it 9-4. Amazingly, Canada had won by the five-goal margin and would strike gold if Sunday's game ended in a tie. Coach Dave King couldn't believe he had been given the goal he needed almost on a silver platter.

The next day Sweden and the Soviets remained tied 1-1 until 9:38 of the third period when a 20-year-old phenom named Mats Sundin scored the gold-medal winning goal for the Swedes.

Canada claimed the silver, the Soviets the bronze and the Americans went home empty.

The Canucks almost won it all – with a little help from their friends south of the border.

Both the Swedes and Soviets were furious that Taylor yanked his goalie.

Needless to say, 1991 was the last year in which a round-robin format was used to decide the medalists. The following season in Prague a playoff system was introduced.

CHAPTER 6
Nuclear disaster in Chernobyl, fall of the Berlin Wall

Earth-shattering events seemed to occur almost every time I was in Europe covering hockey.

The 1986 World Championship was almost over when former Toronto Maple Leaf Billy Harris asked me to get an update on the Stanley Cup play-offs back home. So I called *The Globe and Mail's* Moscow correspondent Lawrence Martin at his Kutozovsky Prospekt office from the lobby of the Cosmos Hotel and learned for the first time about the nuclear disaster in Chernobyl.

There was nothing in the Russian newspaper *Izvestia*, save for a two-inch story that reported there had been an accident at the Chernobyl atomic station when one of the nuclear reactors went out of order.

It proceeded to assure readers that all the necessary measures had been taken to protect those who had suffered and further stated a government commission had been organized to look into the matter.

Total lineage for the story was four sentences.

оллективу Иртышского реч-
параходства предстоит до-
ь населению, народному
тву Западной Сибири
17 миллионов тонн раз-
грузов.
Г. ВСТАВСКИЙ.
СК.

ешите поздравить вас от
Центрального Комитета
его Политбюро, от имени
иума Верховного Совета
и Советского правительст-
олучением наград Отече-

ством большого удовлет-
я сообщаю вам, что Ге-
ный секретарь ЦК КПСС
Сергеевич Горбачев по-
передать вам его искрен-
оздравления и самые доб-
ожелания.
стья, крепкого здоровья
вашим семьям.
решите поздравить всех
наступающим праздником—
международной солидар-
трудящихся — 1 Мая.
* * *
учившие награды вырази-
ердечную благодарность
альному Комитету КПСС,
диуму Верховного Совета
и Советскому правитель-
а высокую оценку их тру-
(ТАСС).

скнм дипломатом.

ООН

Завершилась сессия ЮНИСЕФ

НЬЮ-ЙОРК, 29 апреля. (Корр. ТАСС). Каждую минуту гонка вооружений поглощает в мире около 2 миллионов долларов и одновременно 30 детей умирают от голода и болезней.

Эти статистические данные были приведены на завершившейся в штаб-квартире мирового сообщества сессии правления Детского фонда ООН (ЮНИСЕФ).

Представители развивающихся и социалистических государств выступили на форуме с решительными требованиями остановить опасное наращивание гор оружия, угрожающих миру, а освободившиеся ресурсы использовать в целях развития, в том числе на

нужды подрастающего поколения планеты.

Представитель Советского Союза привлек внимание участников дискуссии к выдвинутой Советским Союзом программе полной и повсеместной ликвидации ядерного оружия к 2000 году. Осуществление этой конструктивной программы, подчеркнул он, явилось бы важнейшим шагом на пути обеспечения мирного будущего для всех детей Земли.

В принятой участниками сессии в связи с 40-летием ЮНИСЕФ декларации содержится призыв ко всем правительствам и организациям отдать все лучшее молодому поколению, заботиться о его здоровье и развитии.

От Совета Министров СССР

На Чернобыльской атомной электростанции произошла авария, поврежден один из атомных реакторов. Принимаются меры по ликвидации последствий аварии. Пострадавшим оказывается помощь. Создана правительственная комиссия.

The Chernobyl nuclear explosion warranted only two inches, at the bottom of the front page, in the government newspaper *Izvestia*.

The worst thing is that the story didn't appear until Wednesday, April 30, four days after the accident.

The lead story on the front page reported Andrei Gromyko, chairman of the Praesidium of the Supreme Soviet, had handed out awards to deserving Soviet citizens in anticipation of the celebration of May Day.

Another piece, which received more play, announced the visit of Politburo member Lev Zaikov to the region of Tula, which is famous for the production of samovars.

Pages 4 and 5 inside blamed the United States for a variety of faults, ranging from the bombing of Libya to what the Soviets called unnecessary nuclear tests in Nevada.

And one-third of the back page, including a large photo, was devoted to the Soviet victory in the World Hockey Championship.

The Communist Party daily *Pravda* reported nothing about Chernobyl, likewise for *Moskovskaya Pravda, Trud, Sovietskaya Rossiya* and other publications.

The accident took place on the morning of Saturday, April 26, the same day Sweden edged Canada 6-5 and the Soviet Union shut out Finland 8-0 in the final round. Fans watched the games oblivious to what had happened.

Experts said anybody within a 500-mile radius could be affected by radiation. The distance from Chernobyl to Moscow by air is 432 miles.

The Soviets defeated Sweden to win the gold medal on April 28. The team went to the Intercontinental Hotel near the Moscow River for a banquet, but as late as that had not been told anything. Everybody was busy consuming platters of beef and battered fish, assorted salads and ice cream while washing it all down with Russian champagne.

The first the Soviet players heard of it was from Swedish fans in Moscow.

When we arrived in Turku, Finland, for a stopover on the way home to Canada, we found out scientists in Sweden and Finland had an inkling something was wrong on the weekend when they noticed radiation levels were 10 times higher than normal.

When I arrived at Pearson International Airport in Toronto on Wednesday night, I was greeted by a CBLT-TV reporter and cameraman anxious to know how things were in the Soviet Union. The interview appeared on the tube later that night.

Incredibly, there still are about 100 elderly people living in the Chernobyl exclusion zone. They left initially but returned.

Large numbers of people took little time evacuating the area near Chernobyl. A forum predicted that exposure to radiation could kill as many as 9,000 people. Greenpeace, on the other hand, put the potential for lives lost at a whopping 93,000.

In spite of this, the population of wild boars, deer and wolves managed to survive and even increase because there were very few farmers left to hunt them.

Soon after the accident, serious efforts were made to protect Moscow by having pilots create rain clouds over Chernobyl and Byelorussia. The goal was to have radioactive material eliminated before it reached places where large numbers of people were living.

The initiative forfeited more than 4,000 square miles of Byelorussia to ensure nobody was adversely affected in the nation's capital.

In April 1989 I was flying home from the World Championship in Stockholm when Alexander Mogilny walked away from the Soviet team hotel in the coastal resort of Dalarno, Sweden, becoming the first Soviet hockey player to defect to the West.

Mogilny was not present at the airport for the Soviet team's journey home after he secretly left a banquet held to celebrate the team's gold-medal victory the night before.

The defection came only five weeks after one of Mogilny's former team-mates, Sergei Priakhin, became the first Soviet national team player to be allowed to leave the country to join an NHL team, the Calgary Flames.

I had asked Soviet assistant coach Igor Dmitriev if I could visit the hotel earlier in the tournament, but he said he didn't think it was a good idea while the team was focusing on winning the gold medal. Team officials might have been suspecting something was going to happen.

When I arrived in Canada Steve Dryden, editor-in-chief of *The Hockey News*, asked me go to Amherst, N.Y., with him to interview Mogilny.

Lena Nilsson, a friend from Sweden, was helping him with his English. She was married to Sergei Fomichev, who formerly lived in the Soviet Union. Both had accompanied Mogilny on the flight to North America, along with Sabres general manager Gerry Meehan and Don Luce, the team's director of amateur evaluation and development.

Mogilny told reporters in Buffalo he had asked Sergei Fedorov to defect with him, but he declined. He called Fedorov a "Mommy's boy".

At the 1989 Worlds, Mogilny had played poorly, scoring no goals in 10 games for a powerhouse club, so perhaps he was being bothered by the decision he was about to make. Mogilny told me later that throughout the tournament, coach Tikhonov kept asking him, "Sasha, what are you thinking about?"

After arriving in the U.S., Mogilny was tried in absentia in the USSR and the court ruled he was a deserter. Rumours were rife that national team captain Slava Fetisov would be sent to North America to try to talk him into reconsidering his decision.

Mogilny joined the Central Red Army club at age 17 and a year later became the youngest Soviet hockey player to win an Olympic gold medal.

Later he had refused to become an officer in the Red Army, which further irritated Tikhonov.

In May 1988, the Soviet national team went to Japan to play a few exhibition games and have a holiday as a reward for winning the Olympic gold in Calgary. Mogilny was not included on the roster.

The story is that he said he did not wish to become an officer in the Soviet army, and this riled Tikhonov. Later in the summer, he is said to have changed his mind and would become a sub-lieutenant.

Tikhonov had actually punched Mogilny on the bench at the Saddledome during the 1988 Olympics after he took a penalty late in the Soviet Union's final game against Finland and the Finns scored on the power play to hand the Soviets their only loss in the tournament, 2-1.

Less publicized, but even more shocking was the incident in which Tikhonov shook a referee and got away with it during a 9-4 Soviet win over Canada in an exhibition game at Hamilton, prior to the 1987 Canada Cup. Incredibly, there was no penalty called against the Soviets and he remained behind the bench for the rest of the game.

While he had many triumphs, Tikhonov's lowest moment came at the 1980 Olympics in Lake Placid when a team of American collegians upset the heavily favored Soviets 4-3 and went on to win the gold medal, relegating the defending champs to second place and the silver. He later admitted he made a mistake by pulling star netminder Vladislav Tretiak after the first period with the score tied 2-2.

The gigantic Izmailovsky Hotel Complex in Moscow was my home for a week in the fall of 1989. It was built for the 1980 Summer Olympics and has 7,500 rooms. Just across the street stands the famous Izmailovsky Souvenir Market, where you can purchase matryoshkas, cheburashkas, fur hats, books and pins at affordable prices.

After a full week of immersing myself in Russian, I dropped into the British Embassy in Moscow on a Friday night to clear my mind and have a couple of beers and a hamburger. That was a tradition for North Americans, who had been living on a steady diet of Russian food for a week.

It also gave me a chance to speak English and give my brain a rest, since I had immersed myself in the Russian language all week.

Displayed on a newsstand was a copy of the London-based *Daily Telegraph* with front page headlines shouting out, 'The Iron Curtain is swept aside: East Germany throws open all its borders.'

Once again, there was scant coverage in the Russian media. The only mention in newspapers was a very short three-inch story.

EAST German border police at Checkpoint Charlie were surprised to learn yesterday that citizens could now travel to the West freely, *writes Douglas Hamilton of Reuter.*

"People are going to read this and say 'there must be some mistake'," said a young guard, shaken out of his normally severe bearing. "It's not good," another said an hour after the decision was announced. "We will lose our jobs."

Traffic was light at the famous crossing, meant for foreign travellers through the Berlin Wall. Pointing towards West Berlin, one East German complained: "I just wanted to see if I could go over there for a look. I intend to come back."

The commanding border police officer, a man about 30, slowly and deliberately read a dispatch about the open borders from the official news agency. "They (the people) will have to read this very carefully. Sometimes you have to read between the lines," he said, pointing to a line saying official permission to travel was still needed.

Asked how many people might want to leave, the officer said he had heard talk that two million East Germans could pack up and move West. He said many may arrive this morning, with or without the necessary papers, and agreed the early shift would be "interesting".

A story in the London-based *Daily Telegraph* focuses on the total surprise of East German border guards at the fall of the Berlin Wall.

When local papers finally did get around to publishing something substantial the Soviet government, which had been slowly softening its brand of communism, endorsed East Germany's decision, but emphasized it had nothing to do with it.

However, it warned about the possibility of instability if East Germans immediately rushed to the West in droves.

Three days later the Monday, Nov. 13 edition of *The Guardian* ran the headline 'Four million flood to the West'.

Some people had taken the extreme risk of jumping from their windows in Berlin to become free in 1961. The wall was planned to be built on land where their houses stood.

It was curious that on the same weekend Helmet Kohl, the Chancellor of West Germany, was paying a visit to the Lower Silesia territory of Poland, ethnic Germans who lived there were asking for more rights. The Allies had given the area to Poland at the end of the Second World War.

The situation was similar to what happened in Crimea in 2014, where ethnic Russians revolted in what then was the eastern part of Ukraine, but later was annexed by Russia.

On the same junket, I covered five games in the Soviet Elite League and was in Moscow on Nov. 7 for the traditional military parade through

Red Square. Although I did not get into the square, I stood on the side-walk as tanks and military machinery made their exit afterwards through Mayakovskaya Square.

It was the first season the Red Army team did not have Slava Fetisov, Sergei Makarov, Igor Larionov and Vladimir Krutov, who all had signed with NHL clubs.

Moscow Dynamo won the championship, halting a remarkable string of 13 straight by the Red Army.

Of all the personalities I met in my travels, none had a more interest-ing tale to tell than Karl Yegorov Watts, for many years the public address announcer for major hockey events at Moscow's Luzhniki Arena, includ-ing the 1972 Summit Series.

While the Soviet Union's best hockey players made their way to North America Watts, many years earlier, had amazingly gone the other way by emigrating from Canada to the USSR, a Communist country.

Watts' parents, Steve and Anne, moved to Canada looking to start a new life in the 1920s. They were born in Poland, but the area where they lived now is part of Ukraine.

Watts was born and raised on a small farm near Winnipeg. As a boy he tuned in to the Saturday night radio broadcasts of Foster Hewitt on a regular basis.

The family lived in Hamilton, Ont., for some time and Karl became a member of the Air Cadets. He even was permitted to pilot a flight.

However, Steve and Anne missed their extended family and, in 1952, they applied to go back home, taking Karl and a brother George with them.

They took up residence in Ukraine, but the boys had no future there and decided to relocate to Leningrad to pursue studies in foreign languages.

Radio Moscow offered both of them jobs in 1959.

Karl also worked for the Voice of Russia World Service and was compelled to read news stories he claimed he did not actually believe. The information was prepared by the USSR State Committee for Radio and Television.

"I simply read what I was given," he told me during an interview at the 1986 World Championship.

Three thousand Canadian hockey fans were urging Team Canada to fight to the finish in Game 8 of the Summit Series, shouting, 'Da, da, Kanada! Nyet, nyet, Soviet!' at the Soviet team. Translation – 'Yes, yes, Canada! No, no, Soviet!'

Some Canadian players were taking the message literally by roughing up their hosts. A fight even broke out between the normally mild-mannered Rod Gilbert and Evgeny Mishakov of the Soviets.

Between periods, Watts was summoned and told to translate into English an announcement from officials of the Soviet Ice Hockey Federation.

"If the Canadians continue to play as they are playing we reserve the right to pull our team off the ice," it read.

Trailing 5-3 at the time, Team Canada rallied to win 6-5 on Paul Henderson's historic goal with 34 seconds left in the game.

The Canadians were so deliriously happy, they invited Watts to their victory celebration, in spite of what he had announced at the start of the third period.

When a 15-part television series called 'Strategy of Victory' was aired, marking 40 years since the Allies conquered Hitler and the Nazis, Watts was asked to read the parts of former American presidents Franklin D. Roosevelt, Harry Truman and Dwight D. Eisenhower.

The Soviet and Canadian teams became bitter foes during the season, but it's hard to imagine the Soviets had a more hated opponent than Czechoslovakia.

The fierce rivalry between the national teams of the two countries was never hotter than immediately after a political uprising against communism in Czechoslovakia was crushed in the summer of 1968.

The 1969 World Championship was scheduled to be played in Czechoslovakia, but because of the invasion the host country had to withdraw.

For the next decade the two countries fought tooth and nail on the ice.

Stockholm was awarded the 1969 championship, and Czechoslovakia was on fire stunning the Soviet team, which had won both the Olympic and World titles the year before, 2-0 and 4-3. Unfortunately for the Czechoslovaks, they lost twice to Sweden and the Soviets were able to repeat as world champions because of a superior goals-for-and-against differential.

Soviet coach Anatoly Tarasov, it was written later, had a mild heart attack during one of the games.

After Soviet goalie Viktor Zinger surrendered the first goal, he was confronted by Czechoslovakia's Jaroslav Holik, who shouted at Zinger, "You are a bloody communist."

At the same time, Holik was goading Zinger by pointing his stick at his face.

Then Josef Golonka, the Czechoslovak captain, stirred the boiling pot when he held his stick up in the air simulating the shooting of a rifle.

A red star on the front of the Czechoslovak jerseys was intended by its government to display loyalty to Moscow. However, prior to their first meeting in Stockholm, it was blocked out with tape by some players, in defiance of the Communist Party.

More than a year before the invasion, Moscow had received a recommendation by the Soviet ambassador in Prague that further matches between the two countries, scheduled for Czechoslovak territory, be cancelled and that Soviet referees and linesmen not do anymore games in Czechoslovakia.

Holik was given a reprimand when he returned home to Prague.

Holik's son Bobby, thanks to an early release from the army, joined the Hartford Whalers in 1990 and played again for Czechoslovakia only twice – at the 1991 World Championship and 1996 World Cup of Hockey.

In fact, Bobby obtained his U.S. citizenship in 1996 and expressed a desire to play for the Americans internationally, since he had given up his Czech citizenship.

But the Americans never selected him and, playing for the perennial Stanley Cup-contending New Jersey Devils by that time, he was rarely available at World Championship time in the spring with the Devils always in the playoffs.

Evgeny Zimin told me many years later the Soviet players did not view the Czechoslovaks as their enemies.

"Our players knew what was going on but they didn't have any influence over the moves of the Soviet government and Communist Party in Moscow," he said. "But in their hearts and their heads they did not agree with the policy of the occupation of Czechoslovakia and the use of tanks against the people of that country."

Interestingly, Zimin said the Czechoslovak and Soviet players continued to speak to each other away from the rink during the tournament.

"The whole Czechoslovak team was invited to the Soviet embassy in Stockholm," he said. "Nobody could feel this tension outside of the rink."

In an interview with Sports Illustrated, Peter Stastny explained the world-wide fraternity of players best when he revealed his reasons for helping Soviet goalie Sergei Mylnikov adjust to his new job with the NHL's Quebec Nordiques in 1989.

"You can't hate the person," Stastny said. "You do not like the politics of his country, but the human being is warm and modest, and he will help this team."

As hot as the rivalry was, there were occasions when the Soviets did favours for the Czechoslovaks whom, despite the political turmoil, they considered their Slavic brothers.

At the 1982 World Championship in Finland, the Soviets clinched the gold medal early and Canada was in line to take the silver if the Soviets defeated Czechoslovakia on the final day.

It was never proved, but many observers believe the Soviets tanked the final game, which ended in a 0-0 deadlock, so that the Czechoslovaks would get a point and earn the silver ahead of Canada.

Alan Eagleson left a blank cheque at the front desk of the Hesperia Hotel in Helsinki to cover destruction by furious Canadian players who ransacked it.

One newspaper reported that at one point Soviet star Sergei Makarov had a clear-cut breakaway, but circled back with the puck rather than driving for the net.

Still, Igor Larionov denied his team didn't try to win.

"We had secured the gold medal already before the match with Czechoslovakia," he said later. "We had no agreement to avoid scoring. You cannot get out on the ice and fool people."

However, when I asked the towering Soviet centre Viktor Zhluktov about the accusations more than a decade later on a visit to Toronto, he smiled and answered through an interpreter, "Well, I guess we can talk about those things now, can't we!"

The 0-0 tie was described in the European press as 'lacklustre' and the game drew jeers from the Helsinki crowd.

It was the first scoreless tie at a World Championship in 34 years. The last time two teams failed to score against each other was in 1948 when Canada and Czechoslovakia drew 0-0 on an outdoor rink covered with snow at the Olympics in St. Moritz, Switzerland.

That one was totally unexpected since Czechoslovakia averaged 10 goals a game and Canada 8.6 in the tournament.

Jimmy Doyle, an American from New York, was selected to referee the Czechoslovakia-Soviet game in 1982, even though he was only 25.

"I was a young official and it took me a while to catch on," he said. "At the end of the second period, it dawned on me what was going on. It became apparent the game was not being played in the normal way. I went off the ice very disappointed at what was happening."

But Doyle could do nothing about it. It was his job only to referee the game and see that the players stuck to the playing rules.

"This was the most significant game I had ever worked. I had done about eight games already in the tournament and most of the games involving Czechoslovakia and the Soviet Union had been very physical.

"This time the speed was there, but the intensity definitely was not. If the Soviets had scored, the Czechoslovaks would have pumped one in very quickly."

Doyle, who now works in the NHL's video replay room in Philadelphia, was given a tape of the game and had it converted into a DVD, but said he hasn't looked at it in 10 years.

Wayne Gretzky, in the only World Championship in which he played, said, "Whether the Soviets threw the game or not is everyone's own opinion. In my opinion they played for the tie. In the last 10 minutes of the game, Makarov and Krutov (the KLM line) were on the ice just once. That wasn't a good sign. They're both communist countries and I think communists stick together. "

Canada had done its part by shutting out Sweden 6-0 in the afternoon. Gretzky scored three goals and eventually finished as the tournament scoring champion. Two Soviet players, Makarov and Viktor Shalimov, who had been tied for the lead going into the last day, naturally got no points.

But as Bobby Clarke said, "It was no one's fault but our own that we didn't win the silver medal. When we tied Italy we lost it."

In that game transplanted Canadian Jim Corsi from Montreal made 55 saves for the Italians in a 3-3 draw. Today he is one of the leaders in the relatively new field of hockey analytics.

Rick Vaive, also playing in the Worlds for the first time, conceded there is no way to prove the Soviets deliberately played to a scoreless tie with Czechoslovakia.

"You can't say for sure that they threw the game. But there's no doubt they didn't play the same way against the Czechs that they played against the other teams."

In the third period fans in Helsinki's Jaahalli whistled loudly to show their disgust at the defensive game both the Czechoslovaks and Soviets were playing.

Soviet goalie Vladimir Myshkin, playing in place of Vladislav Tretiak with the gold medal clinched, was outstanding in goal.

After the game, Soviet coach Viktor Tikhonov called any suggestion that the Soviets threw the game "ridiculous." The Czechoslovaks played very well, he said, and there was just no motivation for his players.

In the House of Commons Terry Sargeant, an NDP Member of Parliament from Manitoba, suggested Canada show its disgust at what had taken place through official channels.

Five years later the skate was on the other foot, so to speak, with the Soviets accusing Canada of laying down in a 9-0 whitewash at the hands of Sweden at the 1987 World Championship in Vienna.

The Soviet Union felt the Swedes were able to score goals far too easily. Their romp over Canada meant the Soviets would have to score at least nine goals against Czechoslovakia to win the gold.

The USSR won 2-1, but it was relegated to the silver medal, a bitter pill to swallow since it went through the tournament undefeated.

The Soviets finished with eight wins and two ties; points earned in the preliminary round did not carry over to the final round.

Asked by a Soviet reporter if Canada dumped the game, Alan Eagleson replied that the Canadians couldn't have played that poorly, even if they had planned it. Coach Dave King, also miffed at criticism by Tikhonov, said it was the worst possible insult anybody could make at hockey players from the land of the Maple Leaf.

Politics has crept into international hockey in many other ways.

Then there is the funny side of on-ice controversies.

Imagine the puzzled look on referee Steve Piotrowski's face when he watched Sweden score a goal with the wrong puck at the 1989 World Junior Championship in Alaska.

The Swedes were trailing the Soviet Union 3-2 with only a few minutes left to play when they scored what appeared to be the tying goal.

However, Piotrowski suddenly realized there were two pucks on the ice. After conferring with his linesmen, he ruled the game puck actually was in the corner of the rink, where Soviet goalie Alexei Ivashkin had directed it when the goal was scored with a second puck that had mysteriously appeared.

Ivashkin had his eyes on the real puck and had no chance to react when the Swedes scored with the second puck.

The Swedes started to jump for joy, but Piotrowski disallowed the goal, the Soviets held the one-goal lead and went on to win the gold medal.

Swedish team manager Kjell Damberg charged on to the ice to protest and had to be ejected from the game.

"It was quite an ordeal," Piotrowski said. "Probably the most compelling moment of the tournament."

Nobody could discover where the other puck came from. They checked Sergei Fedorov's back pocket and found a hole in it.

Nothing ever was proved, but the majority of onlookers suggested the second puck fell to the ice from Fedorov's equipment. He had just returned from serving a penalty and intended to go straight to the players bench, but was forced to get into the play when the Swedes went on the attack.

I once asked Fedorov what really happened but he refused to talk about it.

Sean Draper, son of Canadian team manager Dave Draper, was videotaping games for the Canadian national junior team at the tournament.

"We were using a giant old VCR and trying to get the tape to stop at the right place," said Draper, who now works for the Edmonton Oilers. "We then sent a tape to the University of Anchorage and received still photos back. You can see the puck descend from the pant leg of one of the Soviet players."

Draper said it looked like Fedorov and teammate Alexander Godynyuk collided in front of the net, dislodging the puck.

"There was a pile of tournament pucks in the penalty box," Piotrowski said. "The Russians were big on souvenirs in those days."

Piotrowski and Draper both were summoned to a hearing that lasted three hours the next day and testified they could not conclusively say where the mystery puck originated.

Soviet players traveling for games in Western Europe and North America often were caught shoplifting goods that were not available to them back home.

Among those charged were Slava Bykov, a national team centre, who won two Olympic gold medals and later coached Russia at the 2010 Olympics in Vancouver. The items could be sold back in the Soviet Union for huge sums.

Bykov was caught leaving a department store in Stockholm in 1983 with clothes for his child concealed. Stopped by the store's security person, he said he was just carrying them and fully intended to pay for them. He was searched and the security person could find no money on him.

He had to appear before a magistrate but was acquitted, after spending two days in jail because of lack of evidence. However the Soviet Ice Hockey Federation barred him from playing in the 1984 Olympics in Sarajevo.

Bykov spent two days in jail and was acquitted at his trial, but not before he had answered a question about his occupation and salary.

"I am an ice hockey player on a full-time basis," he said, adding that he earned the equivalent of about $5,000 a year.

The secretary of the Swedish Olympic committee said it was the first time he had ever heard a Soviet athlete admit that he was a professional.

One season a total of 10 Soviet players were disciplined by the Soviet Sports Committee for shoplifting while abroad and had their names published in the newspaper.

In communist times, Soviet players touring Canada often brought Russian goodies like caviar to sell outside the arenas to supplement their meagre incomes. In those days players were given a per diem, but not until the final game of the tour was completed. That was the only time they had money to shop.

Aggie Kukulowicz told this yarn about Anatoly Tarasov, the great Soviet coach who is known as the Godfather of Russian Hockey.

"When he came to Canada one fall as an observer at the Canada Cup tournament, we booked him into the best hotel we could find," he said. "The Soviet Ice Hockey Federation would provide him with enough money to pay for it. But when he got here, he cancelled the reservation, moved into a cheaper hotel and pocketed the difference!"

There is no shortage of anecdotes when it comes to the mixture of sport and politics behind the Iron Curtain.

A few years ago Peter Stastny wrote a letter to IIHF President Rene Fasel describing Juraj Siroky, at that time president of the Slovak Ice Hockey Federation and a member of the IIHF Council, as a secret police informer during the days of communism.

According to the official Slovak Institute dealing with the communist era, Siroky was a high-ranking officer (captain) in the feared Communist STB, the country's counterpart to the Soviet KGB.

"If Mr. Siroky does not abandon all the positions in Slovak ice hockey in three months, I will withdraw from the Slovak Hockey Hall of Fame," Stastny wrote.

Stastny said the STB had either prosecuted or jailed hundreds of thousands of innocent citizens and executed hundreds.

Mystery surrounded Evgeny Zimin, who scored the first Soviet goal of the Summit Series to spark his team to a shocking 7-3 win over Team Canada at the Montreal Forum in 1972.

Strangely, Zimin did not play again in the eight-game series. Soviet officials told the media he was suffering from an injury, but many years later in a story by David Shoalts *The Globe and Mail* speculated he was planning to defect and looking for an NHL club to sign with, therefore was being monitored by the KGB for the remainder of the Canadian half of the series.

Czechoslovak players were supposed to have regular jobs, thereby maintaining their playing status as amateur. But George Gross of *The Toronto Sun* reported in a story in 1980 players were only required to show up one day a week – pay day!

Before the 1988 Olympics in Calgary, Czechoslovak defenceman Drahomir Kadlec was asked about his job as an electrician.

"I can't even change a light bulb!" he replied.

Members of the Red Army club were soldiers, but only in name. However German Titov, who started his hockey career with the Khimik club in Voskresensk, did become a sergeant in an artillery division.

Although he never fought in a war Titov, who later spent nine seasons in the NHL with Calgary, Pittsburgh and Anaheim, had to work 16 hours a day commanding a group of 12 soldiers.

Titov also won a gold medal with Russia at the 1993 World Championship and a silver at the 1998 Olympics.

Just prior to the 1980 Olympics, the Soviet Red Army team played a tour of games against NHL teams, shortly after the Soviet invasion of Afghanistan.

The Soviets had a good record, except for a Sunday night in Buffalo when the Sabres whipped them 6-1 in front of a noisy crowd that booed the Army team loudly when they came on the ice.

Outside the arena, a Ukrainian freedom organization passed out pamphlets entitled 'The Puck'n Red Army – They shoot as well as they skate'.

Also on the cover was a photo of Soviet soliders marching in Red Square with their guns. Listed inside were all the invasions the Soviet army has carried out over the years.

Just two months later, of course, the Soviets were upset 4-3 by the U.S. collegians at the Lake Placid Olympics. The night the Americans won, the fans were literally hanging over the boards in the packed Lake Placid arena. The atmosphere of animosity against the Soviets at that time in history was a major factor in their blowing the gold medal.

In Buffalo, they played like they were intimidated and in Lake Placid they were very nervous.

Today the Soviets' chief rival on the ice is Canada, because it is the best hockey country in world. However, for political reasons, Communist

Party-sponsored newspapers used to give special front-page exposure to games in which the Soviets humiliated the United States.

Arturs Irbe, a native of Latvia who backstopped the Soviet Union to World Championship gold medals in 1989 and 1990, helped form a human barricade in the streets of Riga in 1991 to safeguard radio and television buildings.

Lithuania had made threats of withdrawing from the Soviet Union and government officials in Moscow had ordered tanks into Vilnius, its capital city. Latvians were terrified they might also suffer the same fate.

Irbe declined to play again for the Soviet Union when he was asked to before the 1991 World Championship.

Instead he came to North America, where he fashioned a very respectable career with San Jose, Dallas, Vancouver and Carolina, playing in two NHL All-Star Games.

Irbe said he agreed to play for the Soviet Union because it gave him a chance to play at a much higher level than he ever had before. However, he always kept his head down when the Soviet national anthem was being played, never looked up at the Soviet flag and never sang the anthem.

When Latvia defeated Russia at the 2000 World Championship in St. Petersburg, the Latvian Parliament suspended voting so that lawmakers could watch the game at a bar. Political foes cheered and sang arm in arm when Latvia won 3-2.

Drummers make lots of noise at home games of the KHL club
Dinamo Riga.

The early 1990s was a time of real turmoil in the Eastern Bloc as communism slowly faded away. A Russian league game between Khimik and Spartak had to be called off on Oct. 4, 1991, when tanks appeared in the downtown area of the Russian capital the day before and attacked the Ostankino television station.

The station is located in Moscow's northeast sector, the same area as Spartak's home arena Sokolniki. However, two other games hosted by Moscow Dynamo and Wings of the Soviet on the day of the uprising were played, as scheduled.

It happened just before Boris Yeltsin became the first president of the new version of Russia.

While Soviet coach Tikhonov was widely criticized for insisting that his players live in barracks away from their families, not all of their wives saw the system as the end of the world.

Sandra Gusarov, whose husband Alexei played 11 seasons in the NHL and won a Stanley Cup with the Colorado Avalanche in 1996, took another view.

"Of course I missed my husband," she told me at the 2012 KHL All-Star Game. "But you know what, that was Tikhonov's plan and it worked."

While the Gusarovs lived in Evergreen, Colorado, near Denver, Alexei became interested in hobby car racing and eventually owned a team called Goose Racing on the NASCAR circuit.

International officiating has come a long way. Unbelievably, some players once officiated in the same IIHF tournaments in which they were playing. At the 1949 World Championship, Francis 'Dinty' Moore of Port Colborne, Ont., refereed a half-dozen games when Canada wasn't playing.

Dave Trottier played for Canada and refereed some games during the 1928 Winter Olympics.

Carl Erhardt refereed in eight of the 1936 Olympic matches when Great Britain was not involved.

It was not until well into the 1950s that international hockey developed a pool of dedicated referees.

As a defenceman, Erhardt was known to play more than 40 minutes a game. When Great Britain won its only Olympic hockey gold medal in 1936, upsetting Canada, he was 39 and became the oldest player ever to win a gold.

CHAPTER 7
Working with Ken Dryden and Al Michaels in Calgary

Unless you've tried it yourself, don't tell anybody else how to do it.

That's the lesson I learned when I met Ken Dryden for the first time early in my employment with the ABC television network in Calgary in 1988, the first time Canada hosted the Winter Olympics.

Dryden was interested in what inside information I had about the Soviet team, and for a moment I forgot I was talking to a Hall of Fame goaltender who had faced the Big Red Machine in the 1972 Summit Series, as well as in World Championships and the famous 1975 New Year's Eve 3-3 tie between the Montreal Canadiens and Red Army team at the Montreal Forum.

"Puck possession, as you know, is the name of the game," I instructed my student! "It's like the NFL. When one team has the ball on a scoring drive, the other one can't score. And the Soviets have the puck most of the time."

Dryden quickly got his back up.

"No, it's not," he shot back. "In hockey, the puck changes hands, on average, more than six times a minute."

If my math is correct, that works out to every 10 seconds.

I was stunned that I had been challenged on my view of Soviet hockey success. But from that point on, I resolved to talk less and listen more

My first thrill was when I found out my mailbox was right beside those of Frank and Kathie Lee Gifford. The mailboxes were arranged in alphabetical order, e.g., GIB, GIF. The Giffords were working in the ABC studio.

Al Michaels and Dryden formed the network's broadcasting team, the same as they had been when a spunky bunch of U.S. college players upset the Soviet Union in Lake Placid eight years earlier.

Working as colour man on the second team was Boston University grad Mike Eruzione, who scored the winning goal against the Soviets at Lake Placid in 1980.

Attempting to put viewers in a positive mood from the outset, ABC had asked the IIHF to provide a relatively easy opponent for the U.S. in prime time on the opening Saturday night.

Tournament organizers served up Austria as the sacrificial lamb and the 1988 version of America's best college players won 10-6.

Goalie Brian Stankiewicz, a transplanted Canadian from Toronto, was the victim of the goal-happy Americans. Stankiewicz played for Austria despite stopping a shot that broke his mask in practice the day before.

Stankiewicz has to be one of the unluckiest players in Olympic history. He didn't get to play in the 1984 Games in Sarajevo because his knee was torn up in a collision with U.S. forward John Harrington during an exhibition game.

He finally appeared in five games at the Calgary Olympics and three at Lillehammer, Norway in 1994, but in playing for a non-medal contender faced so much rubber he could have passed for a worn-out tire when it was all over.

Dave Peterson's American squad also threw a scare into both Czechoslovakia and the Soviet Union. But when the Yanks were upset 4-1 by West Germany and failed to qualify for the medal round, we were fighting for air time with Eddie the Eagle, the unconventional but lovable British ski jumper and a rodeo being held next door in the old Calgary Corral with legendary sportscaster Curt Gowdy calling the action.

The early exit of the U.S. hockey team cost ABC plenty in ratings and lost advertising revenue.

The network paid a record $309 million for the U.S. television rights to the 1988 Games, which represented an enormous jump from Sarajevo in 1984, when the figure was only $91.5 million.

While the Saddledome, which was only five years old, hosted most of the games, some were played at the old Calgary Corral next door and the Father David Bauer Olympic Arena.

The Corral also had extremely high boards, which caused some concern.

"The boards were super high," John Davidson once told *The Cochrane Eagle*, a small newspaper in Alberta. "If you jumped off the bench over the boards, it was a road trip to hit the ice!"

Davidson, the former NHL goalie with whom I worked at four Olympics, played his junior hockey there for the Calgary Centennials.

IIHF president Gunther Sabetzki had announced in 1986 that professional athletes would be eligible to compete in all sports in Calgary. The announcement came a decade after NHL players were introduced at the World Hockey Championship.

It was ironic that the first player signed by the Canadian Olympic hockey program was the last player cut before the Olympics. Don McLaren, a peach of a guy from Kitchener, Ontario, stuck with the program until the Olympic year, only to be replaced at the last minute by ex-pros, who wound up failing to help the team.

I knew McLaren because the year before I was riding on the team bus from Chicoutimi to Rimouski following an exhibition game against a Soviet select team. The game was over late and the Canadian players dragged themselves onto the bus, dead tired, and stretched themselves out over two seats to get some rest. I was the last person to board and was embarrassed when there were no seats available.

Coach Dave King hollered for the guys to double up, but no one moved, except for McLaren, so that I could sit down. It's sad that nice guys often seem to finish last.

Defenceman Tim Watters, who had been seeing a lot of the bench with the Winnipeg Jets, credits the Olympics with restoring his self-confidence and prolonging his career. He signed with the Los Angeles Kings the following summer.

King said in the fall of 1987 the NHL gave its teams the right to assist the Canadian and U.S. Olympic teams with players on their rosters.

"But there was a gentleman's agreement that these players could not be superstars," King said. "They had to be approved by the NHL.

"Alan Eagleson, Sam Pollock and others were working towards a best-on-best competition between Canada and the Soviet Union at some point in time."

Canada actually listed two minor league pros, Mark Morrison and Don Dietrich, on its roster one day before the 1984 Olympics, but they were rejected by the IIHF.

"They had played a sprinkle of NHL games," King said. "Hockey Canada was trying to push the pro thing. It was like politics, sometimes you have to run twice before you win.

"But we were almost sure we were peeing in the wind!" he said of the attempt to get the two pros into the Olympics in 1984.

In a *Globe and Mail* article in January 1985, Eagleson revealed the Soviets had told him they no longer cared who plays for Canada, they just wanted to beat its best players. In previous years, the Soviets had objected to the use of pros and together with the Czechoslovaks voted against it.

Calgary released Jim Peplinski and Edmonton Randy Gregg, who had played at the 1980 tournament in Lake Placid, for the 1988 Games. Canada also added goaltender Andy Moog, who was involved in a contract dispute with the Oilers. Serge Boisvert came from Montreal, Ken Yaremchuk from Toronto and Steve Tambellini from Vancouver.

Although Canada had upset the applecart by winning the Izvestia Tournament in Moscow in December 1987, the addition of NHLers appeared to destroy team spirit and King's squad finished out of the medals.

In essence, the Canadian-based NHL clubs provided only players they could easily do without for a couple of weeks. There was a suggestion they feared their European players would revolt because only Canadian players were being released to play.

Nevertheless, Finland had many former NHL players on its roster and was able to win its first Olympic medal.

On the last day, the Finns upset the Soviets 2-1 to clinch a silver. The Soviets already had the gold medal in the bag.

No fewer than 21 Canadian pros were playing for other nations. All of them were minor league or European league stars who had no real chance of making the NHL, but with the aid of dual citizenship they were able to compete in the Olympics for their adopted countries. German goalie Karl Friesen, born in Winnipeg, was the most notable of these players.

Still, a full decade before NHL players started playing in the Olympics, the teams were largely amateur at Calgary. In fact, almost all of the Norwegian players had other full-time jobs.

Right winger Arne Billkvam was a taxi driver and defenceman Petter Salsten was working on highway construction besides attending games and practices in the evening.

Curt Lindstrom, who coached both Sweden and Finland at various times, once owned the largest off-track betting shop in his native Sweden, but sold it after moving to Finland to because he found it too difficult to manage from there.

Even today members of the Slovenian national team own bars and restaurants.

These are the sort of players and coaches who are a pleasure to interview. They receive so little attention during the regular season back home they are totally flattered to meet somebody who is interested in them.

Ten years later in Nagano, Japan, curiosity seekers had a field day watching players from the non-contending nations seeking out the NHL pros they had just played against for autographs outside the arena after the game.

The Soviets won the gold medal in Calgary, to no one's surprise. This was essentially the same team that had competed hard right down to the last minute at the Canada Cup in 1987, taking the Wayne Gretzky and Mario Lemieux-led Team Canada to the brink before losing by one goal.

In the preliminary round, Canada lost to Finland and tied Sweden, therefore beginning the final round with three fewer points than the Soviets and needing a win against the defending champs to keep its hopes of a gold medal alive.

The Soviets, however, won 5-0, all but guaranteeing them the gold. To the surprise of many writers, King chose to start Sean Burke in goal over Moog, a three-time Stanley Cup winner, because Burke had been strong against the Soviets at the Izvestia.

Sweden finished with the bronze medal followed by Canada in fourth.

Calgary also was the site of the first Olympics in which a shootout was used. France and Norway, playing for 11th place, finished regulation time in a 6-6 tie. The French team earned the win by outscoring the Norwegians 2-0 in the shootout. The placement game was played at the Father David Bauer Arena.

My first boss at the Olympics was Draggan Mihailovich, a graduate of the University of North Carolina who had interviewed me for the job at the 1987 Canada Cup in Hamilton.

Mihailovich, a workaholic who turned out to be the best researcher I ever worked with, produced all 120 features the CBS network used 10 years later at the 1998 Olympics in Japan. He now is a producer with the award-winning CBS program 60 Minutes.

Of the five Emmy Awards he has won, perhaps the most gut-wrenching was *The Lost Children,* the tale of 10,000 British children forced to work as slave labourers or sexually abused after being sent to Australia following the Second World War.

ABC aired at least part of between 15 and 20 games, but there were a lot of throws to other venues when the action was at a peak there.

There was never a clear decision made the night before on whether or not we would carry certain games the next day.

I left the broadcast booth late one night with the understanding there would be no games televised the next day and planned to go to Father David Bauer Arena to cover the Canadian team practice.

To my shock, I turned to check a monitor at the practice rink and saw the faces of Michaels and Dryden on the screen. They were broadcasting a game!

Polish player Jaroslav Morawiecki tested positive in a random doping examination during the 1988 Games. The test was taken after Poland defeated France 6-2 in a preliminary round game.

Leszak Lejczyk, head coach of the Polish team, said Morawiecki was the only player on his country's hockey team who had attended a dinner hosted by the Polish community in Calgary earlier in the week and might have eaten something that affected the test. The committee didn't buy it.

The temperature varied greatly in Calgary. It was cold when the Games started, but in the second week a Chinook blew in, the thermometer rose to 63 F and people were walking around in shorts. It had no effect on hockey, but 33 outdoor events had to be rescheduled.

Students from Calgary schools did artwork for visiting members of the media and cards were left in hotel rooms welcoming them. My card showing spectators outdoors in a snowfall came from Celine Del Castilho of Don Bosco School, who was only 9 at the time.

On the final Saturday night I managed to get into the Saddledome for the ladies figure skating final. Canada's Elizabeth Manley got a rousing standing ovation for her program and looked to be a surprise gold medal winner.

But as soon as she scooped her congratulatory bouquets up off the ice and headed off to wait for her marks, Katarina Witt of East Germany came charging out for her warmup, appearing full of confidence.

Witt nosed Manley out for the gold medal, skating a very conservative program and making sure she made no mistakes. She became the first woman to repeat as Olympic champion since Sonja Henie of Norway captured three straight golds in 1928, 1932 and 1936.

I'll never forget the party thrown for the media at the Calgary Convention Centre following the closing ceremonies. A band of electronic fiddlers in cowboy hats greeted us at the door and there were mountains of food inside.

Four years went by like a flash and CBS began a three-Olympics run as American rights holder at the 1992 Games in France. Although they were based in Albertville, the hockey tournament was held in Meribel in the French Alps at an elevation of about 5,000 feet.

Traditionally, both medal game participants purchase Champagne well before the game looking forward to victory.

However, it had either slipped the minds of Czechoslovak team officials or they were being unnecessarily pessimistic.

Between the second and third periods of the bronze medal game, with Czechoslovakia leading the U.S. 3-0, I went down to the dressing room corridor and overheard team trainers lamenting in Czech they had forgotten to buy post-game spirits.

Fortunately, there was a store right across the street from the arena and one of the trainers made a beeline for it. I quickly got on the headsets and notified director Sandy Grossman, who immediately dispatched a cameraman and CBS was able to get a shot of the Champagne being carried into the dressing room before the game even was over.

The Soviet Union had ceased to exist by December 1991 and was replaced temporarily by the Commonwealth of Independent States. However the Soviet Ice Hockey Federation decided to label its entry in the 1992 Olympic hockey tournament the Unified Team

The Unified Team and Dave King's Canadian squad battled to a scoreless tie over the first two periods of the gold medal game, but the former Soviets pulled away in the third to win 3-1.

Even though he was on the 23-man roster, third-string goalie Nikolai Khabibulin didn't get to keep the gold medal he received at the closing ceremonies. It was taken from him by coach Tikhonov. Khabibulin had not played a single minute during the tournament.

At the end of the game the Unified Team players formed a human net and tossed Tikhonov up in the air in celebration to give him a happy sendoff, believing it was his last Olympics. He actually came back for one more.

The medal finally was returned to Khabibulin in a private ceremony during the 2002 Winter Olympics in Salt Lake City, Utah.

Later, that summer, the Red Army club showed up in Toronto unexpectedly looking for exhibition games. I met Khabibulin at the Westbury Hotel and did a little shopping with him on Yonge Street, helping him to pick out a new pair of shoes for his mother.

From an entertainment point of view, you couldn't beat the 1992 quarter-final matchup between Canada and Germany.

The teams fought to a 3-3 tie in regulation time and went scoreless in a 10-minute overtime period. The showdown for the right to advance to the semifinals went to a five-round shootout, with each country scoring twice to leave the game in a deadlock.

Eric Lindros had failed to score when he led off the first round for Canada. Coach King selected the captain also to lead off the second. This time he beat German goalie Helmut de Raaf; Gerrmany's Peter Draisaitl, the father of Leon Draisaitl of the Edmonton Oilers, missed and the Canadians won 4-3.

Later in the evening Germany filed a protest claiming the referee erred in allowing the same shooting rotation in the second round. Indeed it was a mistake. Canada shot first in the opening round, and the rules say the order should be reversed in the second.

However, after talking about it until the wee hours of the morning the IIHF rejected the protest on the grounds that if the Germans had really known about the rule, they would have filed a protest at the time.

Only two of the seven Olympics I worked at were held in a truly winter setting. France was the first.

It was a gorgeous scene with beautiful snow-capped mountains everywhere. Yet the temperature was rather mild, so much so that at noon hour you could actually sit in a T-shirt and shorts at the top of a ski run and soak up the sun.

The 6,500-seat arena was located right beside the finish line for the women's downhill skiing event, which made it convenient to catch some of the action, including Kerrin Lee-Gartner's gold medal run.

The practice rink was located in Courchevel, on the other side of a mountain called Le Sommet de la Saulire, so we had a choice of traveling by bus in a circular route or taking a shortcut by riding the ski lift to the top and skiing down the other side to interview players. The mountain is 9,000 feet high.

I actually did this one day when my bosses assigned me to talk to Tikhonov before the Unified Team's semi-final match with the United States; part of the interview made the CBS Evening News.

Meribel has plenty of snow-covered evergreen trees and the chalets were made out of fresh timber, creating a pleasant scent of pine. It has 45 ski-lifts, drawing skiers from all over the world.

We were housed at the fresh, new log-cabin style Hotel Merilys in the heart of Les Trois Vallées Ski Resort, which featured ski-to-door access.

Getting up to Meribel by bus and back down was very dangerous, but the experienced drivers did an excellent job even though there were no guardrails along some parts of the twisting roads.

Our announcer Mike Emrick slipped and fell on the ice one day, breaking his wrist. When the first cast, applied by a French doctor, proved to be too tight, he visited American team medic Dr. Schaffhausen to get a more comfortable one put on. Getting a cast put on at the same time was a 19-year-old kid named Keith Tkachuk, a rookie with the U.S. Olympic hockey team.

My wife Chris took a week's holidays from her job as a suggestions evaluator at Dofasco in Hamilton to come to France for a few days. We spent Valentine's Day together, had dinner at a restaurant near the arena and I was able to get her tickets for three games.

Experienced chefs from Paris were flown in to prepare the food in the media cafeteria. Tasty sauces were used on almost everything – not the healthiest food in the world but definitely the most appetizing fare I have dined on at the Olympics.

King Karl-Gustav and Queen Silvia of Sweden had their eyes opened when they attended a pre-tournament exhibition game between the Swedes and Americans in nearby Chamonix just before the Olympics.

The U.S. collegians threw their weight around, taking runs at the Swedes; French fans were so upset with the hooliganism they threw empty bottles on the ice at the end of the game, narrowly missing some of players. Swedish newspapers also ripped the Americans printing the word 'SKANDAL' in huge letters in a headline the next day.

Mats Naslund, Sweden's smallest player, was ejected for charging U.S. defenceman Greg Brown into the boards, leaving his feet in the process. American coach Dave Peterson was furious and refused to shake hands with Swedish coach Curt Lundmark after the Americans won 3-2.

CBS got a bargain by paying only $243 million for the U.S. TV rights in France after ABC had to fork out $309 million in Calgary.

Lillehammer, a town of 27,000 a two-and-a-quarter-hour drive north of Oslo, Norway, was the second winter wonderland I worked in. The 1994 Olympics were held there close to Lake Mjosa, Norway's largest lake, where horsedrawn sleighs take visitors for rides on the frozen surface.

It was beautiful not only in the daytime; after dark the spectacular Northern Lights filled the skies.

King Harald V of Norway attended the pre-Olympics media reception, where writers from around the world consumed mountains of salmon and cold scrambled eggs, a Norwegian favourite. The king himself represented his country in sailing at three Summer Olympics.

The hockey tournament in Lillehammer also had a storybook ending. Peter Forsberg's sensational deke on Corey Hirsch in a shootout won Sweden the gold medal 3-2 over Canada. It was the first Olympic gold for the Swedes.

Forsberg drew Hirsch to his left, then deposited the puck on the right side with just one hand on his stick.

Canada had a chance to prolong the shootout but Swedish goalie Tommy Salo stopped Paul Kariya.

The Canadians had been only a minute and 49 seconds away from winning their first Olympic title in 42 years when Sweden's Magnus Svensson scored to make it a 2-2 tie and force overtime.

The Swedish postal service commemorated Forsberg's winning goal by printing an image of the magical play on a stamp, despite protests registered by Hirsch.

Normally, only members of the Royal Family have that honour. There were two photographers hidden in the rafters of Hakons Hall right over the top of the net to capture the moment.

The Canadians, coached by Tom Renney, were very worthy silver medalists. Kariya scored an unassisted goal in overtime to beat the Czech Republic in the quarterfinals and Canada also came from behind to defeat previously unbeaten Finland 5-3 in the semifinals.

Russia sent probably its weakest team ever. NHL players were not yet taking part so coach Tikhonov had to rely on second-rate talent from the Russian and western European leagues.

With Russia trailing 3-0 to Finland in the bronze medal game and looking more like a beer league outfit than a defending Olympic champion, our colour man John Davidson sent me to grab a comment from Anatoly Tarasov, who was at the arena with his daughter Tatiana, a world-class figure skating coach.

The noise was deafening, but I did manage to hear him say in Russian, "I'm not at all interested in this level of hockey" as he pointed to the ice surface. That was the last time I ever saw Tarasov, who died in 1995. Finland went on to win the bronze medal with a 4-0 victory.

Goals for and against differential comes into play big time when two teams finish in a tie for what is only one spot in the playoffs. Some years it was based on the standings of the tournament, but in others it was based on the official IIHF ranking.

It can drive researchers and announcers crazy, and almost led to the only tussle Mike Emrick and I have had at the Olympics.

With the Czech Republic and Russia playing on a Sunday afternoon, I passed 'Doc' an incorrect note during the telecast, forgetting that when one team's differential increases, the other's decreases.

One of my jobs was to scan the crowd for celebrities. I remember Hillary Clinton attended the U.S.-France game in Lillehammer. The First Lady was there to greet all members of the American Olympic team and wish them good luck.

The secondary arena, which had seating for 4,800, was built into the side of a huge rock formation in a mountain in the town of Gjovik, about a 35-minute drive south of Lillehammer. Going through the front door was like entering a cave.

It was so solid that we were told, if a war ever broke out, the Royal family of Norway and the prime minister were to be transported there for their protection.

I was doing the research for CBS, Igor Kuperman for CTV and Tom Ratschunas of Finland, at that time considered the authority on European hockey, for the Turner network, which had purchased a portion of the American rights from CBS.

Eric Shanks, then just 22, was an intern for CBS. Although he was a student at the University of Indiana, where he had worked for and been a victim of basketball coach Bobby Knight's rants and raves, Shanks left school in February of that year for a chance to learn on the job.

Sixteen years later, he was named president of the Fox Sports Network, at the age of 38, leapfrogging over producers and directors he had worked for along the way.

At Fox he helped developed the controversial glowing puck that Fox used for awhile on NHL telecasts, as well as the yellow electronic first-down line that is still used today on football broadcasts.

Norway's population is so small that in 1994 there actually were more Americans of Norwegian descent – five million – than residents of the Norway – 4.2 million. Yet, going into the Sochi Games in 2014, Norway had won more Winter Olympic medals – 306 – than any other country. It also led the way in gold medals at Lillehammer.

A ticket application for events was sent to every home in Norway before the Games. Therefore, even people living north of Arctic Circle had an equal chance to purchase ducats with residents of Lillehammer.

A report by the United Nations ranked Norway as No. 1 in Europe for living conditions. Recently it placed first in the World Happiness Report, based on economics, health, life expectancy, sense of community etc.

In general, Lillehammer was quiet and peaceful, a far cry from 50 years earlier when it was occupied by the Nazis during the Second World War and the town served as the seat of the German High Command.

However, it was expensive. A large pizza in 1994 cost $22, while a similar one in downtown New York went for only $14.50.

Mothers were walking around the town daily pulling their children along snow-packed streets in little sleds, which are called sparks.

Because Norway borders Sweden, Hakons Hall was packed mostly with Swedish fans that had made the easy drive for the gold medal game. Swedish backup goalie Hakan Algotsson's wife gave birth during the Olympics and he was able to go home and still be back in time for the medal games.

Burlington goalie Phil Clancy makes friends with a Swedish tot in January 1985.

Norwegians and Swedes love to tell jokes at each other's expense. The best one I heard in Lillehammer went like this:

"Two Swedish astronauts were sent into space. Several days later one had to leave the capsule to make some repairs. After an hour outside, he was ready to climb back in and knocked on the door. "Who's there?" asked the second Swede!

Brian Savage, a member of Canada's silver medal-winning team in 1994, returned to Lillehammer in February 2016 to watch his son Ryan play for the U.S. in the World Youth Olympics.

Ryan was born in Montreal but was eligible to play for the Americans because he spent most of his young life in Arizona, when his dad was with the Phoenix Coyotes. So he obtained an American passport.

Father and son had watched a replay of the gold medal game about five months before traveling to Norway.

For the first time ever the NHL shut down for two weeks and NHL pros were used at the 1998 Olympics in Nagano

The Czech Republic, also employing 12 players from its own league, surprisingly won the gold medal and the star was goalie Dominik Hasek, who stoned Canada in a shootout in the semifinals as the Czechs won 2-1.

The Czechs were hanging on for dear life in regulation time against a Canadian team that, on paper at least, was superior.

The underdogs slowed the pace of the game down enough to preserve a 1-1 tie and get the game to overtime, which Canada also dominated.

Early in the shootout Robert Reichel's shot hit the post, but the puck still crossed the line, giving the Czechs the lead.

Meanwhile, Hasek stood firm against Theo Fleury, Ray Bourque, Joe Nieuwendyk, Eric Lindros and finally Brendan Shanahan to preserve the win. Lindros had him beaten on a backhand shot, but the puck hit the tip of Hasek's glove and then the goalpost.

Canada had not even practised penalty shots and coach Marc Crawford had to scramble to decide which five players would take part in the shootout.

Somehow Wayne Gretzky, the NHL's all-time scoring leader, was left off the list.

"To say the least, we're devastated," Gretzky said after the game. "It's a strange feeling to play as well as we did, not lose a game and yet be going home on a shootout."

Russia was favored to finally find a way to get Hasek off his game when the two teams clashed for gold. But once again he was brilliant as the Czechs won their only Olympic gold medal with a 1-0 victory.

It was ironic that the only goal of the game was scored by Petr Svoboda, whose last name translates literally from Czech to English as 'freedom'. Svoboda had to defect from the former Czechoslovakia to join the Montreal Canadiens in 1984.

Czech team captain Vladimir Ruzicka stood on the top level of the podium at the medals ceremony as the sounds of the Czech national anthem *Gde domov muj – Where is my home?* reverberated thoughout the Big Hat Arena.

Back home in Prague the folks were going crazy in Old Town Square.

Earlier in the tournament the Czechs had sidelined the U.S. by a score of 4-1 in the quarterfinals. Therefore they had conquered arguably the three medal favourites on their way to securing the gold.

CBS, which paid $375 million for the U.S. TV rights, was bitterly disappointed when the Americans were eliminated. Ratings already were down because of the 14-hour time difference between Nagano and New York.

Canada also failed to medal, falling to Finland 4-2 in the bronze medal game.

Scouts and general managers were so impressed with the skills of the Czech team that a record 21 players from the Czech Republic were selected in the NHL draft that summer.

The Czechs held their victory party at Czech House, located just one block from the Big Hat Arena. Czech beer, considered the best in the world, was flowing like water.

Coach Ivan Hlinka, who as a player had finished second to the Soviet Union in two Olympics, was the first to fill up his mug with Pilsener.

On the street I got an autograph from Jiri Dopita, the only player on the Czech team from Šumperk, the town where I had been detained by the secret police in 1983.

Time was of the essence for the Olympic champions the next day.

President Vaclav Havel sent a plane from Prague to fly the team home for a celebration in Prague's Old Town Square, to be attended by about 100,000 people. All the players, even those who played for NHL clubs, were going there first, even though there were NHL games as early as Wednesday, just three days after the Olympic tournament closed.

Eleven of the Czechs, including Hasek, were from the NHL and their clubs were waiting for them. All of them had to call their general managers to let them know about the plans.

But Czech officials had to scramble to get enough cash to pay for refueling at Irkutsk, in Siberia, before the team could leave Japan. A second refueling stop was required in Kazakhstan.

Ironically, the Czechs were flying home on a Russian-built Ilyushin jet and relying on the Russians for refuelling. Russia was demanding payment of $50,000 U.S. upfront.

The Czechs tried to get the money at the bank in Nagano, but could only obtain Japanese yen. I pulled an American $5 bill out of my wallet and offered to start a fund!

Eventually, the financial problems were ironed out through diplomatic channels and the flight took off.

Just before the Canada-Kazakhstan quarterfinal Don Cherry, wearing a winter coat that reached down to the floor, came down to the players bench to present a photo of Team Canada 1972 to assistant coach Wayne Cashman. Cherry looked like Dracula.

Ron MacLean, reporting from ice level, was trying to get a shot of it on TV, but just then the Kazakh team came out for their warmup and blocked the view of the camera. They appeared to have no clue who the man in the long coat was.

Kazakhstan, which normally does not have a lot of fans at Olympic hockey, got a little bit of boost in Japan. The country's colours are yellow and blue, exactly the same colour Japanese police chose for their uniforms, so it looked like the whole city of Nagano was rooting for the Kazakhs.

Expecting Kazakhstan would not make the playoff round, CBS didn't bother to do biographical player sketches on the team in advance, so when they did qualify, we had to stay up most of the night at the International Broadcast Centre doing the bios.

The game between Slovakia and Kazakhstan also was the last time I saw Slovak general manager Dusan Pasek alive. The Slovaks were favoured to win, but as Kazakhstan took the lead Pasek began to look more and more worried.

Having to play in the preliminary round, which started before the NHL took a break, also was costly to Slovakia. The Slovaks mistakenly left only two spots open on their preliminary round roster, and when their NHL players finally were released and flew all the way to Japan they had to choose only two to dress against Kazakhstan in a game they had to win to advance to the final round.

They chose Peter Bondra of Washington and Robert Svehla of Florida. But Ziggy Palffy, Miro Satan, Jozef Stumpel and others had to sit in the stands and watch the defeat.

Pasek had played for Czechoslovakia in the 1984 and 1988 Olympics, in fact captaining the team in Calgary. He also played briefly for the NHL's Minnesota North Stars.

Kazakhstan pulled off a 4-3 upset, ending Slovakia's chances of making the playoffs. About three weeks later Pasek was found dead in his office in Bratislava with a gun nearby. The cause of death was never determined, but police believe he might have taken his own life.

My first thought when I heard the sad news was that he was totally depressed, as a result of the loss in Japan. However, it was revealed later that he had some gambling debts and those owed money were seeking retribution.

In another great effort Japan, coached by Canada's Dave King, scored in a shootout to beat Austria in a placement game for 13th place to avoid finishing last in the tournament. The roof almost came off the Big Hat Arena when the Japanese scored the winning goal.

I remember the tremendous effort put out by players on the Austrian and Italian teams in the final game of the preliminary round, even though both countries had no chance of advancing. It was a sign of the high degree of pride all players have in playing in the Olympics.

In fact, in the previous eight Olympics dating back to 1972, only two teams – Poland in 1972 and Bulgaria in 1976 – had gone home without earning at least one point in the tournament.

Vancouver Canucks sniper Pavel Bure skated like his blades were on fire, scoring five goals, to lead the Russians to a 7-4 victory over Finland in the semifinals.

The explosive winger had the Finns on their heels from the opening whistle and the game turned into his personal shootout as he dazzled a crowd of 9,000 mostly Japanese fans.

"It was extra special because it was the first Olympics in which NHL players were allowed to play," Bure said. "So all of the best players in the world were there.

"I was always trying to get open for a breakaway. When I got them, I was going so fast I didn't even think about whether I was going to go forehand or backhand."

At the end of the game even the man who built the aptly named Big Hat Arena was tipping his chapeau to the Russian captain and Mount Fuji was threatening to erupt from the noise in the building. Bure's mother Tatiana was in the stands to watch the feat.

"We didn't have time to celebrate afterwards because we had to get ready for the gold medal game," Bure recalled.

Russia lost 1-0 to the Czech Republic in the final, but with nine goals in the tournament Bure was a shoo-in when votes for the best forward were counted. His nine goals matched the output of the entire American team.

"Nowadays, Vladimir Putin rewards our athletes with bonuses and new cars, but in those days we were just happy to be playing for our country. The happiest days of my life were when my children were born. But obviously that day in Nagano is something I will remember for the rest of my life."

A Soviet (Russian player) had not come close to Bure's effort in one Olympic game in 42 years. Vsevolod Bobrov had scored four goals in a 10-3 romp over Switzerland at the 1956 Games in Italy, the first in which the Soviets competed. The nation had won eight hockey gold medals in 11 Olympic Games from 1956 through 1994.

Incredibly, when the International Ice Hockey Federation released its list of top 100 moments in international hockey history in 2008, Bure's amazing performance was not included.

While it was clearly his greatest game, Bure's five goals were not a personal best.

"I remember a game when I was 12 years old playing for the championship of Moscow against a team called Lokomotiv, and I managed to score nine," he said. "We won 30-0."

The last Canadian to score five goals in an Olympic game was Canada's Paul Knox, who bagged his quintet in a 23-0 romp over Austria at the 1956 Olympics. A graduate of the Toronto St. Michael's Majors junior club, Knox played only one NHL game, for the Toronto Maple Leafs, and wound up as a high school teacher in Fergus, Ontario.

An estimated $3,000 worth of damage resulted to rooms in the Athletes Village when a couple of American players went on a rampage. Included were scratched walls, 10 broken chairs, damaged beds and a door with a 20-centimetre gash running through it.

Defenceman Chris Chelios chipped in and collected money from his teammates, then sent a cheque for $3,000 and a letter of apology to the Nagano Olympic Committee.

The host country published an interesting but only four-page program with the team rosters for the particular game printed inside in Japanese. On the cover was a caricature of a hockey player with captions to the left pointing to areas and describing the material used in a hockey stick, a puck and the equipment players wear. It also explained the very basics, that skaters reach speeds of 40 to 60 km/h and player substitutions occur frequently, as often as every 40 to 60 seconds.

I was there the night the tournament committee booted Swedish defenceman Ulf Samuelsson out of the tournament. Samuelsson was born in Sweden, but surrendered his Swedish citizenship when he became a citizen of the United States where he was playing for the New York Rangers. John Davidson, who also was on the Madison Square Garden network broadcasting Ranger games at the time, couldn't believe it when I called him, rousing him out of a nap, to tell him.

Normally, players taking part in the Olympics can have more than one passport, but Swedish law forbids any of its citizens to do so.

Janne Bengstsson, a reporter with the Stockholm daily *Svenska Dagbladet,* was the target of threats by furious readers for writing the story.

But sports editor Per-Olof Olsson said he didn't send reporters to Japan to cheer for Sweden, rather to provide fair coverage of the tournament.

I was right in the middle of the negotiations for the times for the semi-final games. CBC wanted to have the Canada-Czech game at 6:45 p.m. Nagano time, the second game of the doubleheader, because executive producer John Shannon said they were getting very good numbers at 4:45 a.m. in Canada. But CBS wanted it at 2:45 p.m. Nagano time.

Since the American team had already been eliminated, Shannon thought CBS would play ball with him and give them their choice. I was right there when Gary Bettman came out of the meeting and asked Shannon abruptly why he wanted the game at 6:45.

Shannon told him about the positive response in Canada and that he had been talking to Rick Gentile of CBS, who indicated the network would co-operate with him. However, when the meeting ended they announced the starting time for the game would be 2:45. Having paid the most money for broadcast rights, the Americans got their way.

At that point, CBS TV ratings were down 30 per cent from the 1994 Olympics in Norway.

Emrick worked along with former NHL defenceman Joe Micheletti for the Turner network in Nagano, while Sean McDonough, at that time play-by-play man for the Boston Red Sox during the summer, called most of the CBS games with Davidson.

Gary Cohen, who worked first as radio play-by-play man for the New York Mets, then did the same job on TV, called hockey for CBS Radio. Former NHLer Peter McNab handled the colour.

In February, Japanese TV carried video reports of the opening of spring training for teams in the Japanese Baseball League from the Island of Okinawa, where the temperatures are in the low 70s F in February.

I met Masatoshi Kondo for the first time at the Montreal Forum on New Year's Eve 1979 when the Canadiens defeated the Soviet Red Army 4-2. He is a huge supporter of the Habs, who have treated him royally on many visits to Montreal. We have been close but long-range friends over the years, exchanging information about the sport in North America and Japan.

When I landed in Tokyo, Kondo and illustrious Japanese sportscaster Yoshio Nishida, who had called all of Japan's hockey games at the

1980 Olympics in Lake Placid, hosted me for dinner at one of the city's best restaurants.

One night Kondo insisted on taking me to a place that served authentic Japanese food. We sampled squid guts, chicken livers, ground fish stuffed with vegetables, fried tofu, raw horse meat, beef salted tongue and Chinese tea. Thrown in as a snack was what he called in his broken English, "nuts which get worse", better known as 'natto', a dish of pungent, fermented soybeans. The beef tongue and chicken livers were so tough I thought they were from an old boot.

Japanese drummers outside The Big Hat Arena in Nagano in 1998.

The inaugural Olympic women's tournament in 1998 boiled down to a showdown between Canada and the U.S., with the Canadians considered the favourites since they had won every World Championship before that.

As a sideshow U.S. coach Ben Smith and Shannon Miller, coach of the Canadian team, exchanged fighting words at a post-game press conference when Miller accused American players of trying to intimidate the Canadians in a 7-4 preliminary round win by the U.S.

Canada was looking for revenge in the gold medal game, but the Americans came out on top again, 3-1, to become Olympic champions. The U.S. team finished the tournament with a perfect record of 6-0-0 and outscored its opponents 36-8.

As the first women's Olympic champion, the team was inducted into the IIHF Hall of Fame in 2009.

Emrick, who called the gold medal game for the Turner network, said the American win sparked the growth of women's hockey in the U.S.

"I was so thrilled to see the first use of NHL players in the men's tournament and the first tournament for women," he said. "The 3-1 win in the gold medal game by Team USA was exciting. Talking to these female athletes during their exhibition season made you want their sport to succeed at the Olympic level."

The first time the Winter Olympics were held in Japan, in 1972, the northern island of Hokkaido with its winter climate hosted the event. Although Nagano is surrounded by mountains, where the ski events took place, there was no snow in the city and it offered much more moderate weather.

I was lucky to find a Catholic church in Nagano, where Catholics make up less than one per cent of the population. Nevertheless, the church took the time to hand out printed holy cards with a welcome message to all visitors to the Olympics. Most of the people in Japan are Buddhists.

In the cafeteria they had little packages of three candies wrapped in pink Kleenex and tied with a red ribbon to give out to all the men. In Japan, the Valentine's Day tradition is for the girls to give candy to the boys.

When I came down for breakfast one morning, there was a set of dolls on the front counter. I learned that the celebration of Nino Hingyo is held in Japan on March 3. It is a day on which families display a set of traditional

Japanese dolls in their homes and pray for the health and prosperity of young girls.

Besides the traditional eggs, sausages and pancakes, the breakfasts at the media village included cream corn, clam chowder, miso soup, spinach, mashed potatoes and rice. Free saki also was available.

Miso soup, made with miso paste and a stock called dashi, is eaten daily by three-quarters of the population of Japan. The paste is created by allowing soybeans to ferment with salt and koji, a harmless fungus resulting from the fermentation of soybeans. The soup was available in the cafeteria 24 hours a day.

I found the Japanese get very upset if you don't take your shoes off at the door and put on the slippers they provide.

An Olympic journalist's worst fear is losing a credential and it finally happened to me in Nagano. When I went to the accreditation office to get another one, I learned I was in good company.

Waiting there to have hers' replaced was Ekaterina Gordeeva, a two-time Olympic gold medalist in pairs figure skating from Russia who was in Japan working for CBS.

Gordeeva's partner and husband, Sergei Grinkov, had died suddenly from a heart attack while they were practising at Lake Placid in 1995.

CHAPTER 8
Man's best friend supersedes Olympics in Salt Lake

For centuries man's best friend has been a symbol of the old adage, 'You can judge a person's character by the way they treat animals.'

Mike Emrick, who during the 2014 Stanley Cup playoffs started writing personal letters to many of the people he feels have influenced his life in a positive way, is an excellent example. Former high school classmates, neighbors, producers and analysts have been among the recipients.

Emrick was scheduled to call the 2002 Olympic hockey tournament in Salt Lake City for NBC. It would have been his fourth straight Olympics. He had already been TV play-by-play man for CBS and Turner, which owned the American rights at the previous three in France, Norway and Japan.

Just 10 days before the tournament opened Emrick and his wife Joyce, who have no children, came to the realization their beloved Yorkshire Terrier *Katie*, the first dog they ever owned, was in danger of dying.

"We were given a first diagnosis of possible kidney disease in January, but were asked to put her on a special kidney-sparing diet," the Emmy Award-winning broadcaster said. "After trying it for three weeks, she was still ill and in early February another blood test had her in the danger zone.

"I told Joyce we both had to do our best for her. Initially, in Detroit, then later after searching the Internet, I learned they were doing some experimentation with kidney transplantation for dogs at the University of California-Davis. So, we flew her there.

"We had great hope when they said that, at only three years of age, she was a good candidate for a transplant. But, in the days leading up to her transplant she developed other issues and we had to let her go.

"The last gift you can give a dog is to be there at the end. It occurred just as the Games were beginning.

"Initially, I think NBC was surprised when I called them explaining I had to take myself off the Games. But this was family. They understood."

Gary Thorne, the TV play-by-play man for the Baltimore Orioles during the summer, stepped in and did an admirable job, alongside John Davidson. Jim Lampley and Bill Clement were the hosts in the NBC studio, which was located in what normally is a referees room, about 100 feet from the ice surface of the E-Centre.

Before almost every Olympics I worked at there was a huge media scare. Most of it was justified, but my colleagues in the business often went overboard with scare tactics.

Because the 2002 Games took place only five months after 9/11, security was the tightest it has ever been for an Olympics.

Our hotel was only a 12-minute walk from the E-Centre, but we had to leave at least an hour before work started to go through three security checks to get there on time.

The U.S. Army also was part of the security forces. The soldiers were always polite, but it was time-consuming. NBC had recommended spouses not come to Salt Lake City because of the tight security situation.

On the eve of the first game, the airport at Salt Lake was off limits to planes because of the heavy security for the Opening Ceremonies at the University of Utah's Rice-Eccles Stadium.

I was originally assigned to drive to Evanston, Wyoming, about 100 miles to the northeast, to interview Miroslav Satan of Slovakia, who had played 22 minutes as the Buffalo Sabres edged Ottawa 3-2 on Friday night, then flew in the private jet of Sabres owner John Rigas right after the game so he could play for Slovakia the next day.

Satan had played exceptionally well in international competition, leading all goal-scorers with nine at the 1994 Olympics in Norway and topping the list again with 10 as Slovakia won the silver medal at the 2000 World Championship in Russia.

However, at the last minute NBC's director John Shannon decided to have me stay in Salt Lake to secure the final rosters of all teams, which were not set until midnight.

It was essential that Satan get to Salt Lake as quickly as possible. The IIHF has a rule that all teams must have at least 17 of their 23 players registered and in the city of their first game by midnight the night before.

At that point, because the NHL had not shut down for the qualifying round of the Olympics, the Slovaks had only 16 and general manager Peter Stastny was biting his fingernails.

Satan did not arrive in Evanston until almost 5 a.m. while most of his Slovak teammates were still sleeping. He then was driven 90 minutes to Salt Lake and had to catch a few winks before heading to the rink for a 4 p.m. game against Germany.

Although Satan did not arrive until after midnight, he did not turn into a pumpkin! At a special meeting hastily convened, the IIHF agreed to waive the "in the city" portion of the rule on the grounds that Slovakia had gone through enough hardship by trying to put a roster together while NHL games were still being played.

Before the first game in Salt Lake, there was a rumour Slovakia would refuse to play in protest of the manner in which the NHL and NHL clubs handled the release of players.

However, there was no boycott, especially after the IIHF made it clear Olympic hockey tournament entrants guarantee they will play all games and are subject to a heavy fine if they do not.

The airlift was not successful. The Slovaks were upset 3-0 and eventually failed to qualify for the final round.

The Los Angeles Kings had agreed to release Ziggy Palffy for this game against Germany but Stastny made a commitment not to actually put him on the ice because Los Angeles had a bundle of NHL games about that time.

However, the Slovaks fell behind and coach Jan Filc and Palffy made a joint decision that he would play.

The Slovaks got to use Zdeno Chara and Marian Hossa of Ottawa, Jozef Stumpel of Boston and Pavol Demitra of St. Louis in their next game against Latvia, but could do no better than a 6-6 tie and were officially eliminated from medal contention.

Then they were upset 3-2 by Austria and finished 13th out of 14 in the final rankings.

Arturs Irbe was unable to play goal for Latvia because NHL Commissioner Gary Bettman ruled he was an elite player and his team, the Carolina Hurricanes, needed him. In spite of this, Irbe sat on the bench for the full 60 minutes as backup goalie the same night as the Hurricanes were shut out 4-0 by the Sharks in San Jose, just a 90-minute flight away.

Irbe was devastated because the Hurricanes were OK with releasing him for one game. He decided to make a personal call to Bettman. When he got nowhere with the commissioner, he warned he would leave the Hurricanes and travel to Salt Lake City anyway.

Bettman told him that would incur a suspension by the league, one that the IOC would honour. In the final analysis, the Commish maintained the NHL's integrity had to be preserved.

All this would come as news to Belarus defenceman Ruslan Salei, who was serving a two-game NHL suspension when he played in the Olympics in 1998.

Ukraine also suffered from the absence of NHL players for their first game in Salt Lake. But Ruslan Fedotenko of Philadelphia and Sergei Varlamov joined them for the second, an impressive 5-2 win over Switzerland.

Varlamov was so anxious to get there he hitched a ride on the Ottawa Senators airlift, which carried Hossa, Chara and Demitra, following the game between the St. Louis Blues and the Senators.

Colorado general manager Pierre Lacroix, on the other hand, released backup goalie David Aebischer to Switzerland for all three preliminary round games. The previous fall Lacroix had announced Aebischer would not be allowed to play in any of those games, but he had a change of heart after his first stringer Patrick Roy backed out of playing for Canada.

At the press conference following Canada's 7-1 semi-final win over Belarus, Mario Lemieux made Bettman look like a goof by acknowledging publicly he sat out certain NHL regular season games with Pittsburgh and did not dress for back-to-back games, in order to be in good shape for the Olympics. Bettman had denied it when questioned by the media earlier in the week.

The commissioner probably did not want to concede the league's double standard, after it refused Irbe permission to play for Latvia against

Slovakia on the grounds that the Hurricanes would then not be icing their best lineup.

While Canada's 5-2 triumph over the host U.S. in the gold medal game was historic, because it was the first gold in half-a-century for the country that invented the game, the incredible 4-3 victory by Belarus over Sweden in the quarterfinals was definitely the most dramatic.

Belarusian defenceman Vladimir Kopat was simply trying to get the puck out of danger when his high end-over-end flip shot from 70 feet away hit Swedish goalie Tommy Salo and rolled down his back into the net for the winning goal. He was the least likely player on the team to score, managing only two shots on goal in his first six games.

Salei, the only NHL player on the Belarus team, said family members called him from back home after the game and literally were crying on the phone they were so happy.

But after that win, and having played six games in only 10 days, the Belarusian team was so banged up it was literally being held together by glue and was easy prey for Canada in the semifinals and later for Russia, which recorded a 7-2 victory over the upstarts in the bronze medal game. Most of the Belarusians were used to playing just twice a week in the Russian and German leagues.

President Alexander Lukashenko, a huge hockey fan who even practised with the Dynamo Minsk team of the Russian League from time to time, had promised each of the Belarus players $22,000 if they beat Russia in the bronze medal game. They had already earned a bonus, which would be part of the $22,000, for upsetting Sweden in the quarterfinals.

Russian players were offered a bonus of $50,000 for a gold medal, which was exactly double the $25,000 they received for striking gold in Calgary in 1988. However, the Russians lost to the U.S. in the semifinals.

As an alternate jersey the Canadian team chose a gold-coloured replica of the one worn by the Toronto Granites at the 1924 Olympics in Chamonix, France.

But the Canucks lost 5-2 to Sweden the first time they wore it. Mats Waltin, Sweden's captain at the 1980 Olympics in Lake Placid, designed the torpedo system employed by the Tre Kronor in its conquest of Canada.

It designates two forwards as 'super-forwards' to charge into the corners and put pressure on the opposition for 30 seconds at a time. Another two forwards become 'halfbacks' and the only defenceman, called the 'libero', as in volleyball, provides protection for his netminder and trails the play as a pass outlet option when the attack begins.

The decision to honour the 1924 team had created a small outcry in Winnipeg because it ignored the Winnipeg Falcons, who had represented Canada at the 1920 Olympic hockey tournament, which was held as part of the Summer Olympics.

But Canada improved its performance quickly and won the gold medal by defeating the host Americans 5-2. A key factor in Canada's success at Salt Lake City was that the players did not take foolish penalties.

The first time Canada iced a full team of NHL players in the World Championship was 1977 in Vienna. Besides being humiliated by the Russians and failing to win a medal, the Canadian pros behaved like thugs.

Twenty-five years later, it was a different story. Canada went into the gold medal game averaging only 6.48 penalty minutes per game, the lowest of all 14 teams in the tournament.

It was 50 years to the day since the Edmonton Mercurys won the gold medal for Canada in 1952 and 30 years since Canada beat the Soviet Union in the 1972 Summit Series.

Labatt's Breweries paid to fly Bill Dawe and Don Gauf of the 1952 team to Salt Lake City to view the gold medal game.

Theo Fleury waved the Canadian flag proudly on the ice after the game, which was a double victory for him. Almost a year before that he had entered an alcohol rehabilitation clinic in Santa Fe, New Mexico and Team Canada officials thought long and hard about even naming him to the team.

The Calgary Flames winger was thrilled to be an Olympic champion.

"There is a comparison that in the last 50 years there have been 1,500 names on the Stanley Cup and only 23 Canadian Olympic gold medal winners," he said. "I think that puts it all in perspective."

It was an extra special moment for Canadian goalie Martin Brodeur because he and his father Denis became the first father-son goaltending combo to win Olympic medals in hockey.

Denis, who later became a highly respected hockey photographer, earned a bronze medal playing for the Kitchener-Waterloo Dutchmen, who represented Canada at the 1956 Olympics in Cortina d'Ampezzo, Italy. He also was in Salt Lake City to celebrate with his son.

Before the tournament started technician Trent Evans, who works with icemaker Dan Craig, had buried a Canadian loonie at centre ice for good luck.

At that time the Canadian dollar was considerably below par, compared to the American buck. *Toronto Star* columnist Garth Woolsey called burying the loonie "the best 63 cents we ever spent!"

Showing its lack of knowledge of Canadian currency, NBC staffers erred by putting up a toonie on the screen, instead of a loonie, after the game.

At the 2002 Olympics the total NHL salary of all Canadian players was $118.8 million,

One scalper was heard asking $4,500 for a ticket. A sign carried by a fan who came from afar summed things up the best. It read: 'Air Fare $1,400; Tickets $900; A Second Miracle On Ice – Priceless.'

During its telecast, CBC aired a shot of Yonge Street in Toronto. It was empty, with no cars and no people. They were either at home or jammed into sports bars viewing the game. It was reminiscent of Game 8 of the 1972 Summit Series, when a giant bowling ball could have been rolled down the main street of any town or city in Canada, and nobody would have been injured.

I'll never forget the goal Jayna Hefford scored in the women's gold medal game with four seconds left in the second period to make the score 3-1. It gave the Canadian girls some breathing room after they had blown a 4-1 lead and lost 7-4 to the Americans in the preliminary round.

The showdown, which Canada won 3-2, was marred with controversy as American referee Stacey Livingston awarded the U.S. team eight straight power-plays.

In critiquing Livingston's work, *Hartford Courant* columnist Jeff Jacobs described the situation better than anyone.

"As time expired on the American women's hockey team's dream of a golden repeat and chants of 'USA' dissolved into a dull roar Thursday night, the Canadians rushed their crease and bowled over goalie Kim St.-Pierre," he wrote, "It was the hardest anybody got hit all night!"

Hayley Wickenheiser, who called the job Livingston did "atrocious", accused the American team of putting the Canadian flag on the floor of their dressing room and stomping on it, showing it disrespect. She nailed the first accusation but was off the mark on the second. A few days later Bob Nicholson of Hockey Canada apologized for the statement.

The Swedish women's team wisely booked space at Amici's, a fancy Italian restaurant in West Valley City, for a team dinner and marched in wearing their bronze medals after upsetting Finland 2-1. Bill Clement also took the entire studio crew of 13 to eat there.

It was a great triumph for the Swedes. Just three months earlier the Swedish Olympic Committee seriously considered withdrawing the team from the Olympics after it lost 14 straight exhibition games, many by large margins.

However, the Canadians had no place to go. Some players wound up eating at Denny's, a chain restaurant that specializes in breakfasts. Little did they know the place had been closed temporarily shortly before the Games for violations by state food inspectors for the state of Utah!

With my knowledge of French and Russian, I was able to communicate with the players of nine countries. Besides Russia, the players of Belarus, Ukraine, Kazakhstan and Latvia spoke Russian. Those on the Czech and Slovak squads were at least a little bit familiar with Russian.

Besides France, some of Switzerland's players hailing from the western part of the country spoke French fluently. If I had brushed up on my German a little more, it would have taken care of not only Germany's players but also those of Austria and the remainder of the Swiss team.

Robert Reichel of the Czech Republic and Germany's Martin Reichel became the first brothers to play for different countries in the same Olympics since 1960 when Frantisek Tikal played for the former Czechoslovakia and brother Zdenek, who had escaped from behind the Iron Curtain in the 1950s, played for Australia.

Because they suspected Frantisek would fly to Australia with his brother after the tournament, the Czechoslovak secret police monitored him very closely during the 1960 Olympic tourney in Squaw Valley, Calif.

However, the two teams faced each other on opening day and Czechoslovak players went after Zdenek, knocked his shoulder out of place and he was able to compete in only one game. Czechoslovakia rolled to an easy 18-1 victory.

It reminds me of the 22-4 pasting Czechoslovakia gave the hockey club in Butte, Montana, in an exhibition game just before that Olympics.

Soon-to-become daredevil Robert 'Evel' Knievel, who was born in Butte, launched and played for the semi-pro Butte Bombers hockey team in 1959. The team needed publicity and revenue in a hurry, so Knievel invited the Czechoslovaks to town.

Knievel was ejected from the game early in the third period.

However, the visitors came out on the short end of the stick at the box office when it was discovered after the game expense money they had been guaranteed had been stolen.

Fortunately the U.S. Olympic Committee later agreed to look after the expenses and an international incident was avoided.

The Charlotte Checkers of the Eastern Hockey League also employed Knievel's services for a short time.

Although he broke 35 different bones in his body during his career as a stuntman, Knievel survived all of his crashes. He died as a result of pulmonary disease in Clearwater, Florida in 2007, aged 69.

Raimo Helminen of Finland set a new record at Salt Lake by participating in his sixth Olympic hockey tournament. He was 19 when he made his debut at Sarajevo in 1984 and 37 when he completed his Olympic career. He won a silver medal in 1988, as well as bronze medals in 1994 and 1998.

The NBC crew stayed at the Sleep Inn, which was within walking distance of the E-Centre. It turned out to be the worst accommodation of my seven Olympics. Although asking well in advance for a non-smoking room, I wound up with a smoking room with no chance to switch because the place was full.

It was obvious management had allowed smoking in the rooms at one time and tried to get the smell out to pass them off as non-smoking rooms in time for the Olympics. But that just isn't in the realm of modern science.

During the Olympics, the world famous Mormon Tabernacle Choir gave several performances and I was lucky enough to get into one of them free at the historic tabernacle in Temple Square. The theme was American folk songs, including rousing old favourites like *Git Along Home Cindy, Cindy*.

Celebrated conductor John Williams directed the Mormon Symphony Orchestra while the 360-member choir and International Children's Choir sang *Call of the Champions,* the song he composed especially for the Games.

It begins with the choir singing 'Citius! Altius! Fortius!,' the Olympic motto, which translated from Latin means, 'Faster, Higher, Stronger.'

Each of the children, who also sang in foreign languages, was dressed in the colourful ethnic costume of a different country. Christmas lights were purposely left on in the square, making it look like a fairyland.

Another highlight was attending 6 p.m. Mass on a Saturday at the Cathedral of the Madeleine complete with a professional cantor and organist playing the largest pipe organ I have ever seen. It is the only cathedral in the U.S. under the patronage of St. Mary Magdalene.

Very much like Nagano, the grass was green and flowers, bushes and trees were in bloom, giving the 2010 Winter Olympics in Vancouver a flavour of summer.

Even though it was wet and rainy on some days, daffodils and cherry blossoms provided colour to a city that in 2017 was covered with snow at the same time of the year. They were at least two weeks ahead of schedule in 2010.

Vancouver had experienced a record-breaking 31-day period of mild weather, ending on Feb. 9, just a few days before the Olympics started. The city had not been blessed with weather that warm in January and February since 1896.

A bonus was visiting the beautiful Oceanside campus of the University of British Columbia, where some of the practices and games were held at the UBC Doug Mitchell Thunderbird Sports Centre. Father David Bauer coached there in 1962-63, and launched the Canadian national team in Winnipeg the following season.

The pleasant weather and the fact my hotel, the Hampton Suites, was just a 10-minute walk from Canada Hockey Place, provided the most convenience of the seven Olympics at which I worked.

As a result of a tip from lifelong newspaper friend Brian McCristall of Coquitlam, B.C., I secured a contract with Glacier Publishing to write most of the editorial content for the official hockey program that was sold at the two arenas.

I was able to see a dress rehearsal for the Opening Ceremonies at B.C. Place on the Tuesday before the Games opened.

In Vancouver's Chinatown, just a few blocks from Canada Hockey Place, folks celebrated the Chinese New Year with a huge parade.

While eating breakfast in the hotel one morning, I noticed a couple of very serious–looking guys at the next table with earpieces connected to a variety of devices. They turned out to be agents of the U.S. Secret Service and, although they were not willing to reveal it, were in Vancouver to protect U.S. Vice-President Joe Biden, who was arriving later that day for the Opening Ceremonies.

Vancouverites working as volunteers were very hospitable. Other volunteers came from all parts of Canada, some as far as 3,000 miles away.

Residents of the city who weren't interested in the Games rented their homes and apartments for two weeks and escaped to sunny Arizona or California for a vacation.

The organizing committee for the 2014 Games in Sochi rented the entire Science World globe to promote the 2014 Olympics and the Krasnodar Region of Russia. It was renamed Sochi 2014 House for the Vancouver Olympics.

Russian music, food and dancing were featured. Every day from noon until 5 p.m. visitors with proper credentials could meet some of Russia's best athletes, get their autographs and have their pictures taken with them. Videos of classic matches between Canada and Russia from the past were screened in a special theatre.

The Olympic flame in Jack Poole Plaza was a huge attraction for spectators, but initially there were many complaints that good views of it were being hampered by the chainlink fence that surrounded it. Eventually, officials opened a platform that provided a clear view of the flame through Plexiglas.

The streets, especially Granville and Robson which were turned into pedestrian malls, were alive every night with entertainment and well into the wee hours of the morning.

Despite the fun atmosphere, I got a hint of what was to come during the Stanley Cup playoffs in 2011, with Canadian fans baiting and trash-talking Americans following Canada's 3-2 overtime win in the gold medal game.

Violent crime rose 17 per cent during the Games, mainly as a result of assaults on police officers during protests in the downtown area.

Vancouver was the only Olympics in which I could not find a hockey ticket unless I was willing to fork out a minimum of $500. The TV networks used to provide free tickets to employees who wanted to arrange for family members to see a game, but they cut that out promptly when benefactors started to re-sell the ducats for a profit.

Earlier in the tournament, scalpers had been asking as much as $4,000 for a pair of centre ice aisle seats for the Canada-Russia quarterfinal match at Canada Hockey Place. Tickets for the gold medal game in Vancouver were going for $5,000 each or more.

However on the second last day, through a friend from Europe, I came up with a single for the bronze medal game between Finland and Slovakia and my wife Christine was able to attend.

She rooted hard for Slovakia, the birthplace of her father Johnny, but the Slovaks blew a 3-1 lead in the third period and the Finns won the medal with a 5-3 victory. From the NBC box at centre ice, I could hear her whistling loudly, with her fingers in her mouth, above the roar of the crowd when Slovakia scored.

On some days our crew broadcast five games, airing three of them live from Canada Hockey Place and commenting on two more by monitor from UBC.

That meant starting work with a meeting at 9 a.m. and finishing at midnight. Bedtime, at the earliest, was 1 a.m. I saw 33 games live in Vancouver. There were six days with five games a day to cover.

Emrick and Eddie Olczyk called most of the games, with Kenny Albert working on the second crew. I was assigned to the studio, where Bill Patrick, Mike Milbury and Jeremy Roenick were on the panel.

Pierre McGuire and Joe Micheletti were behind the glass and at ice level, respectively.

Author Denis Gibbons was chief researcher for the NBC Olympic hockey broadcast tandem of Mike Emrick and Eddie Olczyk.

Cammi Granato, captain of the U.S. women's Olympic gold medal-winning team in 1998, worked on the studio desk for the women's games, with A.J. Mleczko, a teammate from 1998, handling colour commentary.

I was sent to the main NBC studio in the International Broadcast Centre (IBC) for the Czech-Russia game, which started at noon on a Sunday or 3 p.m. in prime time on the East Coast.

Later that day Canada and the U.S. squared off in a preliminary round game in front of a full house at Canada Hockey Place. When the Americans took a 2-1 lead on a pair of goals by Brian Rafalski in the first period, NBC immediately fetched Al Michaels by limousine from the IBC and he got there just in time to see the U.S. win 4-3.

Michaels arrived with an entourage, including producer Sam Flood, and stayed to do a wrap-up. NBC was thrilled with the viewing audience it got in prime time.

Of all the games I've worked for American television in seven Olympics, about the only thing I've ever seen pre-empt a hockey telecast was the Daytona 500, which usually is held on the second Sunday of February.

Roenick had been with Russian superstar Alexander Ovechkin the night before the Canada-Russia game and reported the Washington superstar was unusually nervous about the quarter-final showdown.

The Canadians came out like they were shot out of a cannon. In the 7-3 win, they scored six goals on 23 shots in just over 24 minutes of play.

With still more than two minutes to play the large crowd started to chant, 'nah, nah, nah, nah; nah, nah, nah, nah, hey, hey-eh goodbye.' Christie Blatchford, a columnist with *The Globe and Mail* at the time, described it as the 'unofficial national anthem.'

By laying an egg against Canada, Russian players relinquished not only a chance to win a gold medal but also $100,000 each and a luxury car, which had been promised by Vitaly Mutko, the Russian Minister of Sport. The cash was to come from the Russian government and the automobile from the Olympic Athletes Support Foundation.

It was the first time in 50 years Canada had beaten the Soviets or Russians at the Olympics. The last time it happened was in 1960 at Squaw Valley, Calif. when Canada, represented by the Senior A Kitchener-Waterloo Dutchmen, won 8-5. Yet neither team won the gold medal there. It went to the underdog Americans.

Afterwards I bumped into legendary NHL coach Scotty Bowman in the corridor and asked him if he was surprised by how easily Canada disposed of the Russians.

"No," he said. "They've (Russians) only got about four or five players who could make our team. Our players are way better."

Based mostly on clashes from the past between the two hockey powers, I was initially shocked by his response. However, I was in no position to dispute it. Canada had thoroughly dominated.

In spite of the loss, I thought Pavel Datsyuk and Evgeni Malkin had relatively good games for Russia. But Ovechkin was completely bottled up by the Canadians, the Russian defence was porous and the goaltending of starter Evgeny Nabokov was below par.

Emrick said Sidney Crosby's overtime winning goal against the U.S. in the gold medal game is his most memorable moment from the six Winter Olympics he has worked.

"The Crosby goal had all the elements of great theatre," he said. "The storybook match in the home country of hockey's ancestry, an earlier loss to the U.S., a change in goalies from Brodeur to Luongo, a gallant performance in the gold medal game by Ryan Miller, later named game MVP, a late goal by Zach Parise that forced overtime and so much riding on Canada to win it all.

"I loved Vancouver. There was a joy of spirit that was universal within the city."

Most of the 50,000 young girls registered to play hockey in Canada tuned in and got more inspiration for the future when the women's gold medal game was played.

Marie-Philippe Poulin scored both goals and Shannon Szabados recorded the shutout as the Canadian women won their third consecutive gold medal, blanking the U.S. 2-0 with the entire men's team looking on from high in the stands.

It was a disappointing loss for the Americans, but women tend to get over these disappointments a lot more quickly than men. They may shed a few tears at the time, but they rarely hold the grudges their male counterparts can carry for a long time.

Canadian centre Jennifer Botterill and American defenceman Angela Ruggiero had been roommates at Harvard.

The Canadian girls, including game star Poulin who was only 18, celebrated on the ice after the game by smoking cigars and drinking beer and Champagne.

Later, Hockey Canada apologized for any embarrassment the incident might have caused the IOC or the Canadian Olympic Committee, but in the final analysis the majority of the country regarded it as just Canadians being Canadians

There were three sets of twins competing in the women's hockey tournament – Julia and Stefanie Marty of Switzerland, Laura and Sara Benz of the same country and Jocelyne and Monique Lamoureux of the U.S.

While they were obviously rooting for Canada, fans in Vancouver adopted a second team. Slovakia became one of their darlings because of the fabulous tournament Pavol Demitra of the Canucks put together. Others chose Sweden with Vancouver's Sedin twins in the lineup and, if they were really ready to put all animosities aside, there were the Americans with Ryan Kesler of the Canucks showing well.

On the women's side, Canadian supporters also tended to side with the Slovaks, who were competing in their first Olympics and drew some pity after being shellacked 18-0 by Canada on the opening Saturday night. Prior to the Games, Slovakia became the lowest-ranked women's team ever to gain an Olympic berth.

China also drew a following because 43 per cent of Metro Vancouver residents have an Asian heritage, the highest percentage for any city outside the continent of Asia.

The Slovak men's team had its best Olympics since making its debut in Norway in 1994, where it won its group and made the quarterfinals. This time Demitra led the Slovaks all the way to the semifinals. Canada eliminated them, but only by a score of 3-2 and with the underdogs buzzing around the Canadian net for the tying goal in the dying seconds.

Switzerland also played surprisingly well in Vancouver. The Swiss threw their weight around against Canada to the extent that the score was tied 2-2 at the end of regulation time and it took a goal by Crosby in a shootout to win it for the Canadians.

It also was the eighth Olympic gold medal for the Canadian men, tying them for first all-time with Russia and the Soviet Union.

Although no NHL players were barred from playing in the tournament this time, officials in Denmark were upset NHL clubs refused to release the best Danes available for the qualifying tournament, which was held in Oslo, Norway in February 2009.

The Danes claimed there should have been an agreement in place between the NHL and IIHF compelling clubs to make players available.

Mikkel Boedker, Jannik Hansen and Frans Nielsen, regulars with Phoenix, Vancouver and the Islanders, respectively, remained in North America. As a result, Denmark lost 5-3 to Norway in a game that could have punched its ticket to Vancouver.

European leagues shut down from Feb. 3-11 and Norway was able to use its best players. Germany and Latvia won the other two qualifying tournaments.

Kim Pedersen, general manager of the Danish Ice Hockey Association, said there was a lot of resentment in his country. Denmark has never qualified for the Olympics and this was its best chance.

"We don't fault the NHL clubs for wanting to hold on to their players," Pedersen said. "We do, however, wish an agreement existed between the NHL and the IIHF so that our best team was available to play in the qualification."

One of the thrills of my life was meeting Gordie Howe in the corridor prior to the gold medal game. When I asked for an autograph, he quickly pulled out a signed hockey card, gave it to me and said: "This will be a helluva lot faster."

Robert Bernath of Agassiz, B.C., summed up the feelings of 30 million Canadians about the double gold-medal triumph in a letter to the editor of *The Vancouver Province*:

"Our father," he wrote, "who art in Canada Hockey Place, hockey be thy name. Thy will be done, gold to be won, on ice as well as in the stands.

"Give us this day our hockey sticks and forgive us our penalties, as we forgive those who cross-check against us.

"Lead us not into elimination but deliver us to victory.

"In the name of the fans, Canada and the holy puck.

"Amen."

CHAPTER 9
The new order of world hockey

While I was sports editor of *The Independent*, the newspaper in Georgetown, Ont., the OHA Intermediate A Georgetown Raiders hosted the national team of Yugoslavia for an exhibition game in February 1978. Our editor Hartley Coles, to whom I owe everything in my journalistic career, came up with the novel idea of printing a front page welcome story in Croatian.

Our guests were impressed and were very polite with their comments. What we didn't realize is that almost all of the players were from Slovenia in the northern region of the country!

Nevertheless, the visitors told us the thought was there.

In those days Yugoslavia played in the B Pool of the World Championship and was using a tour of Canada as a preparation for that event, which they would host in Belgrade in March. It also was part of their effort to qualify for the 1980 Olympics in Lake Placid.

The Raiders, who had won the OHA championship in 1976-77, defeated the Yugoslavs 9-5 in front of a sellout crowd at Gordon Alcott Memorial Arena.

But Yugoslavia dissolved gradually in the 1990s and by 2002, as a new country, Slovenia had improved so rapidly it won three games in six starts at the A Pool World Championship in Sweden.

Eleven years later Slovenia qualified for the 2014 Olympics in Sochi for the first time.

Slovenia had only 148 registered players in the country when it qualified for Sochi, the lowest number of any country in the history of the Games.

In just their second game at the Olympics, the Slovenians pulled an upset by defeating Slovakia 3-1. They later shut out Austria and surprisingly made it to the quarterfinals before losing 5-0 to Sweden.

The victory over Slovakia may have caused some confusion on the wire services, even to the extent of some operators awarding the win to the Slovaks, because the names of the two countries are very similar.

Besides the resemblance in names, their flags look so much alike that Slovenia actually considered changing its. The only difference is Slovakia's bears a cross with two horizontal crossbeams, while an image of three mountain adorns Slovenia's. The colours are the same – blue, red and white.

If mistakes in fact were made in reporting the score, they weren't the first.

During a presidential campaign in 1999, George W. Bush, then governor of Texas, told a reporter from Slovakia he had learned a lot about the country when its foreign minister paid a visit to Texas.

The truth is that it was Janez Drnovsek, the prime minister of Slovenia who dropped in at the Bush ranch!

Several times over the years host countries have played the wrong national anthem of the visitors during state visits and international hockey matches.

The first clue there were more than four good teams in Europe came at the 1982 World Championship in Finland: The Czechoslovaks lost to the West Germans for the first time in 45 years.

At the same tournament the Italian team, dressing 17 transplanted Canadians, upset the U.S. 7-5 and surprisingly tied a Team Canada that included Gretzky, Bob Gainey, Bill Barber and Darryl Sittler, 3-3.

At the 1994 Olympics in Norway I asked Italian team manager Peter Holzner if that was Italy's greatest day on ice, expecting him to answer yes.

To my surprise, he said the biggest event in Italian hockey history occurred at the 1993 World Championship when his team tied Austria and avoided relegation to the B Pool.

The catch is that Italy was scheduled to host the 1994 World Championship and would have been totally embarrassed not to have qualified for the tournament.

Non-contending nations also are keen on staying in the A Pool because they share in the large pool of revenue.

On a 23-man roster at the 1994 Olympics in Lillehammer, the Italians had 12 Canadian-born and two American-born players. One of them, defenceman Bill Stewart, was eligible to play for Italy only because his wife's parents were born there and he had played enough years in the Italian League to meet a requirement of the IIHF.

The organization's leniency in these matters was criticized by hockey fundamentalists. However, there's no question it helped smaller countries climb the world rankings ladder more quickly.

The French, Austrian and West German teams at the Calgary Olympics in 1988 were strengthened by Canadians with dual passports; France had seven, Austria five and West Germany four.

Today hockey has developed in these same countries to the point where they use homegrown players almost exclusively.

Bob Nicholson, former president and CEO of Hockey Canada, said the World Championship A Pool was expanded to 12 teams from eight in 1992 primarily for two reasons.

"The main reason was that the IIHF really felt the calibre of the Central European teams had improved and they would be competitive," he said. "Also, a lot of corporate dollars for the championships were coming from Central Europe."

Switzerland made its breakthrough by qualifying for the bronze medal game at the 1992 World Championship in Prague, tying both Canada and Russia along the way.

The Swiss hired Ralph Krueger, a native of Winnipeg in 1998, and he guided them to the bronze medal game again. Included was a stunning 4-2 victory over Russia, Switzerland's first win against the Russians in 13 tries at the World Championship and Olympics.

In 2000, Norway recorded its first victory over Canada, 4-3, at the World Championship in Russia. In that game, Canada was ahead on the scoreboard for only one minute and 33 seconds.

The next outsider to pose a threat to the hockey powers was Denmark, which returned to the A Pool in 2002. Just one year later the Danes beat the U.S. 5-2 and tied eventual gold medal champion Canada 2-2 at the Worlds in Finland.

It was a far cry from Denmark's first A Pool appearance in 1949 when it lost 47-0 to Canada, represented by an amateur club the Sudbury Wolves, with every Canadian player scoring three goals.

While the surprise victories and ties were achieved against Canadian and American teams deprived of their best players because of the NHL playoffs, the established countries certainly sat up and took notice at the 2006 Olympics in Torino where Switzerland's Martin Gerber made 49 saves to shut out the defending champions from Canada with a star-studded lineup 2-0. The Swiss also upset the Czech Republic 3-2.

At the 2013 World Championship, Switzerland went undefeated before losing to host Sweden in the gold medal game. Krueger relied heavily on Roman Josi, a Nashville Predator who was named the top defender in the tournament.

Today these nations are supplying the NHL with quality players. In the 2016-17 season, for example, there were 13 Swiss players, 11 Slovaks, nine Danes, five Germans, four players from France, three Austrians, two from Norway and one from Slovenia.

Pierre-Eduard Bellemare, the only player from France on the Team Europe entry at the 2017 World Cup of Hockey, has at least one happy memory of playing against Canada. The Vegas Golden Knights winger scored the most memorable goal of his career on May 9, 2014, in Minsk, Belarus, in a shootout as France shocked Canada 3-2 on the opening day of the World Championship.

When the Soviet Union broke up at the end of 1991, Belarus, Kazakhstan, Latvia and Ukraine, all former republics of the Soviet Union, formed their own teams and in most years two or three of them have been good enough to qualify for the World Championship tournament's top level.

The Czech Republic and Slovakia also started icing separate teams in 1993 following the breakup of Czechoslovakia.

Russians make up 40 per cent of the population of Kazakhstan and 33 per cent of the population of Latvia. These two countries benefited tremendously from the input of Russian-trained coaches.

At the 1992 World Junior Championship in Germany, Soviet players started the tournament with the Cyryllic letters CCCP (Union of Soviet Socialist Republics) on their chests in the last week of December. But with the USSR ceasing to exist on Jan. 1, 1992, the team switched its name to Commonwealth of Independent States and changed jerseys before going on to win the gold medal with a convincing 7-2 win over Canada.

The 1992 gold medalists had six players out of a 22-man roster (27 per cent) from other republics of the Soviet Union – two each from Latvia and Ukraine and one each from Kazakhstan and Lithuania. Players from these republics were no longer available to Russia from 1993 forward.

At the 1993 World Juniors, playing without the extra help, Russia was humiliated 9-1 by Canada and finished sixth overall. Surprisingly, though, at the senior level Russia was still able to win the gold medal at the 1993 World Championship in Germany.

The season before in France, playing under the name 'Unified Team', the former Soviets won another Olympic gold medal for Viktor Tikhonov. The team wore jerseys with no emblem on the front.

All but four players from that team later left to play in the NHL. The gold medalists played under the flag of the Olympics and the Olympic anthem was used as their own at the medals ceremony.

Traditionally, these former republics contributed about one-third of the players on the Soviet national junior team and made up about 20 per of the Soviet national team.

Players from other republics had a choice of playing for the new country, since they were actually born in that area, or sticking with Russia. Darius Kasparaitis, a native of Lithuania, selected Russia.

On the other hand, Arturs Irbe and Sandis Ozolinsh opted to go with Latvia and Dmitry Khristich with Ukraine, even though they had already played for the Soviet Union internationally.

Latvia and Ukraine had always had teams in the old Soviet Elite League – Dynamo Riga from Latvia and Sokol Kiev from Ukraine – and the Soviets had managed to grab some good players out of Kazakhstan in the past.

To illustrate how attitudes towards compensation were gradually changing in the Soviet Union and Czechoslovakia in the 1980s and 1990s, every player on the gold medal-winning team for the Soviets at the 1988

Olympics in Calgary received 12,000 rubles, which equated to $25,000 U.S. At the 1992 Olympics in France, all Czechoslovak players received a new car, albeit a tiny Skoda, for winning the bronze medal.

The Soviets' reward for winning the gold medal at Sarajevo in 1984 was 7,000 rubles, per player (about $15,000 U.S.). So the government in Moscow had become more generous in four years.

The average worker in the USSR was earning only 3,000 rubles, about $6,000 U.S., at that time and an average player in the Soviet Elite League just 6,000 rubles, about $12,000 U.S.

Czechoslovakia ceased to exist on Jan. 1, 1993. At the 1993 World Juniors the two nations played together for the last time, but under a slightly different name – Czech and Slovak Republics. Traditionally, Slovak players made up about 20 per cent of Czechoslovakia's national team, but Peter Stastny told me there was always discrimination against Slovak players in the selection process because most of the time the coaches were Czech. He said there were a lot of other Slovak players who should have been chosen.

Between 1945 and 1992 only 66 Slovak players were selected to play for the Czechoslovak national team out of 408, which works out to just 16 per cent.

The IIHF made a decision that because Czechs made up the larger section of the country and that region always had the most players on the national team, they would get the automatic berth for the 1994 Olympics in Lillehammer the country had earned by placing third in 1992 in France.

So Slovakia had to start out in the C pool of World Championship play and work its way up.

The Slovaks got up to the A pool in the fastest way possible. They finished first in the C pool in 1994 and first in the B pool in 1995. They made their international debut in the A pool at the 1996 World Juniors in Boston and the 1996 World Championship in Austria.

There was a different qualifying process for the Olympics. In order to gain a berth in the 1994 Olympics, Slovakia had to play in a qualifying tournament in Sheffield, England, in August 1993.

They won that and in their first Olympics finished first in their group at Lillehammer before losing a tough game in overtime to Russia in the quarterfinals. The Slovaks even beat Canada 3-1 in the preliminary round.

Peter Stastny had effectively retired following the 1992-93 season, but made himself available for the tournament in Sheffield and many NHL players took part because they had so much pride in their new nation. Stastny later returned to play briefly in the NHL with St. Louis.

"Slovakia having its own team was always a dream for us," Stastny said. "Now we had a chance. We were less developed than the Czechs. In those days, all our resources went into developing projects like the Prague metro. But the relationship has never been better since we split into two countries. Before that time, all decisions came from Prague."

It was Stastny who coaxed the IIHF into allowing Slovakia to play in the Olympic qualifying tournament in England.

"I had the privilege of being our flag bearer at the Opening Ceremonies in 1994," he said. "And when we won our division, I was getting faxes of congratulations from all over the world."

During a mini-tournament in France prior to the 1994 Olympics, his younger brother Anton was ejected from a game and suspended by the IIHF after he hit a referee following a controversial call. Therefore, he could not play in Lillehammer.

I remember talking to Peter about it at a practice in Lillehammer. He was blaming the Slovak Federation for not standing up for its players and trying to get Anton reinstated.

At first I couldn't believe what he was saying, since his brother had hit a referee, but later I realized it showed how close the Stastny brothers are.

The lyrics to the Slovak national anthem, which were scripted in the revolutionary 1840s, urge all countrymen to wake up from their sleep and adopt patriotic feelings.

"It is lightning above the Tatra mountains, thunders are savagely striking. Stop them my brothers, indeed they disappear and the Slovaks will revive," the opening words go.

The words appropriately describe Slovakia's quick rise to hockey prominence as a nation.

The Slovaks continued to get better, and at the 2000 World Championship in St. Petersburg, Russia, they made the final against their former brothers, although the Czechs won.

Finally, Slovakia won its first gold medal at the 2002 World Championship in Sweden. The Slovak junior team had already won a bronze medal at the 1999 World Juniors in Winnipeg where they held Canada to a 0-0 tie in the preliminary round and beat Sweden in the bronze medal game with future NHLer Ladislav Nagy scoring three goals.

At the 2006 Olympics, the Slovaks upset Russia 5-3, the U.S. 2-1 and Sweden 3-0. Unfortunately, they came up short in the quarterfinal, falling 3-1 to the Czechs.

Matej Buckna, a Canadian coach of Slovak origin, helped to develop ice hockey in the Slovak region of the former Czechoslovakia. A native of Trail, B.C., Buckna moved overseas in the 1930s and made a major contribution to the game.

At the 1997 World Championship, Latvia surprised the eventual gold medalist Canadians by tying them 3-3 in their first post-Soviet appearance at the top level of international play.

On Independence Day in Latvia in 2000, Latvia defeated Russia 3-2 at the 2000 World Championship in St. Petersburg, ending Russia's hopes of making the quarterfinals.

In 2005, Latvia rallied from a two-goal deficit with six minutes to play and upset Belarus 5-4 to qualify for the 2006 Olympics. The victory is called the 'Miracle In Riga'.

Belarus, once known as 'White Russia', also proved it had some hockey talent. The Belarusians upset Russia in 2000 at St. Petersburg, then at the 2002 Olympics in Salt Lake City they pulled off one of the most monumental upsets in Games history by eliminating Sweden 4-3 in the quarterfinals.

The coming-out party for Kazakhstan, in a sense, occurred at the 1998 World Junior Championship in Finland. Nikolai Antropov, a future Toronto Maple Leaf, led the new kids on the block to a totally unexpected 6-3 victory over Canada in a playoff for seventh place. Canada's eighth-place finish was its worst ever.

Little more than a month had passed when Kazakhstan also took a major step forward at the senior level by qualifying to play Canada in the quarterfinals of the 1998 Olympics in Japan by knocking off heavily favoured Slovakia.

Canada once had so little regard for the non-contending European hockey nations that it would dress the minimum 17 players against them in the preliminary round of the World Championship, keeping roster spots open for better players to arrive as their clubs were knocked out of the NHL playoffs.

Hockey has developed worldwide, however, and easy wins against Germany, Slovakia, Switzerland, Denmark, Norway, France, Slovenia and Austria, the eight nations supplying players to Team Europe at the World Cup of Hockey, are no longer a foregone conclusion.

However, primarily through Hockey Canada's Program of Excellence, Canada made the necessary adjustments to confirm its position as the top hockey nation in the world.

The major improvement Canadian teams have made is in the area of discipline. Canada's teams always had the best skills but blew many medal chances in the 1970s and 1980s with goon hockey and subsequently played most of their games shorthanded.

Canada's average skill level also is much higher today than in the 1980s.

The national teams of the Czech Republic and Slovakia now are in decline because most of their good young prospects left the country to play in North America. It has made preparing teams for IIHF championships a much harder job.

Anyone stupid enough to question Canada's depth in player talent should know the land of the Maple Leaf is a major supplier of talent to European clubs, as well as to college teams in the United States.

Ralph Slate, one of the Society for International Hockey Research's best statisticians, counted 673 Canucks playing overseas in the 2016-17 season and he conceded there are many second and third division leagues he doesn't even follow.

Peter Kathan, coach of the German team at the 2014 Olympics, described the difficulties his country has in competing at the top level against the best teams in the world.

"Our government needs to realize that Canada, the U.S., Sweden and Finland spend more money on hockey than us, have more players and are quite simply better than us," he said. "They drive a Porsche, we drive a Volkswagen, so it is obvious who will win the race!

"But when the ones driving the Porsche continue to get support and the ones with the Volkswagen don't, we will need 100 years to catch up."

The German national team often has been strengthened by so-called 'Volga Germans'. Either they or their ancestors were born in Russia along the Volga River but moved to Germany.

A lot of Germans left their homeland and took up residence in the Volga Valley in the 18th century. In Germany they had been persecuted for their religious beliefs. Besides that, they were facing high taxes and deterioration of their farmland

Eventually, thousands of them crossed the Atlantic, taking up farming in Kansas, Nebraska, North and South Dakota. A portion of North Dakota was referred to as 'the German-Russian triangle'.

Those who remained in the Volga Valley were persecuted again by the Russians after the First World War started. Many were sent to Siberia, but others were lucky enough to be able to go back to Germany.

Eduard Lewandowski, who was born in Krasnoturinsk, Russia, and played for Germany in four World Championships and the 2006 Olympics, was among the Volga Germans.

Another German national team player, Boris Blank, who was born in Kazakhstan and participated in three World Championships, said his parents were called Nazis and wound up in Siberia.

The intricacies of securing eligibility to play for a country internationally are illustrated in the case of Arnaud Briand, who played for France in four Olympics, serving as team captain in Salt Lake City. He was born in Sydney, Nova Scotia, while his family was living in the islands of St. Pierre and Miquelon, which are inside Canadian territory but are protectorates of France. He had played some hockey in Sydney, Nova Scotia before emigrating to France.

Kazakhstan lost a good player in 2004-05 when the IIHF ruled that goalie Evgeny Nabokov could play for Russia, even though he was born in Kazakhstan and had represented Kazakhstan at previous IIHF tournaments. Forty per cent of the population of Kazakhstan is Russian and Nabokov falls into that category. He also holds a Russian passport.

Nabokov had returned to Russia after an NHL career that saw him selected to play in two All-Star games. He also backstopped Russia to a gold medal at the 2008 World Championship in Quebec City.

However, he did not play well in the KHL, and when his family could not adapt to life in Russia, they asked to go back to the U.S. where he closed out his career with the New York Islanders.

A player who has previously participated in an IIHF competition can switch national eligibility only once in his lifetime. He must be a citizen of the new country of his choice, and have participated in the national competitions of that country for at least four consecutive years.

During this time he cannot play for his previous country or have transferred to another country. He must have an approved international transfer card dated and approved at least four years before the start of the competition in which he wants to play.

In 2017, the IIHF granted Kasparaitis the right to play for Lithuania, where he was born, even though he has previously played for the Soviet Union and Russia. Kasparaitis, who is now 44, will have played the required four seasons in the national league of Lithuania by 2018.

Even the 1999 pilgrimage to the Holy Land I took with my wife Chris and a group organized by Dr. Vicky Tam, the organist at Holy Rosary Church in Burlington, had a hockey angle. While in Jerusalem, I interviewed Sergei Matin, at that time President of the Israeli Ice Hockey Federation.

I visited the Canada Centre, the international size ice rink where the Israeli national team trained in Metula, very close to the border of Lebanon. It was a stop on a bus trip we took past fields full of mines left there from the 1967 war on our way to the Golan Heights.

The arena is so close to the border that it once was hit by rockets fired by the fundamentalist group Hamas in Lebanon.

At that time there were only three other ice rinks in Israel, and each of them was only 30 metres long by 15 metres wide. Nevertheless, there was a hockey league with six teams competing.

To my surprise, I learned almost 50 per cent of the national team players were Jews, who emigrated to Israel from the former Soviet Union or other Eastern Bloc countries where they had some training in hockey.

In fact, at that time there were 1.5 million ex-Pat Russians living in Israel.

Nowadays ice hockey is still fighting for recognition in the Middle East country where the Negev Desert covers more than half of the land. Yet organizers of the Maccabiah Games in the summer of 2017 were willing to hold the hockey tournament in Jerusalem's Pais Arena, which has seating for 10,000.

Roger Neilson brought his years of experience coaching in the NHL to Israel in 1997, launching a hockey camp in the summer. Later, former Montreal Canadiens and Quebec Nordiques coach Jean Perron was hired to lead the Israeli national team for five years. Guy Carbonneau and Jacques Demers both have taken a turn at coaching teams in Israel.

In 2015 David Levin, who was born in Israel, was selected first overall in the Ontario Hockey League import draft by the Sudbury Wolves. He is ranked for the 2018 NHL draft and hopes to be the first player born in Israel to play in the League. His father is a former pro soccer player in Latvia and his mother is Russian.

Levin was only 12 when he moved to Canada to live with his aunt and uncle to improve his hockey skills. Within four years he was invited to Hockey Canada's U-17 summer development camp.

Max Birbraer, a Jew who was born in Kazakhstan, was selected by the New Jersey Devils as the 67th overall pick in the 2000 draft. He was good enough to play three seasons with the Albany River Rats of the AHL.

Israel is now producing more homegrown players and took the best of them to the Olympic qualifying tournament in Estonia in 2015. The team did not qualify but managed to beat Bulgaria 5-2. It was the first victory for an Israeli team of players born solely in that country.

In the same vein, Belfast, Northern Ireland, once was not the safest place in the world to watch a hockey game. But the Belfast Giants, who play in Great Britain's Elite Ice Hockey League, decided to make things better.

The team developed a slogan, 'In the land of the Giants, everyone is equal' and made it clear it would not tolerate any sectarianism. This in a nation where Protestants and Catholics have been at loggerheads for decades.

For example, fans are not allowed to come to games wearing the colours of any particular community. The Giants were careful to choose red, teal and white as their team colors, avoiding any green or orange which might tie the club to either Catholics or Protestants.

Jim Van Der Meer, a 37-year-old defenceman from Caroline, Alberta, who has 482 NHL games under his belt, suited up with the Giants in 2016-17.

Meanwhile, it's noteworthy that the Republic of Ireland in the south recorded its first hockey victory on St. Patrick's Day, March 17, 2004. The Irish clobbered Armenia 15-1 at the Division 3 World Championship in Iceland.

With only two covered ice rinks in the south at the time, and most of its players living in Dublin, the shamrock crew stole a page from Anatoly Tarasov's book by practising at midnight three times a week on an under-sized outdoor ice pad.

During the 2017 Asian Winter Games in Japan even Iran made its debut on the international hockey scene. The Iranians did not compete for the championship because at the last minute many of their players were declared ineligible. However, they still got their feet wet by playing friendly games.

Mika Zibanejad of the New York Rangers spent his youth in Mashhad, Iran, before moving to Sweden and becoming a hero by scoring in overtime to bring the Swedes their first World Junior Championship gold medal in 31 years.

You could fry an egg on the streets of the capital city of Tehran during the summer when the temperature rises into the 30s C. But during the winter it's cold. Three small rinks have been constructed in Iran over the last few years.

The growth of hockey has initially led to some ungodly scores. In 1998, South Korea slaughtered Thailand 92-0 and Kazakhstan clobbered Iceland 63-0. Slovakia embarrassed Bulgaria 82-0 in a women's match in 2008.

There have been so many player transfers in both directions across the Atlantic that you can't tell who's playing and where they're from even with a program.

During the 2016 Spengler Cup, TSN announcer Greg Sansone made a small goof. With Canada leading Dynamo Minsk of the KHL 3-2 in the dying minutes, he proclaimed, "The Russians don't often pull their goalie early," forgetting that the Minsk club was coached by Canadian Craig Woodcroft and had three Canadian players – Matt Ellison, Rob Klinkhammer and Ben Scrivens – in its lineup. Furthermore, the club is from Belarus.

Many North American announcers could create a lot more interest in their telecasts by delving into the origins of European names.

Just pronouncing the last name of Finnish defenceman Reijo Ruotsalainen, a two-time Stanley Cup winner with Edmonton, created many headaches for them. It was an information gem, however, when some of them found out the literal translation of his last name from Finnish to English is 'citizen of Sweden'.

That, they joked, made him ineligible for play for his country!

At the 1988 World Junior Championship in Moscow, the Swedish team drove play-by-play men to distraction by dressing three players with exactly the same first and last names – Stefan Nilsson.

In 1975 the Atlanta Flames drafted Torbjorn Nilsson from Sweden when they meant to select Kent 'Magic Man' Nilsson. They had to keep quiet about the mistake for a year before they actually were able to pick Kent in 1976.

Silence is golden. The 'Magic Man' had three seasons of 40 goals or more in his bag of tricks.

Patric Kjellberg, who played 394 NHL games with Montreal, Nashville and Anaheim, startled the media when he arrived in Canada with the correct pronunciation of his last name SHELL-berriyeh. Perhaps it was to cover up his summer job as a detective with the Stockholm city police force!

In the case of giant-sized Buffalo winger Yuri Khymlev, who was born in the Soviet Union, they did their best with HIM-ah lev when it is really HMEEL-yove.

After the Oilers signed Miroslav Satan in 1999, he took such a ribbing from teammates who were calling him all sorts of devilish things he considered applying for a legal name change. But it never happened.

Apparently, he was satisified with the shuh-TAN version announcers use, rather than the correct SHAH-tahn from the Slovak language.

Sometimes names that are almost impossible for English-speaking announcers to pronounce have a certain irony about them

The literal translation of Pobedonostsev, a member of the Ukrainian national team at the 2005 World Championship, is 'winner', but Oleksandr turned out to be a loser after he tested positive for an illegal substance during the tournament and was disqualified!

I respectfully disagreed with John Shannon, who directed hockey for NBC in Salt Lake City, when he instructed his cameramen not to bother taking any shots of foreign-language signs in the crowd.

Deciphering their meaning, as well of those of cheers from spectators, can add a lot of spice for viewers.

'Go, Canada, Go' is the familiar chant of Canadian fans urging their team on to victory. European nations also have their favorites.

The most famous, 'Shybu', which literally is the accusative case of the word for puck in Russian, urges players to 'go, get that puck'.

Dating back to hockey's earliest years in Czechoslvakia, fans screamed 'Cesi do toho', meaning 'Let's go, Czechs'.

One of my all-time favorites is 'Hopp Schwiiz', basically 'Go Switzerland'.

Russia failed to make the final at the 2016 World Cup of Hockey, but it wasn't the fault of team boosters who posted the age-old slogan 'Glazomyer, Bistrota, Natisk! – Nauka Pobyezhdat' on the wall of the team dressing room.

It was spoken by Alexander Suvorov, a great Russian military commander of the 18th century, and roughly translates to 'Precise shooting, speed and pressure on the attack is the science of winning'.

CHAPTER 10
Lokomotiv air crash depletes European rosters

When a tragic air crash claimed the lives of all the players on the Lokomotiv Yaroslavl team in September 2011, Russian officials faced the monumental task of replacing the team.

KHL President Alexander Medvedev wanted the team to keep playing in the KHL immediately and suggested each of the 23 other teams in the league contribute three players to a pool from which the replacement team would be chosen. His idea was for the contributing teams to cover the salaries of the players picked for one season

However, Lokomotiv executives said the city needed time to heal and returning to the KHL so soon was not realistic.

"Yaroslavl was in mourning," said Andrei Tutarikov, an employee of the Region of Yaroslavl who arrived at the crash scene just 20 minutes after the plane went down. "And to play in Arena 2000 and dress in the same locker rooms would have been very difficult. Nobody entered those locker rooms from the day of the crash until the end of October."

Lokomotiv president Yuri Yakovlev recommended the club maintain its team in the Russian junior league while having its top team join the Russian Major League, one level below the KHL, by December.

Some of the best players from the junior club were promoted to the Major League team. The club was then allowed to sign free agents and select young players born between 1989 and 1994 who had been playing with clubs in the KHL or Major League.

Those clubs were allowed to protect two players. The final decision on moving to Yaroslavl was then left to the individual player selected. If he was willing to make the move, his club lost him without compensation.

For awhile in the fall of 2011, the only hockey in Yaroslavl was provided by Loko, the city's club in the Russian Junior League.

The rebuilt men's team finally returned to the ice in the Major League in December. The Major League is approximately the equivalent of North America's AHL.

Yaroslavl did not have a KHL club again until the following season, 2012-13.

Lokomotiv fans would hang banners in the arena bearing the words, 'Pomnim, lyubim, skorbim – vsyegda v nashix syerdtsakh', which translates to 'We remember, we love, we mourn – always in our hearts.'

There were suggestions the new Lokomotiv club be given a bye into the Major League playoffs, but in the end club executives felt this would be unfair to the rest of the teams in the league.

Therefore it was decided the team would qualify for the playoffs, or not, based on its winning percentage over the rest of the season. The patchwork club, in fact, posted a record of 13-6-3 in the regular season and made the playoffs.

The doomed plane was supposed to carry Lokomotiv Yaroslavl to a KHL game in Minsk, the capital of Belarus.

An investigation showed when the aircraft landed in Yaroslavl to pick the team up the forward chassis hit the tarmac. The pilot thought it was a minor problem and no repairs were done.

After the players had boarded and the plane took off again, the captain and first officer decided to change places, which is a serious violation of aviation rules.

The final death toll from the crash was 44.

Sixteen of those killed were Russian players. Some of the others, like Pavol Demitra of Slovakia, Ruslan Salei of Belarus and Karlis Skrastins of Latvia, had previously played in the NHL and were considered legends in their respective countries.

An investigation determined the pilot incorrectly stepped on the brake pedals during takeoff before raising the nose wheel of the aircraft.

The KHL immediately ceased using the outdated Yak-42 aircraft and switched to more modern models. In addition, in-flight regulations were tightened up considerably.

It was not the first such violation in Russia. Yet North American players, who are out of a job, are willing to take risks to earn a living.

Matt Ellison, a native of Duncan, B.C., was drafted by Chicago in 2002 after putting up big numbers with Red Deer of the WHL in 2002-03, scoring 40 goals and 96 points in just 72 games, and being named rookie of the year in the Canadian Hockey League.

Ellison signed with Dinamo Riga for the 2008-09 season after short NHL stints with the Blackhawks and Philadelphia Flyers.

Dinamo's first two games were in Khabarovsk in the Far East of Russia, near Japan, a 10-hour flight from Riga.

"First of all we had to stop in Novosibirsk to refuel, then when we were about an hour away from Khabarovsk the pilot announced the weather was poor and we wouldn't be able to land," he said. "We turned around and flew about 400 miles, landing in Mongolia. We couldn't get off the plane because we didn't have visas and we had a game that night."

Realizing his players were very tired, coach Julius Supler took all of them up to first class so they could get some sleep.

"Some players were sleeping across the seats and some on the floor when all of a sudden the plane took off again," he said. "We got to Khabarovsk four hours before game time, got a snack and went straight to the arena."

The frightening day ended happily when Ellison scored the fourth goal in a 4-2 Dynamo win.

In August 2012 the national junior teams of Canada and Russia opened a four-game exhibition series to mark the 40th anniversary of the 1972 Summit Series. The series, which opened in Yaroslavl, also honoured the memory of those who lost their lives in the 2011 air disaster, including Pavel Snurnitsyn and Maxim Shuvalov, two candidates for the 2012 World Junior Championship.

It was fitting that Kirill Kapustin, a close friend of some of the Lokomotiv Yaroslavl victims, was the star of Russia's 6-3 win in Game 2 at Yaroslavl. He scored three goals and came very close to netting a fourth.

Following the crash, Kapustin paid this tribute to his former teammates:

"I have a strong desire to win the (KHL's) Gagarin Cup now, to win the youth championship and dedicate the victory to my friends, who died," he told the website *Russia Today*.

Byron McCrimmon, father of Brad McCrimmon the Lokomotiv coach who was killed, accompanied the Canadian junior team to Russia and laid flowers at a memorial before the series started.

As early as 1950, 11 players from the Soviet Air Force team VVS also had been killed in an air crash near Sverdlovsk.

In between those two catastrophes, the Soviet (Russian) player pool was diminished by a series unfortunate deaths of several players.

The dynamic Valery Kharlamov died in 1981 at the age of 33 in an auto accident. He missed the inaugural Canada Cup tournament in 1976 because of a separate car accident, in which he broke both ankles, and was not even selected to the roster for the second in 1981 because coach Tikhonov was introducing younger players. In fact, he was killed while the Soviet team was in Canada preparing for the 1981 event.

Just four years later, the same thing happened to Slava Fetisov's 18-year-old brother Anatoly, who some scouts said might have been better than the legendary defenceman. Anatoly was a leading prospect for the 1985 NHL draft.

If all the Soviet players who died before their time or under tragic circumstances had been spared, the statistical history of world hockey might have to be rewritten.

Besides Kharlamov, another seven veterans of the Summit Series were no longer around when the 40th anniversary was celebrated.

Valery Vasiliev was captain of the Soviet Union's 1981 Canada Cup championship team. But in 1972 he was a goat of sorts when he misplayed a puck that made its way to the stick of Paul Henderson for the winning goal in Game 8. Heart and kidney failure, as well as pneumonia, ended his life in 2012 at the age of 62.

Vasiliev had experienced chest pains at the 1978 World Championship in Prague and was informed later by doctors he actually suffered a heart attack.

Gennady Tsygankov, who was blamed by coach Vsevelod Bobrov for Henderson's winning goal in Game 7, died in February 2006 at the age of 59.

The photo of Soviet captain Viktor Kuzkin wearing a white Stetson was published in many Canadian newspapers and magazines. Kuzkin also will be remembered as one of the few Soviet players who was always smiling. At the age of 67 he died of a heart attack in 2008 while diving in the Black Sea at a resort in Sochi.

Evgeny Paladiev was the victim of Peter Mahovlich's end-to-end rush for a highlight-reel goal in Canada's 4-1 win at Maple Leaf Gardens in Game 2 of the 1972 Summit Series. He died from heart trouble in 2010 at the age of 61.

In another memorable goal in Game 2, Yvan Cournoyer 'undressed' legendary Soviet defenceman Alexander 'Rags' Ragulin, who was just 63 when he died in November 2004.

Vyacheslav Solodoukhin, who played in only one game, was only 28 when he fell asleep in his car with the motor running, in a closed garage.

Some Soviet newspapers described the death as accidental asphyxiation, others called it a suicide. The death occurred in October 1979, only seven years after the 1972 series concluded.

Although he did not play in the series, backup goalie Alexander Sidelnikov died in 2003 at the age of 53

Boris Aleksandrov, the flashy winger who scored the tying goal in the Red Army's famous 3-3 tie with Montreal on New Year's Eve 1975, was killed in a head-on auto collision in Russia at the age of 47 in 2002.

In 1997 Valentin Sych, then president of the Russian Ice Hockey Federation, was shot to death in the suburbs of Moscow while he was driving his car just before flying to Finland for the World Championship.

Police believe Sych had aroused the ire of some in Russia because at that time the federation was making an exorbitant profit with the government allowing it alcohol and tobacco import exemptions.

During the NHL lockout in 2004-05 Sergei Zholtok, a Latvian who had played 588 NHL games for six different clubs, suffered a heart attack and died in the dressing room with only five minutes left in a game between HC Riga 2000 and Dynamo Minsk. He was only 31.

Speculation about why so many great athletes had their playing careers and retirements cut short ranges from body fatigue as a result of the strenuous training they did 11 months of the year when they were young, to the possibility they were using steroids. Some observers suggest they couldn't adjust to retirement away from the rink and became slaves of alcohol. The answer would be different in every case.

Evgeny Belosheikin, named best goalie at the 1986 World Junior Championship, took his own life at the age of 33 in 1999 after a battle with the bottle.

New York Rangers prospect Alexei Cherepanov was a young lad of 19 when he died from a heart attack during a game in Chekhov, near Moscow, in October 2008. He was a first-round pick of the Broadway Blueshirts the year before and would have played in his third World Junior Championship in Ottawa after Christmas that year.

It took 45 minutes for paramedics to get him to a hospital.

After his death, the league made it mandatory for all arenas to be equipped with defibrillators, aspirators and tracheotomy kits.

The KHL also ordered testing of all young players and prohibited three top prospects, whose electrocardiograms had detected heart irregularities, from playing temporarily.

One of them, defenceman Dmitry Vorobiev, had been drafted by the Toronto Maple Leafs in 2004 and played on Russia's World Championship gold medal team at Quebec City in 2008.

Goalie Vadim Zhelobnyuk, a bronze medal winner at the 2009 World Junior Championship in Ottawa, and Spartak defencemen Dmitry Vishnevsky were the others.

However, all three later received health clearances and are still playing today.

Other outstanding Soviet players lived miserable lives before dying before their time.

In an era when European players rarely got involved in fights, winger Evgeny Mishakov had to defend himself in a scrap with Rod Gilbert in the third period of Game 8 of the Summit Series.

In retirement Mishakov went through hell. He required operations on both knees, was a victim of alcoholism and eventually passed away when he was 66 in 2007.

He didn't even get to the operating table because he had so many other problems, even though Dr. Lowell Van Zuiden, a Canadian from Calgary, said he would operate without charging a cent.

Ron Ellis, a member of Team Canada 1972, said he would try to raise $15,000 for Mishakov's travel and after-care expenses with the help of the committee that looks after marketing for Canadian alumni of the Summit Series.

Later, Igor Larionov and Slava Fetisov created a fund to help retired Soviet players.

Some of the Soviet Union's most illustrious players went to work as gravediggers in their retirement because the pensions they were receiving added up to only $80 a month. Wages for this menial cemetery work actually were above what the average guy on the street was earning.

Conditions have changed tremendously for the better, though, and today players in the KHL lead comfortable lives, even if many North Americans aren't ready to believe it.

Imports who signed with the Dynamo Riga club in Latvia in 2010 were quite happy living in the ultra-modern Panorama Plaza skyscraper.

"The biggest difference here from North America is there's not much fast food." Chris Holt, a goalie from Vancouver, told me. "If you go out for the evening to have a nice sit-down experience, you're there for the whole night."

Jaromir Jagr tipped the scales at the heaviest of his career when he left the NHL to play for Avangard Omsk in 2008.

"I found out quickly that, if you're going to play in this league on the big ice surface, you've got to lose some pounds," he said. "You have to skate more, there's not a lot of play along the boards."

Sergei Brylin, who earned two Stanley Cup rings with New Jersey, maintained a home in the U.S. while playing for SKA St. Petersburg in the KHL.

"The skill level there is pretty good," Brylin said. "The top four or five teams could easily play in the NHL."

Six-time Vezina Trophy winner Dominik Hasek found the KHL, with its puck possession-style of game, an ideal place to wind down his career, even though his club Spartak Moscow was not a championship contender.

"There's less shooting here, which I like!" Hasek told me.

More young Russian prospects are choosing to stay at home to pursue a professional career.

That's not to say the league does not rely heavily on imports. There were only nine Russians among the top 20 scorers in 2016-17. In some years there have been as few as five. Rounding out the top 20 in 2016-17 were four Canadians, two Americans and one player each from the Czech Republic, Denmark, Finland, Slovenia and Sweden.

More than one-third of the league's 700 players at any given time are non-Russians.

The NHL was mildly concerned when the KHL was launched in the fall of 2008. While the new league has never attracted the flow of former NHLers it had hoped to, it has provided a living for a lot of players whose contracts were not renewed.

A new arena, which seats between 12,000 and 14,000, was built in Astana, Kazakhstan, where former Los Angeles Kings defenceman Kevin Dallman plays for the Barys club.

Ray Emery, who played in the city of Mytischi near Moscow a few seasons ago, said one of the major adjustments he had to make was getting used to squads of cheerleaders dancing on platforms to the sound of rock music right behind his net in some buildings.

One drawback for players is the enormous distance between other venues. Dynamo Riga, in the west, is 6,800 kilometres from the eastern-most, Amur, in the city of Khabarovsk near the border of Japan. That adds up to a lot of time in the air.

Also, Russian clubs start training early. For example, in the summer of 2016, CSKA Moscow's players arrived for training camp on July 3 and worked on dryland training for a week. The club traveled to Finland for a second two-week training camp in the town of Kemi, on the shores of the Gulf of Bothnia, only 57 miles south of the Arctic Circle. They then returned to Moscow on July 25 for a pair of exhibition games.

The next camp took place in Sochi from Aug. 2-12, and at the conclusion CSKA participated in the Sochi Hockey Open tournament with three other clubs, SKA St. Petersburg, HK Sochi and the so-called Russian Olympic team, which essentially is the Russian national B team.

If that wasn't enough, the club then flew back to Moscow to play in the annual Mayor's Cup pre-season tournament from Aug. 15-18 with Spartak Moscow, Dynamo Moscow and Vityaz Chekhov.

Finally, the KHL regular season began on Aug. 22 with CSKA playing Metallurg Magnitogorsk, in Magnitogorsk, in a replay of the previous season's Gagarin Cup final.

In the old Soviet Elite League, teams that failed to make the playoffs or were eliminated in early rounds continued to practise for about a month in anticipation of next year. They had only the month of July for vacation.

Today it is not uncommon for European players under NHL contract to train during the summer with their previous clubs at home.

When Tarasov was training the Central Red Army team in the 1960s, there was a huge shortage of indoor rinks in Moscow, so the players went outside.

They had outdoor ice pads located at the foot of the Lenin Hills in the shade of tall trees so the sun couldn't get at them when the temperature started to rise in early spring. To get on the ice before it melted, the players would get up at 3 or 4 in the morning to practise.

Russian clubs in the modern era have money because a lot are sponsored by oil and gas companies and the country has lots of natural resources. However, over the last two years some have been suffering because of a reduction in the price of oil by almost 50 per cent. Several clubs were behind in paying their players in 2016-17.

When Dynamo Moscow incurred debts of two billion rubles ($35 million U.S.) over two seasons recently, the KHL declared all 42 players on its roster unrestricted free agents in July 2017. The players hadn't been paid in three months.

Dynamo officials claimed the debts resulted from an employee embezzling funds.

There were two options for the players. They could re-sign with the club under its new ownership for the same amount they were making before, or for a new contract which could be higher or lower. Or they could sign with another team.

Veteran goalie Alexander Eremenko, 37, not wanting to move at his age, re-signed. On the other hand the club's best defenceman, Mat Robinson of Calgary, inked a new deal with cross-town rival CSKA Moscow.

The financial collapse of the team was a huge surprise to Russian hockey fans. In 1999 a Moscow newspaper had described Dynamo as 'wealthy and prosperous'. Dynamo and CSKA were just two of four teams based in the capital that had the means to continue to operate following the breakup of the Soviet Union and subsequent reduction in funding from the government.

"They know where and how to get money and the people who belong to this organization are considered very clever," the article said.

Billionaire Arkady Rotenberg, a close friend of Russian President Vladimir Putin, owned Dynamo when it won KHL championships in both 2012 and 2013. However, he sold the club in 2015.

The possibility of a 30-per cent pay cut for players even was discussed at a league meeting in 2016.

Nevertheless, someone always seems to come up with enough money to pay the players in the long run.

As in the NHL, some KHL clubs are richer than others. The difference is that in Russia there is greater disparity.

When I went there for the KHL All-Star Game in 2011, season tickets for games of the Atlant Mytischi club, near Moscow, could be obtained for 1,260 rubles, averaging only about $1.50 per game. The most expensive tickets at the CSKA ice palace in Moscow were going for $50.

When the Allan Cup champion Chatham Maroons played exhibition games in Moscow in the fall of 1960, tickets for the games at the Lenin Palace of Sports in Moscow were only $1.50 and sold on a first come, first served basis, so earlybirds got the best view. The first three or four games were sellouts, but by the fifth game the fans were disappointed with the quality of the Chatham team and it was only half-full.

However, the average salary in the Russian capital in the summer of 2010 was in the area of $1,000 (U.S.) a month when the newspaper *Sport Express* ran a story saying tickets were too expensive.

"To buy a car or go to a hockey game?" the story headline screamed.

"There is no comparison in the standard of living in Russia and North America," the story read. "For many people where KHL clubs are based, admission to hockey games is too expensive. For them, it is a serious problem for the family budget."

Strangely enough, though, while KHL clubs in Siberia and the Far East usually draw full houses, clubs in Moscow continue to have big-time trouble at the gate.

In the 2010-11 season Dynamo Riga in Latvia was averaging between 8,000 and 9,000 fans in a building that accommodates only 10,300. However, more than 11,000 Latvians somehow jammed their way in for an exhibition game against the Phoenix Coyotes.

Still, the CSKA club in Moscow sometimes had as few as 2,500 bums in the seats.

Support for the game is growing in Russia, but I once read a notice on a Russian sports website informing readers that a KHL game, originally scheduled to be shown that day, would be pre-empted by the telecast of a biathlon competition!

In the 2016-17 season, Dynamo Minsk in Belarus topped all teams in the KHL with an average gate of 13,230. CSKA was fifth from the bottom with just 3,287, despite finishing first in the Western Conference.

If you're attending a KHL game, don't expect to have to line up for tickets. There is so much competition for the entertainment dollar in the Russian capital that arenas are rarely filled.

When former Detroit Red Wings assistant coach Barry Smith guided SKA St. Petersburg to a first-place finish in the regular season in 2009-10, almost every home game was sold out. But the team was ousted in the first round of the playoffs, leading to a parting of the ways between Smith and the club.

The next season attendance was only in the range of 5,000 to 12,000, even though SKA finished in a tie for second place in the Western Conference.

Fans in St. Petersburg like a frontrunner; it's not that the club fails to offer entertainment value. The SKA fan club sits at one end of the rink chanting and waving banners with its mascot 'Firehorse'. There are attractive cheerleaders waving pom-poms in every aisle.

The choice of a horse for mascot goes back to the club's tradition as the Sports Club of the Army because of the horses Russian military personnel once rode.

SKA officials said attendance at hockey games suffers if the Zenit St. Petersburg soccer team has a home game the same night. At that time Gazprom, one of the country's huge producers of natural gas, sponsored not only the hockey club but also the soccer club and basketball team.

Dave King became the first Canadian to coach in the KHL when he signed with Metallurg Magnitogorsk of the Russian Superleague, the KHL's predecessor, for the 2005-06 season. Later in 2013-14 Mike Keenan, who guided the New York Rangers to their first Stanley Cup in 54 years in 1994, coached the same Metallurg club to the Gagarin Cup, emblematic of the KHL championship. He also was named the league's coach of the year.

Keenan now has been hired to lead the Chinese club Kunlun Red Star, which plays in the KHL. China will host the 2022 Winter Olympics and there's a good chance he also will coach that team. Chinese officials have told him they want regular shifts for at least five Chinese players, so they will develop their skills.

In its first year in the league, 2016-17, Kunlun Red Star used 11 players from Finland at various times of the season. The team acquitted itself well by finishing eighth in the Eastern Conference and making the playoffs.

When King was fired as coach in Magnitogorsk, just eight games into his second season in Russia, he said he was completely caught off guard.

Even after reflecting for six months, he had no idea why he was fired, but said he was always paid on time.

The former NHL coach wrote a book entitled *King of Russia: A Year in the Russian Superleague* about his experiences.

Generally, he enjoyed it. During the Olympic break in his first season there, the team traveled to Dubai for a combination training-holiday, with players and their wives staying at a resort where the temperature was 75 F.

Magnitogorsk produced steel for half the Soviet tanks in the Second World War.

Valery Bragin was at the peak of his coaching career when he found a pink slip among the other papers on his desk.

Bragin had coached Russia to a gold medal at the 2011 World Juniors in Buffalo and a silver at the 2012 WJC in Alberta.

He was a national hero when he was fired by Sergei Fedorov, general manager of the CSKA Moscow club. Bragin had been on the job for only seven months.

At the end of the 2016-17 season no fewer than 11 bench bosses had either been fired or resigned.

Smith said Russia is not an easy place to work and coaches have to know going in that they could be dismissed at any time.

"It's a totally different mentality there," he said. "They expect so much back from the money they're spending. And it's 'win now', they don't have any patience. It's not just that you're not winning, it's that you're not doing it by enough goals."

Although it was Smith's own decision to leave when his contract expired, he said he is aware of some fired coaches not receiving full compensation.

"And there's just nothing you can do about it," he said.

Wayne Fleming, Canada's head coach at the 2001 and 2002 World Championships, knew better than anyone how unpredictable owners and general managers in the KHL can be.

Anatoly Bardin, general manager of Avangard Omsk, entered the team's locker room at the end of the second period with Avangard losing 1-0 to Vityaz Chekhov and told Fleming he would not be coaching for the final period.

Fleming got in his car and drove home but at a meeting with Bardin and captain Alexander Svitov the next day both told him they wanted him to continue as coach.

Former NHL goalie John Grahame was cut loose by the same team in the 2008-09 season amid allegations he was drunk in a local nightclub after a game.

Grahame claimed he was set up by club officials anxious to get rid of him without compensation.

It's far from the norm, but a game between Ak Bars Kazan and Moscow Dynamo in Moscow in the league's first season was suspended when Dynamo fans set off flares when their team scored late in the first period. Billowing clouds of smoke filled the arena and people had to put scarves over their faces to protect themselves. Alexander Ovechkin, who was in Russia to visit his ailing grandfather, was there to watch it all.

The league ordered the game replayed and, at one point, considered having it take place behind locked doors with no fans. However, officials relented and spectators were allowed to see it.

The KHL hired the Boston-based Ketchum Sports and Entertainment company to do its marketing in North America, but after Russian troops moved into Crimea at the eastern end of Ukraine in 2014, the company did not renew its contract with the league.

In the 2009-10 season when buyers for the Phoenix Coyotes franchise were being sought, KHL president Alexander Medvedev sent two letters to his NHL counterpart Gary Bettman indicating an interest by Russian investors in purchasing a franchise, but received no reply.

Geography, apparently, was not part of the curriculum when NHL Vice-President Bill Daly was going to college.

Medvedev said he would send Daly an atlas after the vice-president announced a few years ago NHL teams definitely would not travel to Siberia. Bettman had expressed grave concern about the freezing temperatures.

"Let him take a look at where Siberia starts on the map," Medvedev said. "We (Russia) have good airline carriers and air traffic control in our country. They (NHL) themselves travel far and wide for games in North America. For logistical purposes, of course, it would be better to play the games in the European region of Russia. However, from Moscow it's only a two-and-a-half-hour flight to Omsk."

The KHL president could have added that in the 21st century the Siberian region, which covers 77 per cent of Russia, now has modern cities with all the amenities the West once claimed as its own.

It's a small example of the ignorance that still exists in North American about the world's second best professional hockey league

In 2012, the KHL announced it would play two league games in the new Barclay's Centre in Brooklyn, N.Y. in January 2013. The arena is owned by Russian billionaire Mikhail Prokhorov, who also owns the Brooklyn Nets basketball team.

Fetisov, who played in the New York area for the New Jersey Devils, was the first to come up with the idea.

"There are 100,000 Russians living in the immediate area of New York," he said.

However, the games were cancelled in October, 2012. Speculation arose that it was because the NHL lockout ended just about the time the games were to be played. But Medvedev's explanation was that fans in the two Russian cities where the games ordinarily would have been played complained too loudly that they were being shortchanged.

KHL teams come and go. When one leaves, it's usually for financial reasons. However, the league lost the Donbass team from the city of Donetsk in Ukraine in the 2014-15 season because of the turmoil after Russia annexed Crimea.

During the playoffs in 2014 the club had to move some of its home games to Prague and Bratislava.

In May, 2014 the arena Donbass was playing in was torched after looters made off with a bundle of equipment.

With a $65-million budget to sign players during the NHL lockout of 2004-05, the Russian Superleague club Ak Bars Kazan was nicknamed 'New York Rangers East'.

In the first round of the Russian Superleague playoffs the Kazan club, with 12 locked-out NHL players in uniform, lived up to the Rangers' reputation for post-season failure by falling 3-1 in a best-of-five series with Lokomotiv Yaroslavl.

Goaltender Nikolai Khabibulin, center Vincent Lecavalier and winger Brad Richards of the 2004 Stanley Cup champion Tampa Bay Lightning signed lucrative contracts to play for Ak Bars (Snow Leopards) during the lockout. Although Richards did not dress in the playoffs because of an injury, the club also had goaltender Fred Brathwaite, defencemen Darius Kasparaitis, Alexei Zhitnik and Ruslan Salei, and forwards Ilya Kovalchuk, Dany Heatley, Alexei Kovalev, Alexey Morozov, Slava Kozlov and Denis Arkhipov in uniform.

Russian hockey also has its novelties. NHL stars were there when the team decided to put its overall speed to the test.

Invited to play a friendly match against the local bandy club on an outdoor ice surface measuring 328 long by 164 feet wide, the Ak Bars players found themselves sucking wind as they were shellacked 7-2.

In the early 1990s Howard Baldwin, owner of the Pittsburgh Penguins, sank money into the Central Army Sports Club to try to boost attendance and the team became affectionately known as the Russian Penguins.

The Penguins used North American marketing techniques, starting to sell beer at the games and even having strippers between periods. It helped boost attendance to about 5,000 per game for awhile, but the novelty wore off and they reverted to about 2,000.

During the 1980s, when the Army club was dominant, many times they would draw only about 1,000 fans to games in Moscow, because fans knew the games would be a slaughter and refused to buy tickets.

There have been other attempts at partnership between Russian and North American clubs, but they were short-lived. Torpedo Yaroslavl had an agreement with the Las Vegas Thunder of the IHL, but it ended early after players the Russian club sent to Las Vegas for development were given very little icetime.

The Detroit Vipers of the IHL attempted to co-operate with the Moscow-based club Wings of the Soviet in 1997, with the Vipers providing the Wings with North American-style sports marketing.

Under the Communist government, the four Moscow-based clubs – CSKA, Moscow Dynamo, Spartak and Wings of the Soviet –received the most government funding. CSKA was sponsored by the Red Army and Dynamo by the Ministry of Defence.

In the late 1980s, Perestroika started during the presidency of Mikhail Gorbachev, changing the whole picture. The four Moscow clubs were compelled to turn to private sponsors and large factories and enterprises began to throw big money into previously non-contending teams like Metallurg.

CHAPTER 11

Sub-tropical climate comfortable setting for Sochi Games

Visions of Siberia's vast territory of ice and snow were all I could conjure up when I heard Russia had been awarded the 2014 Winter Olympics. I had been to St. Petersburg twice in the middle of winter and taken about a week to thaw out.

What I didn't realize is the region in the south that includes Sochi has a sub-tropical climate, sitting on the coast of the Black Sea.

Over the three weeks I was there, the temperature ranged from 50 to 65 F, and even pushed 70 a couple of days. Palm trees were growing everywhere and a few hardy folks even took a dip in the ocean.

Workers were sticking boxed plants into the ground near the two ice hockey arenas right up until the opening ceremonies. A lot of people weren't even wearing jackets.

Meanwhile, back home in Burlington my wife Chris was battling freezing temperatures and ice-covered sidewalks trying to walk our little dog Polo every day.

Although the Games were billed as Sochi 2014, they were actually held in Adler, about an hour's train ride to the east.

Adler is just one of four districts that make up the Greater Sochi area, which actually borders the Black Sea for a distance of 120 kilometres. The Olympic park was sandwiched between the Black Sea, lined along its shore by an interlocking brick walkway, and the snow-capped Caucasas Mountains

The Athletes Village was located close to the coast. Five sports venues – the Bolshoy Dom for ice hockey, Shaiba Arena for ice hockey, Ice Cube for curling, Iceberg for figure skating and Adler Arena for speedskating – were situated in a huge circle along with the Fisht Olympic Stadium, site of the opening and closing ceremonies, two ice pads for hockey practices and one pad for skating practices.

In the middle of it all was the Olympic torch and an outdoor stage for medal presentations.

Metal fencing closed off areas not open to the public, creating a sort of maze for first-time visitors.

Directly across from Canada House, in the middle of the Olympic Park, a small cemetery was preserved with a fence around it. Interred there were the bodies of Old Believers of the Orthodox Church. Their ancestors had left Russia many years before after suffering discrimination for their beliefs.

However, Czar Nicholas II extended an invitation for them to come back to Russia where some became farmers close to the Black Sea in the early 1900s. The cemetery, which dates back to 1915, was off limits to any renovations by the organizing committee for the Games.

The circular Olympic Park once was the site of sanatoriums, built during the rule of Soviet dictator Josef Stalin, whose goal was to impress upon nations in the Western world how much he was prepared to do to make sure his laborers lived a healthy life.

Still standing in Sochi today is the dacha where the Soviet dictator used to go as a sort of a retreat to escape the threat of assassins, to relax and ease his pains. Visitors can rent a room for $450 a night. Not far from there is the presidential residence currently used by President Vladimir Putin.

According to stories, Stalin used to retire to a movie viewing room where he watched westerns and Charlie Chaplin movies. He normally sat in a high-backed sofa, which was stuffed with horsehair. He hoped the extra padding would stop a possible assassin's bullet.

On the northern edge of the Olympic Park the official opening of the Russian Orthodox Church Khram Nerukotvornovo Obraza Christa Spasitelya (Temple of Christ the Saviour) took place a few days before the Games, causing a temporary traffic jam for buses carrying journalists to the International Broadcast Centre.

The NBC crew stayed at the Azimut Resort Hotel on the shores of the Black Sea, just a 15-minute walk from the hockey arenas.

Travel agents estimated it would cost anywhere from $8,000 to $12,000 for a room in Adler for six nights during the Olympics. Less than a day after the Games closed, rooms could be rented for $100 a night.

While people in remote parts of Russia exist on a meagre diet, I'm ashamed to say I put on almost 10 pounds, as the local organizing committee tried to put its best foot forward for visitors from the West.

My typical breakfast included orange juice, oatmeal topped with walnuts, prunes or peaches, scrambled eggs, sausages, mushrooms, fried potatoes, crepes, roasted tomatoes, baked beans, cheese, croissants and green tea. I could also order an omelette, if I desired.

The Sochi area had a real feeling of Central Asia to it as well. One night a dinner was held to promote the first European Games, which were held in Baku, Azerbaijan, in 2015.

It was only a three-mile walk to the fence that constitutes the border between Russia and the autonomous republic of Abkhazia, which is part of Georgia. Like the Niagara Peninsula, Abkhazia is a huge producer of peaches, many of which we consumed at breakfast each day.

In the Emmy Award-winning TV game show 'What's My Line?', blindfolded panelists tried to nail down the occupation of guests by peppering them with questions. Sometimes the clock ran out and the questioners were shocked to see the face of a celebrity they knew very well when they removed their eyecovers.

A similar thing happened to me in the steam room of the hotel. The temperature was about 110 F and I couldn't see six inches past my nose for steam when I entered the bath.

On the other side of the room I saw two legs, which looked like they belonged to an elderly man, dangling down from the cedar bench. But the face and upper body were completely covered by steam.

"Are you working for NBC?" I asked. "No, CBC," came a voice from the fog.

Just another of the national broadcaster's many cameramen, I presumed. So, I prodded to see what the mystery man's specific job was.

"I'm the star of Hockey Night In Canada," he replied.

Don Cherry, the 'Star of Hockey Night In Canada' with author
Denis Gibbons in Sochi.

And that's the truth, and nothing but the truth, about my chance meeting with Don Cherry, who turned 80 just a week earlier, on the shores of the Black Sea, 10,000 miles away from Canada.

Former figure skating gold medalist Katarina Witt, who shone at the 1988 Olympics in Calgary, was in our breakfast room most mornings.

The interesting thing is that during my first Olympics in 1988, there were no hockey games on the final Saturday night, so I got into see the women's singles figure skating final.

When I talked to Witt in Sochi and asked her about charging out onto the ice in Calgary before her performance, she said she was not at all trying to make a statement, she was just very nervous after Canadian Elizabeth Manley had made a splendid effort and was afraid the gold medal was going to escape her.

Because I had been there, I was able to have an interesting conversation with her about what transpired.

Witt won the gold medal, but had to skate under tremendous pressure following Manley's superb effort. Manley won the silver and Debbie Thomas of the U.S. took the bronze.

What made it more intriguing is that Witt was born in East Germany, which at that time was still under communist rule.

I still have her autograph and I have to tip my hat to ex-NHLer Eddie Olczyk for pointing her out.

Every die-hard fan in North America has heard the tale of how Herb Brooks addressed his team of collegians before their historic upset of the Soviet Union at Lake Placid in 1980. After firing them up in the dressing room before the game, he closed with the words, "This is your time!"

On the day of the Russia-U.S. game in Sochi, the newspaper *Sport Express* ran its own follow-up headline for the game preview - 'Eto nashe vremya' – which translates to 'This is our time.'

At first glance, I thought it referred to the 7-3 shellacking Canada gave the Russian team, eliminating it in the quarterfinals of the 2010 Olympics in Vancouver. The host nation, I speculated, was in effect saying, 'Things will be different this year.'

But Emrick, with his excellent recall, pointed out the words were linked to the Brooks pep talk 34 years earlier.

More so even than their loss to Team Canada in the 1972 Summit Series, the Russians had never lived down the defeat in Lake Placid.

Likewise, they were so confident about winning the gold medal in Sochi, they took the unusual step of having their entire team present at the pre-tournament press conference.

The last time anybody in Russia could recall anything similar was in 2000 when the entire team faced the media after the World Championship in St. Petersburg to apologize for a dismal 11th-place finish under coach Alexander Yakushev.

Asked if he foresaw any difficulties, Ilya Kovalchuk joked, "Starik Khottabych will get us through", a reference to a Russian fairy tale character.

Khottabych is an old man with a beard who can get anything he wants by just pulling one hair from his beard. He is something like Aladdin with his magic lamp and is a favourite of Russian children.

Alexander Ovechkin was quoted as saying the 2014 Winter Games were a $50 billion investment in one event – men's hockey. It is his dream to become an Olympic champion, since his mother was a two-time gold medalist in basketball at the Summer Olympics.

Russians who had bought up a bunch of tickets for games not involving their country in advance stood in the Olympic Park holding signs indicating they were ready to trade plenty of them now for a chance to see the host country play.

Ticket prices to events in Sochi were more reasonable than Vancouver. Fans could actually buy a ducat for 500 rubles (at that time $16 U.S.). Putin also promised that 50 per cent of all tickets could be purchased for under 3,000 rubles (at that time $96 U.S.).

In Vancouver, scalpers got as much as $2,500 each for tickets to the men's gold medal game between Canada and the U.S.

In 2014, the average Russian wage was less than $12,000 a year. The best seats to a KHL game were worth $20.

The Russians' first setback in Sochi came during the first week against the Americans, against whom they so dearly wanted revenge.

With the scored tied 2-2 in the third period, defenceman Fedor Tyutin blasted a shot from point past Jonathan Quick to apparently give the Russians a 3-2 lead. However, American referee Brad Meier ruled that the goalpost had come off its moorings before the puck went in and disallowed the goal.

The game went to a shootout and T.J. Oshie became the first player to score four times in an Olympic shootout as the Americans edged the Russians 3-2. Coach Dan Bylsma actually used him six times in the shootout, which lasted eight rounds.

Oshie accepted congratulatory Twitter messages from 130,000 people afterwards, including President Barack Obama, whose missive read, "Never stop believing in miracles."

Russian fans derided their own players by whistling loudly as the defeated hosts stood in a circle at centre ice after the game.

In the house were Russian President Vladimir Putin and Al Michaels, who called the Miracle On Ice Game in Lake Placid in 1980 for ABC, but now is employed by NBC.

In one replay, it seemed that Quick pushed the goalpost off its moorings.

After the game, Russian defenceman Slava Voinov, who was a team-mate of Quick with the Los Angeles Kings, told the press, "He does that all the time in the NHL." Quick, on the other hand, denied it.

A headline in a Russian newspaper read, "An American referee and the puppet international federation deprived us of a deserved victory."

In Moscow, Russian supporters gathered outside the U.S. embassy, yelling "Make soap out of the ref!" as they used a cheese grater to shred soap into a bucket.

Before the Games, Putin had paid a visit to the Olympic site where he did some skiing in the mountains to see how the runs were and played in a friendly hockey game with retired stars like Slava Fetisov and Pavel Bure, as well as Alexander Lukashenko, the president of Belarus.

The president, who stayed on a government yacht 'Olympia' during the Games, also had visited the U.S. Olympic House on the afternoon of the Russia-U.S. game. The Bolshoy Ice Dome was packed to the rafters with fans waving the red, white and blue Russian flag.

$186 million was spent to transform a cargo port into a marina capable of berthing large yachts. Paul Allen, who co-founded Microsoft with Bill Gates, had his 303-foot yacht 'Tatoosh' tied up there.

Just before the Olympics, the KHL players on the Russian team had trained in Kazan, Russia, while they were awaiting the arrival of their NHL colleagues. Olympic team coach Zinetula Bilyaletdinov, who had guided Ak Bars Kazan to the first Gagarin Cup championship in 2009, had scheduled games of bandy outdoors as part of the preparation. But a cold spell hit Kazan and the plans were scrapped.

Nevertheless, the Russians qualified for the quarterfinals and were matched against a relatively reasonable foe in Finland.

The night before the game, at a special dinner in the arena's VIP room, 145 of Russia's hockey legends were inducted – 60 of them posthumously – into the Russian Hockey Hall of Fame.

Olga Khymlev, a former tennis star at Boston College who was working for NBC as an interpreter, accepted a plaque for her father Yuri, a member of the 1992 Olympic gold medalists who later played in the NHL for Buffalo and St. Louis.

The great hockey history of the Soviet Union and Russia was toasted and celebrated, only to have the 2014 Olympic team fall 3-1 to Finland the next day, bursting the bubble for supporters of the host team.

Bilyaletdinov surprisingly started Simeon Varlamov of the Colorado Avalanche in goal against the Finns, even though Sergei Bobrovsky of the Columbus Blue Jackets was his number one man. The coach finally replaced Varlamov after the score became 3-1.

With the Finns leading 3-1 after two periods, the hosts came out on the ice for the third looking withdrawn and ashened-faced. They were thinking, in effect, 'We choked against Canada in Vancouver four years ago. Here we go again.'

Russia's Olympic medal drought now extends back to Salt Lake City in 2002 when they beat upstart Belarus for the bronze. Even more amazing, the Russians have been outscored by a 17-10 margin in their last six Olympic playoff games, dating back to their 2-0 quarter-final victory over Canada at Torino in 2006.

Ovechkin, Bobrovsky, Pavel Datsyuk, Andrei Markov and Anton Belov were the only players who came out to speak to the media

Undoubtedly hurting the most on the Russian team were superstars Ovechkin and Evgeni Malkin, who four years earlier had threatened to walk out on their NHL clubs and play in the Sochi Olympics, even if the NHL made a decision not to go.

Russian fans left the building with their heads down and their national flags dragging on the soaked pavement.

The next day Russian players sat stunned in the airport, not saying anything, as they awaited the flights that would take them back to the U.S. and their regular jobs in the NHL.

Flames still were soaring from the Olympic flame, but the fire had been extinguished in the souls of Russian team backers. Productivity at workplaces in the host country the next day hadn't been that low in a long time.

Legendary Russian announcer Nikolai Ozerov's comment, "Takoi hokkei nam ne nuzhen' 'This kind of hockey we don't need,' – during the 1972 Summit Series when Canada's NHL stars were taking runs at Soviet players – were repeated in a headline of the newspaper *Sport Express* on Feb. 20, 2014, the day after Russia was eliminated in the quarterfinals.

Translated from Russian, another headline on the front page
of *Sovietsky Sport* after the loss to Finland, reads 'The nation is
offended.' The photo shows Russian players on their knees.

My first stop after breakfast every morning was the Russian store located
in the basement of the International Broadcast Centre (IBC), where I purchased the previous day's Russian sports newspapers.

The gigantic building accommodated the TV networks of nations from
around the world. NBC, the American broadcaster, got about a quarter of
the space but a significant portion was occupied by the host broadcaster.

Also located in the basement of the IBC were shops providing almost
everything a journalist would need to survive – a grocery store, pharmacy,
bank, a post office and a McDonald's fast-food outlet.

To add flavour to the telecasts, I photocopied prominent headlines so
they could be put up on the TV screen during game previews.

During the second week in Sochi, *Sport Express* ran the headline 'Where
is the Red Machine?'

Even with the Olympic Games going on, the newspaper usually devoted 50 per cent of its pages to soccer. The Russian Premier League plays a schedule starting in late summer and running until the following spring.

Boris Mayorov, a three-time Olympic gold medalist in hockey, gave a full-page interview to *Sport Express* headlined 'Six coaches', in which he questioned the need for the Russian team to have a head coach and five assistants.

"In our day," he told me, "Arkady Chernyshev was our head coach and he had only one assistant – Tarasov, and we won nine World Championships in a row.

"Why do they need six coaches? What the hell do they all do? They're just contradicting each other."

Russia's early exit in the quarterfinals was so devastating that many were calling for a foreign coach to be hired to replace Bilyaletdinov. Finn Jukka Jalonen was talked about, but both President Putin and Sports Minister Vitaly Mutko spoke out against it.

In the end Oleg Znarok, who spent most of his career playing and coaching in Latvia but was born in Russia, succeeded Bilyaletdinov for the 2014 World Championship two months later.

By finishing out of the medals in Sochi, Russian players missed out on receiving $120,000 and a new Mercedes GL SUV that all of the country's gold medalists in other sports received. The gifts came from the Russian Olympians Foundation, a consortium established by Russian businessmen in 2005.

For comparison's sake, the United States Olympic Committee paid its athletes $25,000 for a gold medal, $15,000 for a silver and $10,000 for a bronze.

Kazakhstan led the proposed medal payment rate at $250,000 for a gold, but has not had a gold medalist at the Winter Olympics in 20 years.

Of course, not all athletes benefit quite so handsomely. Dario Cologna of Switzerland won two golds in cross-country skiing. His reward from his hometown Davos – which hosts the Spengler Cup, the longest running international hockey tournament annually – was a pig, which he named 'Sochi'!

In December 1984, I traveled to Finland with the Burlington Cougars bantam team, which was competing in the Finnair Cup tournament. Starring for the Jokerit Helsinki club was a 14-year-old lad named Teemu Selanne. Thirty years later I had the honour of seeing the future Hockey Hall of Famer play his final Olympic game, earning a bronze medal, and retiring from Olympic play as co-holder of the record for most Olympics by a hockey player with six and as Olympic hockey's all-time leading scorer.

Raimo Helminen of Finland, who had a short stint in the NHL with the Rangers, Minnesota North Stars and Islanders, also appeared in six Olympics.

At 43, Selanne also became the oldest player to score a goal in Olympic hockey and the oldest to win a medal, beating out Igor Larionov, who won a bronze with Russia at the age of 41 in Salt Lake City.

More exciting, between the second and third periods of the bronze medal game in Sochi against the U.S., I met Teemu's wife Sirpa and his father Ilmari, who told me he had been at that very Burlington-Jokerit game in 1984. Sirpa was attending her fourth Olympics.

Finland was leading the U.S. 2-0 at the time and Sirpa said she was looking forward to Teemu's bringing home another medal. The Finns added three goals in the third for an easy 5-0 victory.

"We already have three Olympic medals, but we have four children," she said. "We very much need another one!

"I'm praying that we win. I hope this is the end. I might be the only person in the world who is hoping that. I have a big list of chores for him."

As a boy Selanne also played minor hockey in the town of Rauma, which for many years was a twin city of sorts for Burlington teams that went overseas to play.

Just three months earlier Chris Getzlaf was named most valuable Canadian in the Canadian Football League's Grey Cup game while playing for the Saskatchewan Roughriders in a 44-25 win over the Hamilton Tiger-Cats.

Now he was strolling in the corridors of the Bolshoy Ice Dome, cold beer in hand, ready to cheer on brother Ryan of Team Canada.

Only non-alcoholic beer was sold at the arenas in Adler but Chris offered me one of his own, smuggled into the ice palace in a bag, before I interviewed him.

Canadian athletes staying in the Olympic Village were not deprived, however. Molson Coors, one of the Canadian Olympic Committee sponsors, sent a beer fridge over to the village and athletes could get a free cold one by scanning their passport in the machine.

At hotel bars, imported beer was going for 250 rubles, about $8. Russian beer was only 100 rubles, about $3.

While we worked the U.S.-Czech quarterfinal at the Shaiba Arena, we kept an eye on the progress of the Canada-Latvia game at the Bolshoy Ice Dome on a monitor and could not believe our eyes with the two teams tied 1-1 and only 13 minutes left to play.

Before the game an expert had calculated Canada had 25 NHL players earning a combined salary of $156 million, while the Latvians had only one from the NHL – Buffalo's Zemgus Girgensons - with a stipend of just $894,167.

After Canada's narrow 2-1 win, Latvian coach Ted Nolan said he believes there are more ice rinks in his hometown Sault Ste. Marie than in the whole of Latvia.

Kristers Gudlevskis of Latvia, who had spent most of the season with Syracuse of the AHL, almost pulled a rabbit out of the hat by stopping 55 of 57 Canadian shots. He was in the Tampa Bay Lightning farm system. Just the year before Gudlevskis had been playing for the Florida Everblades of the lowly East Coast Hockey League (ECHL).

Gudlevskis had appeared at the Lightning's training camp the year before with an out-of-date collection of equipment he was given in Latvia.

On his mask was the image of Lady Liberty clasping gilded stars on top of the Freedom Monument in Latvia. It was designed to honour soldiers who laid down their lives for their country between 1918 and 1920 in the Latvian War of Independence.

Latvia had hired Nolan, who also was coaching the Buffalo Sabres at the time, for the Olympics. He had a difficult time even identifying his own players, since he hadn't been in Europe since a pre-Olympic training camp the previous summer.

The gold medal game was anti-climactic. For the first time in 62 years a Canadian team repeated as Olympic champion when Canada shut out a Swedish team, undermanned by injuries, 3-0.

The Canadians had previously done it in 1948 with the Ottawa RCAF Flyers and in 1952 with the Edmonton Mercurys.

It was Canada's ninth Olympic gold medal in hockey, which gave it the all-time lead ahead of the Soviet Union (Russia) with eight.

The Olympic final was seen on CBC-TV by more than 15 million viewers in Canada, despite being shown at 7 a.m., Toronto time, because of the nine–hour time difference. The average audience for CBC during the tournament was 8.5 million.

The figure for the gold medal game was down one million from the Canada-U.S. final in Vancouver four years before that. However that game was aired on a Sunday afternoon.

Once again Canadians proved they are the most dedicated hockey fans in the world.

I've worked at seven Olympic tournaments, and it was the first time I had seen a team go undefeated and untied. At the other end of the scale no team has gone through the whole tournament without earning at least one point in those seven events. I missed the 2006 Olympics in Italy for health reasons.

The roof of the Bolshoy Ice Dom lit up at night and even provided a running score of the game going on inside.

With the final score 3-0 flashing brightly, Canadian fans hooted and hollered in the Olympic Park well into the wee hours of the morning.

Key contributors to the gold medal triumph of the Canadian men were, left to right: Drew Doughty, Ryan Getzlaf, Jonathan Toews and Sidney Crosby. In front is goalie Carey Price, who allowed a total of only three goals in the five games he played.

Jonathan Toews and Patrice Bergeron, both two-way stars in the NHL, were particularly effective in a checking role as Team Canada smothered any Swedish offensive attacks. The Canadians surrendered only three goals in six tournament games. That was the lowest total since Canada gave up none in what was a three-game Olympics in 1928.

Canadian goalie Carey Price shut out the opposition for the final 164 minutes and 19 seconds of the tournament.

At one time Canadian coaches believed the larger European ice surfaces made it easier to score goals. Over time, though, they came to understand that with completely different shooting angles than in North America and a longer distance to get to the net, goalies have the advantage.

That proved to be true in Sochi, where a total of 11 shutouts were recorded. There also had been 11 the last time the Olympics were held in

Europe, in Italy in 2006. On the other hand, there were just seven on the NHL rink in Vancouver.

The Sochi Olympics also will be remembered for depleted rosters. Going into the tournament, more countries had players decline to play because of injuries than at any other event. Many more like Canadian sharpshooter John Tavares fell by the wayside with injuries when play got underway.

Five players who had won the Hart Trophy as the NHL's most valuable player – Crosby, Corey Perry and Martin St. Louis of Canada, along with Ovechkin and Malkin of Russia – did play, but strangely produced a total of just three goals – one each by Crosby, Ovechkin and Malkin.

Drew Doughty, who was a standout on defence for Canada, said he was enjoying himself and was sad to see the Olympic experience come to an end.

NHL players stayed two to a room in the Olympic Village. In the NHL all, except newcomers on rookie deals, get their own rooms on the road. But the players specifically asked to stay in the village.

In spite of what Doughty said, the gold medalists didn't stay around to celebrate. They headed straight from the Bolshoy Dom to the airport and were in the air shortly after that, their NHL clubs anxiously waiting for them to return.

It was left to the women to record the most dramatic finish.

A meaningless preliminary round game in which Canada defeated the U.S. women was viewed on the CBC by 5.6 million Canadians. The previous year's Grey Cup, won by Saskatchewan over Hamilton, drew fewer, 4.5 million.

When the two North American hockey rivals clashed again with the gold medal at stake, the Americans carried the play and were leading 2-1 late in the third period when Canadian coach Kevin Dineen pulled goalie Shannon Szabados for an extra skater.

Kelli Stack of the U.S. fired the puck the length of the ice, only to have it hit the goalpost dead-on and bounce directly out.

Then, with only 55 seconds left on the clock, Marie-Philippe Poulin tied the score 2-2 to force overtime.

Poulin played the role of heroine again when she scored the gold medal-winning goal at 8:10 of the extra period.

Canadian defenceman Laura Fortino cut her hockey teeth playing for the Stoney Creek (Ont.) Sabres and earned a hockey scholarship at Cornell University.

Her parents, Ignacio and Ivana, were tucked away in a corner of the rink opposite our NBC broadcast position. When Laura faked a shot, then made a perfect pass to Poulin for the winning goal, I quickly cranked out my telephoto lens and got a shot of them giving each other a victory kiss.

Laura Fortino, who set up the winning goal by Marie-Philippe Poulin, shows off her gold medal.

Back home in Hamilton, students at Bishop Tonnos high school, where Fortino played as a teen, had crowded into the school gym to view a screening of Canada's earlier 3-0 win over Finland. A special guest seated in the front row was the retired Bishop of the Roman Catholic Diocese of Hamilton, Anthony Tonnos, for whom the school is named.

This time the Canadian women confined their imbibing to the dressing room of the Bolshoy Dom. They had been criticized in the media for drinking champagne and smoking cigars at centre ice following their gold medal win over the Americans in Vancouver in 2010.

Two days later most of the players came back to the Bolshoy Ice Dome to cheer the Canadian men to victory against Sweden.

For the most part it was a disappointing tournament for Americans Phil and Amanda Kessel, who didn't get the gold medals they were after. The first brother-sister combo ever to play in an Olympic hockey tournament, nevertheless, were outstanding individually. Phil tied for the men's tournament scoring lead and Amanda finished in a second-place tie on the women's side. Their father Phil Sr. was drafted by the Washington Redskins in 1981 and played quarterback briefly for the Calgary Stampeders.

Ironically, Matt Duchene and Tara Watchhorn, who both won gold medals for Canada, on the men's and women's teams, respectively, had once played together for the Central Ontario Wolves novice Triple-A team, which plays out of Lindsay, Ont.

Prime Minister Stephen Harper, author of the book *A Great Game: The Forgotten Leafs and the Rise of Professional Hockey*, and a member of Society for International Hockey Research, won a case of beer in a bet with U.S. President Barack Obama on the women's gold medal game.

A.J. Griswold (nee Mleczko), an Olympic gold medalist for the U.S. in 1998 who worked as colour commentator with Emrick for the women's games, was in tears at the end of the game. A graduate of Harvard, Griswold not only had the inside scoop on everything going on with the American team, she passed it along to the millions of NBC viewers with clarity and authority. Natalie Darwitz, a three-time World Championship gold medalist in hockey out of the University of Minnesota, and Kathryn Tappen, who ran track and cross-country at Rutgers, also did excellent work on the women's tournament.

With the Bolshoy Ice Dom and Shayba Arena only a five-minute walk apart, it was possible to watch a period at one building, scoot over to the other for the second and be back where you started for the third.

It was quite common to see goalies dressed in their masks and full equipment walking to practice with skateguards on.

The arenas had already been christened when they hosted the 2013 World U-18 Championship in April 2013. Coincidentally, Russia fell short in that competition also, losing 2-1 to Finland in the bronze medal game and settling for fourth place.

Canada, in a preview of the Olympics, won the gold medal with former NHL coach Don Hay behind the bench.

I worked at 36 games altogether in Sochi, between men's and women's play in two weeks.

Canada House and the U.S. Olympic House sat side by side, but only athletes and members of their families with proper credentials were allowed in to enjoy refreshments.

The Olympic Village was just across the road from the Bolshoy Ice Dom, so many players either walked or rode bicycles provided by the village to their games. NBC cameras caught American players, dressed in jackets and ties, arriving on bikes for their semifinal match with Canada.

Between periods of games at the smaller Shayba Arena Vera Vodupyanova, a quick-witted Russian announcer, kept fans entertained with games and contests, speaking in both Russian and English. One segment included an on-the-spot marriage proposal.

The modern Olympic Park, planned to wow visitors, had very little to offer in the way of Russian culture, except for hordes of flag-waving Russian fans. There were a few stage shows, but music at the arenas featured the latest North American pop tunes. Not once did I hear the quick tempo Russian favourite *Kalinka*, even though it is played often in North American arenas.

Many of the young volunteers weren't even born when the Soviet Union broke up in 1991 and they have no recollection of communism. The newest Russian word I learned from them was 'kruto', which means 'cool', in the sense of 'impressive'.

Youths from all parts of the world's largest country (geographically speaking) and nearby countries came to the Olympics to volunteer. I chatted in Russian with teens from Novosibirsk and Omsk in Siberia, Arkhangelsk, near the Arctic Circle, Narva in Estonia and Lviv in Ukraine. I even met a young man from South Africa, who noticed a job opening online and responded to the ad.

The 25,000 volunteers, who wore bright multi-coloured uniforms, were cheerful and courteous. Although sometimes a bit short on details, they were extremely eager to help visitors.

And they were young. Statistics showed the average age was only 23, down considerably from 45 at the 2010 Olympics in Vancouver.

They were happy to work long hours for nothing other than free room and board and a chance to experience the Olympics and a subtropical climate.

A total of 32 nations applied for entry in the men's hockey tournament, while 24 started out on the women's side. Among the bottom countries on the list on the men's side were Bosnia-Herzegovina, Israel and Mexico.

The top nine men's and top six women's nations, according to the 2012 IIHF Men's and Women's World Rankings, respectively, qualified automatically. Three more men's teams and two women's teams were determined through a series of qualification tournaments during the 2012-2013 season, starting in the autumn of 2012 and ending with the final qualifications in February 2013.

Russian soldiers salute as the flags of the men's hockey medalists
Canada, Sweden and Finland are raised.

What separates Olympic hockey tournaments from World
Championships is the participation of athletes from other sports. In Sochi
a special section was set aside in one corner of the Bolshoy Ice Dom for the
2,856 athletes, many of whom came in droves in their brightly coloured
national team track suits to cheer for their country. It gave the tournament
a sort of American collegiate atmosphere.

Every Olympics, it seems, offers a new education. In Russia, the nations marched into the stadium during the Opening Ceremonies in alphabetical order – not according to the Roman alphabet, rather to the Cyryllic. Therefore, Canada came in with the K's (as in Kanada) and the U.S., normally near the end, moved up to the S's (as in Soyedyony Shtatov Ameriki).

While the venues and hotels were state of the art, I found a slightly different situation when I had to walk about three miles to the little seaside village of Blinovo in search of some distilled water for my C-pap machine, which I use to control my sleep apnea. I was told it was available there in a pharmacy.

In the end, I visited five aptekas (pharmacies), most no bigger than a Tim Hortons drive-through, before I found what I wanted.

In this little village about two miles from the hotel, I discovered a statue of Lenin still standing prominently in the Park of Culture and Recreation for children. Life went on almost as it did in the former Soviet Union under communism a quarter-of-a-century earlier. Residents, obviously too poor to own a car, crowded their way onto buses to go to work.

There were a lot of stray dogs roaming around looking for food and I saw two sadly walking around on only three legs.

Emrick, a huge lover of pets, admired those who tried to help them.

"I will never forget all the trouble that some of the athletes went to in rescuing them," he said. "David Backes (U.S. centre) told me the day before the game with Canada they had two dogs that were actually living in their apartment. They had given them a bath and fed them.

"They were just like any other dogs. They just want food and attention.

"He was able to get both back to the U.S. but went through a lot of red tape to get vaccinations done before he got them out.

"At one point, before a period, I was able to tell David's story and convey the message he had for fans in the U.S. – 'It may be exciting to adopt a dog rescued by an Olympic athlete, but there are dogs in shelters everywhere in the U.S. that need you, too.'

"If you remember nothing more about this Olympic athlete, remember that," Emrick added.

"I did not expect the sickening treatment of dogs by some in Russia," he said. "There were heroic stories of rescues by some of the athletes, but I am used to better."

The Toronto Star told the story of Howard Baggley, a freelance radio engineer from Mount Albert, Ont., north of Toronto, who befriended a stray puppy after leaving some meat for it outside.

Curled up on the lawn, it looked like it might be dead, but it was just asleep.

From that point on, the dog made a habit of waiting for him at the bus stop when he came home each day. Naming him 'Sochi', Baggley secured an international dog passport for him and flew home to Canada with him.

Luckily, Russian billionaire Oleg Deripaska later committed to building a shelter for stray dogs in the nearby town of Baranovka.

On my walk to the border of Abkhazia another day, along the ornate brick pathway laid in decorative colours, I encountered a man who turned out to be Sergei Proskuryakov, assistant deputy director of the Ballet Company of the Mariinsky Theatre, now the largest ballet company in the world. His troupe was in Adler rehearsing for the closing ceremonies.

I also saw Cossacks in heavy winter coats and fur hats patrolling the walkway along the coast of the Black Sea, close to the border of Russia and Abkhazia, which broke away from Georgia in the early 1990s.

Cossacks on patrol near the border of Russia and the autonomous Republic of Abkhazia.

Fisherman were casting their lines along the shores of the Black Sea and occasionally dolphins soared through the air over the waves.

Before the Games there were reports that as many as three potential terrorist bombers were already living in Adler. They wanted to get revenge on Putin for keeping the region of Chechnya under this thumb, the rumours went.

Fears that Sochi would be targeted were raised after two suicide bombers killed 34 people in Volgograd on consecutive days in late December.

But I felt safe, except for the fact I skipped the opening and closing ceremonies, fearing something could happen.

Putin established a ring of steel around the whole Olympic area.

Russian coast guard cutters patrolled the Black Sea coastline every day to guard against possible terrorism. The Navy always has been an important component of the country's defence system and worked with the Allies during the Second World War.

Bill Fitsell of Kingston, Ont., served in the Canadian Navy on supply ships to Murmansk, Russia during the war.

Fitsell said he didn't see any hockey games himself, but in the book *Far Distant Ships,* published in 1950, author Joseph Schull reported players from HMCS Algonquin beat a team from HMCS Sioux and in turn were trounced by reps of the Port of Murmansk, with the final game being played with Russian equipment and under Russian rules in December 1944.

Some historians say the game they were playing actually was bandy, still this was almost two years before the first Soviet league game was played in 1946.

In 2015 Russia named two ships from its Northern Fleet the *Anatoly Tarasov* and the *Viktor Tikhonov.* It was the first time in history two legendary Russian sports figures had been honored in this way.

Each day in Sochi we were subject to bag checks and body scans, but it was certainly no worse than what I experienced in Salt Lake City in 2002, one year after the 911 disaster at the World Trade Centre.

A total of 42,000 police officers and 10,000 Ministry of the Interior troops were deployed at the Olympics.

Before traveling to Sochi, NBC issued a memo making us all aware that Russian law allows the government to monitor all communications.

The penalty for loaning credentials to an unaccredited visitor is automatic ejection from the Olympic Park. That is for all but Russia's elite athletes, apparently. Hockey legend Vyacheslav Starshinov, a gold medalist at the 1964 and 1968 Olympics, was spotted wandering around the Bolshoy Ice Dom with a card draped around his neck reading 'Alexander Maltsev', his close friend and former Soviet national teammate.

The riot and fires set in Kiev's Independence Square by opponents of Ukraine's Russian-backed President Viktor Yanukovych occurred on Feb. 19.

Ukrainian athletes, who chose to remain in the Olympic Park after the violence broke out in Kiev, asked the IOC for permission to wear black armbands while competing, but the request was denied.

The athletes did, however, attach black ribbons to Ukrainian flags hanging from the balconies of the Olympic Village. Sergei Bubka, an Olympic pole vault champion now on the IOC, sympathized with them, but maintained the wearing of black armbands would be a violation of the Olympic charter.

Putin called the protests foreign-backed terrorism and Russian Foreign Minister Sergei Lavrov said the West had encouraged the protesters.

It was difficult to believe that 600 miles away 82 people had died in the protest. The fires in Kiev's city square were shown on Russian TV, unlike two previous momentous events that occurred during two of my six previous visits to Russia.

The accident at the nuclear plant in Chernobyl in 1986 and the fall of the Berlin Wall in 1989 warranted only three-inch stories in the newspaper when the Communist government was in power.

Shortly after the Sochi Games Slava Fetisov claimed there was no Russian involvement in Crimea. Russian people who were living there and also spoke Ukrainian were fighting for 'their land', he said. Fetisov said Russia was trying everything it could to stop the conflict.

President Obama placed sanctions on two Russian billionaires who had purchased a major hockey arena in Helsinki, Finland, as well as a 49 per cent stake in the Finnish club Jokerit Helsinki, which now plays in the KHL. Gennadi Timchenko and Boris Rotenberg are dual citizens of

Russian and Finland and both were awarded huge contracts to build some of the infrastructure for the Sochi Olympics.

The Russian government paid for only part of the $51 billion it cost to stage the Olympics. The rest was provided by companies owned by the state and oligarchs cosy with the government.

In 2007, the Russians estimated the Olympics would cost $12 billion, but it wound up coming in at about $51 billion. That contrasts with only $7 billion to stage the Vancouver Games four years earlier.

At the closing ceremonies, the Games' polar bear mascot shed a fake tear as he blew out a cauldron of flames extinguishing the Olympic torch that burned outside the stadium.

During the closing, I was fascinated by the marching military drum corps of the Russian Army and the dozens of grand pianos floating around the stage as a pianist played favourites by the composer Rachmaninoff.

KHL President Alexander Medvedev was at the Games, but it was surprising the fledgling league did not have more of a presence during a time when it had shut down for almost a month to allow players from all countries to train and play for their Olympic teams.

Less than a month after the Olympics closed, Medvedev announced there would be a new team representing Sochi in the league starting in the 2014-15 season. Pavel Bure was the first general manager of the team, which chose the nickname Dolphins, after the mammals who swim in the Black Sea.

Some games in the 2018 World Cup of Soccer are scheduled to be played in the Krasnodar Region.

The long-term plan is to turn Sochi into a year-round destination – a snow-and-ice paradise in winter and a Cote d'Azur-style destination for tourists in the summer.

The Olympic Park now is the annual site of the Russian Grand Prix, a Formula One race. Just before the 2015 KHL All-Star Game in Sochi, one of the players Dennis Parshin got into a race car and took a spin around the track, which goes for 5.9 kilometres around the 2014 Olympic venues

Would the Pittsburgh Penguins allow Crosby to do that? I wonder!

CHAPTER 12
Women sacrifice more to go for gold

The Canadian women whoop it up following their stunning come-from-behind victory over the U.S. in the gold medal game.

When women's hockey was introduced into the Olympics at Nagano in 1998, CBS aired a highlights package of the U.S. team's gold medal win, but because of the 14-hour time difference with New York there was no prime time live telecast.

Sixteen years later, CBC reported 5.6 million Canadians tuned in for a meaningless preliminary round women's game in Sochi between Canada and the U.S., which the Canadians won 3-2.

Then a whopping 13 million Canadians watched at least some of the exciting Canada-U.S. match for the gold medal, which ended with Marie-Philippe Poulin scoring the winning goal for Canada in overtime.

That's how far the women's game has come in its continuing drive for recognition.

The U.S. team took a giant leap forward in March 2017 when it reached an agreement with USA Hockey that could result in national team players receiving in the neighbourhood of $70,000 a year in compensation.

The American players had threatened to boycott the 2017 World Championship in Plymouth, Mich. if their demands for better financial arrangements were not met.

While they receive $1,000 a month during the six months before an Olympics, the players said they were barely surviving for the rest of the time during the four-year Olympic cycle.

I've had a chance to work with five former members of the U.S. team, including A.J. Griswold (nee Mleczko), Cammi Granato, Alana Blahoski, Natalie Darwitz and Lisa Brown-Miller. Perhaps they were born too early to benefit from the agreement, but as pioneers of a new Olympic sport and as knowledgable commentators they laid the groundwork for it.

Sport Canada already was paying elite female players $18,000 a year. Depending on their needs they also had access to another $6,000 annually from the organization's Excellence Fund.

Because Canada won the gold medal at Sochi, each player also was awarded a bonus of $20,000.

In support of the American women, NHL players were threatening to stay away from the men's 2017 World Championship, which was co-hosted by France and Germany.

The Edmonton Oilers once dropped $18,000 just to celebrate New Year's Eve with their families at Osteria de Medici, a fancy Italian restaurant in Calgary!

Becky Kellar, a three-time Olympic hockey gold medalist with Canada, took extreme measures to stretch the dollar on the $18,000 she was receiving in the summer of 2009.

Kellar, a native of Hagersville, Ont. who now resides in Burlington, was so keen on going for her third Olympic hockey gold medal in Vancouver that she shipped her car out to Western Canada and flew to Calgary with her two sons, Owen and Zach, so she could train with the Canadian team.

Meanwhile, her parents Wayne and Shirley drove to Alberta where they shared a rented home with Becky and their grandchildren, looking after the boys while she was at workouts and games. Kellar's husband Nolan Duke remained in Ontario to run the family business.

In January 2006, Kellar's wedding and engagement rings were stolen from the Canadian dressing room during an exhibition game in Medicine Hat, Alta. Besides the sentimental value, that put an extra financial burden on the family.

Two-time gold medalist Vicky Sunohara, now head coach of the women's team at the University of Toronto, also found it hard to make ends meet. She retired from the Canadian team in 2008 after giving birth to twins, but did not qualify for maternity leave from the federal government's employment insurance program.

Russia's Yekaterina Pashkevich, who in Sochi at the age of 41 became the oldest woman ever to compete in women's Olympic hockey, broke out laughing when a Russian journalist, unfamiliar with the amateur status of players in the U.S, asked if she remembered her first contract in America.

"I played for nothing," she replied. "Not a cent!"

Pashkevich emigrated to the U.S. at the age of 22 and, after playing hockey for Assabet Valley, a senior women's team in the Boston area, took up American football and starred as a linebacker and running back with the Manchester (N.H.) Freedom of the Independent Women's Football League. She also coached the women's hockey team at Massachusetts Institute of Technology (MIT).

Sweden's Danijela Rundqvist, an Olympic silver medalist in 2006 and bronze medalist in 2002, hopped across the Atlantic to play for the Burlington Barracudas of the Canadian Women's Hockey League in 2010 because she wanted to compete against the best players in the world.

Rundqvist led the Barracudas in scoring with 11 goals and 15 points in 22 games, playing on the same team as Kellar. Rundqvist had a reputation as a feisty player and had more than one nasty clash with Canadian star Hayley Wickenheiser.

Incredibly, Rundqvist started playing in the Swedish Women's League at the age of 13 and was only 17 when she made her Olympic debut at Salt Lake City in 2002.

She once worked in customer service for Stadium, the largest sports company in Sweden, but became a full-time hockey player in 2009. Including the money she could have made working back home, she estimates coming to Canada for the year cost her about $25,000.

After the Swedish women won their first Olympic medal – a bronze – at Salt Lake City in 2002, each of the players received $1,500 from the Swedish Ice Hockey Federation.

Rundqvist, therefore, was quite surprised when they initially received nothing for upsetting the U.S. in the semifinals and winding up with a silver medal at Torino in 2006.

"Money is very important for us," she said. "I called the federation to see if we would be getting something, and they said, 'No'.

"I just wanted them to show some appreciation for what we did," she said.

The federation later did an about-face and gave each of the silver medalists $1,500.

Rundqvist, who now is retired and too old to take advantage of it, has suggested asking NHLers with their multi-million-dollar salaries to sponsor players in women's leagues might not be a bad idea.

Several members of the German women's team at Sochi were in a sense part of the country's army. Sportforderung der Bundeswehr (Sports Promotion of the Federal Army) is a program supporting participants from a wide variety of sports.

Athletes are employed and paid by the Ministry of Defence but exempt from conventional army duties. Therefore, they can focus on their sport while earning an income. The Chinese women's team has become accustomed to training in Canada and playing exhibition games against senior and university teams to prepare for the Olympics. Often they are based in Markham, Ont., which has the largest Chinese community per capita in the province.

When the Chinese played in Vancouver in 2010, many members of the city's huge Asian community came to Canada Hockey Place to support the team, yelling 'Zhong gwah dweh zhah yo', which translates to 'Team China, Go'.

The Chinese, who train in the city of Harbin in the far north of the country, have nicknames for their players, the same as North American teams. Liu Zhixin is called 'Kaka' after the famous soccer player from Brazil. Teammates call Zhang Mengying 'Lucky' and Huo Cui's monicker is 'Baby', because she is very small.

For the most part, it's easier to interview female players. They're not smothered with attention year-round like NHL pros, they're polite and appreciate having you take the time to learn how they made it to the Olympics.

Most of them are either enrolled in university or have graduated and are very articulate.

The Benz family of Switzerland is a shining example of people who put education first.

"Well, my father Daniel and mother Caroline are both doctors," Laura Benz of the bronze medal-winning Swiss team told me in Sochi. "My brother Dominic and I are both studying to be doctors and my sister Sara is going to school to be a lawyer."

Other than that the twin sisters, who have played for their country at two Olympics, come from an ordinary, run of the mill family!

European players always impress me with their knowledge of languages.

Kristina Petrovskaya, a defence player with the Russian team, studied English at the Boston Academy of English before enrolling at the University of Minnesota-Duluth, where she played on a hockey scholarship.

Sometimes the strangest things happen in the world of women's hockey. Nadezhda Alexandrova, one of the Russian goalies, was dropped from the team in Sochi because she found out just two weeks before the Games in a medical exam that she was pregnant!

Alexandrova had been voted best goalie at the 2013 World Championship in Ottawa, leading Russia to a bronze medal. She returned to play for Russia at the 2017 World Championship in Plymouth.

Russia not only has a professional women's hockey league, its national team players have turned to picking up extra money by modeling and posing for Internet pictures.

The old American stereotype of Russian women – the lady with the square jaw and coke-bottle glasses reading the evening news on TV – took a jolt during the Sochi Olympics when *Sport Express* published photos to go with its ranking of the five best-looking players on the country's Olympic team.

Canadian and American players take it for granted family members will be there to support them in important international games, but some players from Russia don't have the same luxury.

Among the crowd at Russia's 4-1 win over Germany in Sochi were Iya Gavrilova's parents, who had never seen her play an international game before, even though she was 26. They are from Krasnoyarsk in Siberia, 2,500 miles away.

"The national team usually plays abroad, or in Moscow or elsewhere far from Siberia, and they simply couldn't afford to come and watch me play," said Gavrilova, who also played at the University of Calgary. "I was so thankful they finally could get here. It wasn't easy for them to get off work, even for something like the Olympics."

Canadians with dual passports always are key contributors for European countries. They are players who aren't good enough to make the Canadian Olympic team but are more than happy to just be playing in the Olympics.

One of the most pleasant to interview was Natalie Babonyova from Oshawa, Ont. Although she was born in Canada and played college hockey at Yale, her father was born in Poprad, Slovakia, at the foot of the High Tatra Mountains, and her mother in the town of Bardejov near the border of Poland.

Slovakia qualified for the women's tournament in Vancouver, even though it had only 288 registered female players in the country.

CHAPTER 13
Looking forward to the Olympics in South Korea

When South Korea takes the ice for the men's Olympic tournament in PyeongChang its team will be reinforced by imports, most of them from Canada.

Chances are slim that the hosts will qualify for the playoffs. If there ever was a time for an Asian miracle on ice, however, it's now with the NHL deciding not to shut down in the middle of the season so that players can live the Olympic dream.

Plenty has been written pro and con about the owners' decision to sit this one out. It's curious, though, that they're still interested in taking a break in the schedule in 2022 when China is the host. The prospect of selling products to the country's more than one billion people is mouth-watering for them.

South Korea has earned 53 Winter Olympics medals altogether, most of them in short-track speed skating. However, it has yet to participate in an Olympic hockey tournament.

Because its men's and women's teams are ranked only 21st and 22nd in the world, respectively, the IIHF deliberated for a longtime before even granting them automatic berths, according to tradition.

The latest IIHF statistics show South Korea has 2,675 players registered, but only 171 are adult men and 319 of them women.

Jim Paek, the first Korean to play in the NHL, was named coach of the men's team in July 2014. He played three-and-a-half seasons in the NHL for Pittsburgh, Los Angeles and Ottawa, earning Stanley Cup rings with the Penguins in both 1991 and 1992.

Paek served as an assistant coach of the AHL Grand Rapids Griffins for nine years. The Detroit Red Wings farm club won the Calder Cup in 2013, and while he was there, he had a hand in grooming Gustav Nyquist, Tomas Tatar and Anthony Mantha, three of the NHL team's top five scorers in 2016-17.

Paek's father was a doctor in South Korea but found it difficult to work there in the 1970s with martial law in effect at the time. He accepted a job at Sick Children's Hospital in Toronto and moved his family to Canada after Jim was born in Seoul.

Because he didn't have enough money to return to school and get a Canadian licence, Paek's father eventually launched a hospital supplies company. It required him to travel back and forth to South Korea and Jim started to operate hockey clinics there, as well as arrange for high school teams from the Asian country to visit Canada.

Most of the homebrews on the South Korean national team come from the country's three professional clubs in the Asia Ice Hockey League. They are very good skaters but, as with most teams in the Asian league, they lack size.

Three players with AHL experience – Brock Radunske of New Hamburg, Ont., Michael Swift of Peterborough and Bryan Young of nearby Ennismore – obtained their South Korean passports five years before the 2018 Olympics. Swift and Young are cousins.

Two more – goalie Matt Dalton of Clinton, Ont. and Eric Regan of Ajax – became eligible to play for South Korea in 2016 and Alex Plante of Brandon, Man. obtained his South Korean citizenship in 2017. Dalton and Regan have AHL experience. Plante, a first-round pick of Edmonton in 2007, appeared in 10 NHL games with the Oilers.

Up to that point, for the most part, only those of Korean nationality were entitled to citizenship.

Paek is getting coaching help from former NHLer Richard Park, a Korean national who has played for the U.S. in four World Championships, serving as captain of the team in 2006.

Sarah Murray grew up in a home where coaching was a daily conversation. The daughter of former NHL coach Andy Murray, who guided Canada to World Championship gold medals in 1997, 2003 and 2007, has the challenging job of getting the South Korean women's team ready for the Olympics.

Goalie So Jung Shim played at St. Francis Xavier University in Antigonish, N.S., then with the New York Riveters of the National Women's Hockey League in the U.S. Forward Danielle Im, a two-time Ontario University Association champion with the Laurier Golden Hawks, pursued graduate studies and played for the Ryerson University Rams in her hometown Toronto in 2016-17.

By coincidence, sisters Hannah and Marissa Brandt will be playing for separate countries – the U.S. and South Korea, respectively.

Marissa, who was born in South Korea, was adopted by Greg and Robin Brandt of St. Paul, Minn. The Brandts eventually had their own daughter, Hannah, and the two girls grew up playing hockey.

While Marissa played NCAA Division 3 hockey at Gustavus Adolphus College in St. Peter, Minnesota, Hannah accepted a hockey scholarship to the University of Minnesota, where she became team captain in her senior year. She also has won two gold medals playing for the U.S. at the World Championship.

In the 2012-13 season, Hannah averaged two points per game as a freshman to lead the Golden Gophers to the Division 1 championship with a perfect record of 41-0. She earned two more national championship rings in 2014-15 and 2015-16.

Gustavus Adolphus just missed making the Division 3 championship game in 2012-13, losing by one goal to eventual champion Elmira in the semifinals and wound up its season with an excellent mark of 27-2-1.

At the end of her senior year, Marissa was invited to try out for the South Korean team.

China, meanwhile, already is looking past PyeongChang to the 2022 Winter Olympics it will host. The Chinese made it clear from the outset they're serious about icing a legitimate team when they hired Mike Keenan to coach Kunlun Red Star, the Beijing-based club in the KHL, for the 2017-18 season.

Keenan, who is fifth in wins on the all-time list of NHL coaches, became the first Canadian to coach a KHL Gagarin Cup champion, Metallurg Magnitogorsk, in 2014

There also is a good chance Keenan will be selected to coach the Chinese Olympic team in 2022.

Kunlun Red Star had just five Chinese players on its roster when it made its KHL debut in the 2016-17 season. But the team surprised a lot of critics by finishing eighth in the Eastern Conference and making the playoffs, mainly through the efforts of imports, including a team-leading 11 players from Finland.

Russian Andrei Makarov, formerly property of the Buffalo Sabres, shared the goaltending chores with Tomi Karhunen, a native of Oulu, Finland.

Former Toronto Maple Leaf Alexei Ponikarovsky also played in China, but had a below-par season with only seven goals and 14 points in 52 games.

North Americans on the team have very little experience. Defenceman Brett Bellemore played two seasons for the Carolina Hurricanes. Forward Sean Collins, a graduate of Cornell University, was a late pick of Columbus in 2008, and eventually played 21 NHL games for the Blue Jackets and Washington.

American Chad Rau, who played at Colorado College, also appeared in nine NHL games with the Minnesota Wild, after being drafted by Toronto in 2005.

Collins scored the first goal in the club's history in a 2-1 victory over Amur Khabarovsk.

Kunlun Red Star uses the 18,000-seat LeSports Arena in Beijing for the majority of its home games. It was the site of the basketball tournament during the 2008 Summer Olympics.

Although the Beijing facility already is the largest in the KHL, a few games also have been played in Shanghai.

China tried to qualify for the 2018 Games in South Korea but lost badly to Serbia, Spain and Iceland in the early rounds of the tournament.

Hockey also is on the rise in Hong Kong, which used to be a colony of China.

Former NHLer Barry Beck is general manager of the Hong Kong Academy of Ice Hockey and has been a major force in developing youth hockey there.

There now are 1,500 youth hockey players, a huge jump from only a handful 10 years ago.

Beck also coached Hong Kong's national team at the 2016 IIHF Division 3 World Championship in Istanbul, Turkey.

To determine the 12 participating nations for the 2018 Games in South Korea, the IIHF awarded automatic berths to the top eight countries in its 2015 world rankings – Canada, Russia, Sweden, Finland, U.S., Czech Republic, Switzerland and Slovakia.

South Korea also was given an automatic berth as the host nation. The final three slots, which went to Germany, Norway and Slovenia, were filled by the winners of qualifying tournaments held in September, 2016.

Canada, the U.S., Finland, Russia and Sweden were recipients of automatic berths in the women's tournament, along with host South Korea. Japan and Switzerland each won qualifying tournaments in February 2017 to nail down the final two spots.

As in Nagano, Japan, in 1998 North American broadcasters face a big challenge in providing coverage for their viewers since there is a 14-hour time difference between PyeonChang and cities in the Eastern Standard Time zone of Canada and the U.S.

CHAPTER 14
Our view of world hockey still evolving

The attitude of Canadians towards the international game has changed immensely over the last half-century. Some adjustment still is necessary, however.

If you value Canadian history, you'd think the 100th anniversary of its first hockey association would be accompanied by widespread publicity.

Hockey Canada did its part by holding the 100th annual meeting in exactly the same French Corridor room of Ottawa's Chateau Laurier as the inaugural on Dec. 4, 1914.

The historic hotel, which was officially opened by Prime Minister Wilfrid Laurier, donated use of the ornate French Corridor room at the time.

The Centennial meeting in 2014 was followed in the evening by a gala at the Ottawa Convention Centre.

The local media, however, didn't bite even with oodles of hors d'oeuvres, pastries and gallons of beer available.

The ink-stained wretches were 20 miles away at the Canadian Tire Centre in Kanata where the Ottawa Senators were honoring Daniel Alfredsson for his long and faithful service by retiring his number 11 jersey.

Neither the *Ottawa Citizen* nor the *Ottawa Sun* carried a single word about the ceremonial meeting and gala the next day. Meanwhile, *The Sun* devoted 15 of its 24 sports pages to Alfredsson's jersey retirement.

The NHL and its high-powered marketing still rule the roost.

Canada, too, seems to have difficulty identifying its roots.

In one of its bulletins in 2002, the IIHF called Canada the 'country that bleads maple syrup' in a headline about its success in the gold medal game of the Olympics in Salt Lake City.

Maple syrup is sweet and poutine (French fries with melted cheese and gravy) is to die for. Many, in fact, do from clogged arteries after eating it!

Both are well-known Canadian culinary treats with established ties to the founders of the land.

So it was indeed curious when promoters were planning a bill of fare for the World Cup of Hockey Fan Village that would include the national dish of each participating country they chose a grilled cheese sandwich for Canada!

"But sir, the aged cheddar cheese was made right here in Canada," protested a waitress when I challenged the choice.

Did Sir John A. MacDonald dip his sandwich in ketchup? I rather think he was eating his cheese with a baguette in 1867.

Among the other national dishes served up at the Fan Village were Swedish meatballs with lingonberry sauce, Czech slanina (back bacon), Russian shashlik (meat on a stick) and pierogis, and smoked Southern-style spare ribs with cole slaw, representing the United States.

There's a little bit of Europe in almost every neighborhood of Canada.

Chatting up hotdog vendors can present Canadians with a new global experience. They're friendly and usually ready to talk about their life before coming to North America.

Gourmets interested not only in the taste of the food, but also its presentation can sample the famous "Rose of Prague" hotdog at a stand in Burlington.

In the true Czech style, the wiener is cross-cut, making it appear to have petals like a rose and providing ample crevices to fill with mustard, relish and onions.

In short, the personal development that comes with reaching out to immigrants and soaking up the culture of other countries is invaluable.

After four decades of involvement in international hockey, the games have become less and less important to me and meeting new friends from around the world now is paramount.

I once was shocked when an instructor passing along tips at a newspaper seminar made the statement that sports is a limited interest area.

I disputed the claim, pointing out the only section of the newspaper you can't find to read in the coffee shop every morning is sports.

However, the truth is there a lot more people in the world with other interests than the typical blue-collar worker who drops into Tim Hortons.

When we face The Creator at the Pearly Gates, he isn't going to ask how many goals we scored. The question is going to be, 'Did you set some goals and did you reach them using the talents I gave you?'

David Booth, a Michigan State graduate who played in the NHL for Florida, Vancouver and Toronto, said it best in a piece he penned for the Hockey Ministries International website while playing in the KHL.

"Having the opportunity to live and play throughout Russia has opened my eyes to how much I take for granted in life," he wrote. "Playing in the NHL blessed me with so much, but it also gave me a sense of entitlement.

"I was incredibly frustrated when I first came to Russia. We didn't fly first-class on planes or out of private airports. We were required to spend our home game days in a hotel. The sidewalks and roads hadn't been fixed since the foundations were laid so many years ago.

"When I looked back on how frustrated I was, it struck me how these things would not even cross a Russian's mind. Now I understand how to live and enjoy these differences and just how much I needed them in my life."

Alex Westlund, a graduate of Yale seconded the motion in a 2003 interview with Szymon Szemberg of the IIHF.

"If I had passed on this opportunity, I would have regretted it for the rest of my life," said Westlund, a goaltender who played in the Far East city of Khabarovsk, Russia.

I once asked Ulf Nilsson if he had any regrets about his NHL career.

"Probably the amount of time I wasted playing cards in hotel rooms," he replied.

That also sums up my argument.

CPSIA information can be obtained
at www.ICGtesting.com
Printed in the USA
LVHW02s1243281217
561038LV00005B/5/P

9 781525 508042